Forever

PRAYĀGA

The Site of Kumbha Melā

In Temporal and Traditional Space

Forever

PRAYĀGA

The Site of Kumbha Melā

In Temporal and Traditional Space

D.P. Dubey

Aryan Books International
New Delhi

For My Parents
Pt. Ramadhar Dubey
and
Smt. Patiraji

FOREVER PRAYĀGA: THE SITE OF KUMBHA MELĀ
In Temporal and Traditional Space

ISBN: 978-81-7305-719-9

First published: 2001
(with the title: Prayaga: The Site of Kumbha Mela, ISBN: 978-81-7305-203-3)

Second edition (with additions): **2025**

Published by
Aryan Books International
Pooja Apartments, 4B, Ansari Road, New Delhi - 110 002
Tel.: 23255799, 41099562
E-mail: aryanbooks@gmail.com
www.aryanbooks.com

Printed in India

PREFACE TO THE SECOND EDITION

Much water has flown down the river Gaṅgā from the day this book was first published at the beginning of the first Kumbha Mela of the millennium. Kumbha Mela is the largest peaceful congregation of pilgrims on the earth, during which participants take a dip in the sacred waters of the Gaṅgā, Godāvarī and Śiprā rivers in rotation. UNESCO during its 12th session held in December 2017 at Jeju, South Korea, inscribed Kumbha Mela on the Representative List of the Intangible Cultural Heritage of Humanity. The mela has also witnessed incidents of tragedy in the recent past. About 50 pilgrims were killed and more than 150 injured in a stampede and drowning on the main bath day as lakhs of devotees thronged the banks of the Gadāvarī for a holy dip at Nasik in 2003. A dozen pilgrims died and many were hurt in a stampede during the main syāhī bath at Haridwar in 2010. A stampede broke out at the Allahabad Railway Junction killing 45 devotees and more than 300 injured when a huge crowd surged forward to board the train. The devotees were on their return journey home after taking a holy bath at Sangaṃa on the main bath day in 2013. Lapses in crowd management and strategies for security led to mishaps in 2003, 2010 and 2013. The then State Urban Development minister, ignorant of mela's importance, was chief in charge of management. This mela also witnessed the nature-fury in the form of a strong storm followed by heavy rains leaving the tent city devastated and deserted after the main bath day. This Kumbha mela at Prayāga became the victim of a political game to ignore the centuries-old astronomical tradition of holding it at the first option when Jupiter enters the zodiac Arics and the sun and moon are in Capricornus. The mela was held at the alternative astronomical conjunction of stars and zodiac in 2013; the U P state legislative elections were to take place in early 2012. No akhāṛā authorities and traditional pundits dared to question the decision of the state government. To the common public, however, 2012 was the Kumbha Mela year, more than ten million pilgrims took a bath on the amāvāsyā day; they came, bathed and silently left the mela ground, much to the relief of the unprepared Magha Mela administration. Kumbha Mela at Prayāga should be celebrated in 2024 on the first astronomical position, but it will be held in 2025 in accordance with the alternative astronomical position due to scheduled elections for parliament in the preceding year. The 45-day mela in 2025 will start on 14th January and come to an end on 12th February, the main bath day (amāvāsyā) is on 29th January.

Much to our delight and satisfaction the state government at the initiative of Chief Minister Yogi Adityanath approved the renaming of Allahabad to Prayāgarāja on 16th October 2018 in fulfillment of the demand of the general public. To casual visitors, Prayāga appears to be a place wholly preoccupied with religion at the confluence of rivers and is considered to possess certain intrinsic power and efficacy for spiritual purification. Unlike Vārāṇasī, Ayodhyā, Mathurā, Purī or Ujjain, Prayāga is non-sectarian in the religious world. There are no great and grandiose temples. Whatever shrines do exist there, are poor, insignificant and shabby; the 19th century Gangoli Śivālā on the left bank of Gaṅgā at New Jhusi and the three-storied Śaṅkar Vimān Maṇḍapam in draviḍa style of architecture at Triveni bund near the fort are tolerably good to look at. No specific deity presides over Prayāga, because the significance of this tīrtha is associated mainly with water. The most sensitive space is the vast sandy tract of land around the confluence where any ritual performed accrues immense merits of *bhukti-mukti* (worldly pleasure and release from rebirth). What is most striking about rituals performed is that they have nothing at all to do with shrines or image worship. True sanctity resides in the unseen energy associated with the sacred waters of the confluence as well as the holy ground itself.

The book was well received by readers and remained out of stock for a long time. Credit goes to Shri Vikas Arya, the publisher, for bringing out the second edition for the benefit of scholars and the public. I am thankful to him for evincing a keen interest in taking up the publication and completing it neatly and expeditiously. There is no change in the main body of the text, only two appendices have been added at the end. I hope it will be well received by the readers again.

Prayagraj
August 15, 2023

D.P. Dubey

CONTENTS

FOREWORD

The study of sacred places in South Asia has been remarkably intensified in recent years. Important books on Benares (Diana Eck), Madurai (Christoph Fuller), Ayodhyā (Hans T. Bakker) and other *tīrthas* have been published. However, the cultural history of Prayāga has for long been a neglected chapter in the historiography of India, although Prayāga (Allahabad) is perhaps the most mentioned *tīrtha* in the Purāṇas, mentioned even more than Kāśī (Benares).

A study on this place is therefore highly welcomed by all who are interested in comparative research on holy places. Devi Prasad Dubey is highly qualified to write such a study, having been brought up near Allahabad and well trained in the cultural history and geography of India. He combines several articles on various topics to a fruitful study of Prayāga which can give the reader a grasp of what he calls Prayāga's "personality".

To most people, Prayāga is known for its *triveṇī* and the *kumbhamelā*. However, Dr. Dubey discusses not only these aspects, he also deals with the important subject of ritual suicide at Prayāga, with the structure of its sub-*tīrthas* and with the controversial historicity of the *akṣyavaṭa*-tree.

Dr. Dubey is interested in history, mythology, ritual, ethnography and sacred geography. Nevertheless he carefully limits his conclusions to the topics of the chapters. I am sure that his book will stimulate further research on Prayāga so that another lacuna on the rich map of South Asia's sacred geography can be filled. I wish Dr. Dubey's monograph success and many readers.

Prof. Dr. Axel Michaels
Professor of Classical Indology & Sanskrit
Director, South Asia Institute
University of Heidelberg, Germany

PREFACE

Western encounter with Indian history and culture projected many institutions of Hindu civilization, including the *tīrthas*, *melās* and rites and rituals performed therein, as curios of human past. This led to the rise of a number of descriptive and, at times, mystery mongering research works about things of the wonderland that India was thought to be. The first exposition of Indian *tīrthas* consisted of the works of hundreds of authors and researchers who had tried to describe the socio-religious and politico-economic significance together with academic and ascetic glory of various pilgrimage centres of this country. Needless to say, foreign scholars have given the lead in this direction and Indian scholars followed suit. It may also be pointed out that most of these studies were characterised by the sociological and anthropological rather than historical and cultural approach. Indologists may be given the credit of initiating the second approach, at first, casually but later seriously. One is here reminded of the observation of Milton Singer ('Text and Context in the Study of Contemporary Hinduism', *The Adyar Library Bulletin* 25, 1961: 276), who raised doubts about the appropriateness and adequacy of the anthropological studies on *tīrthas* of India. He is supported by the famous sociologist, Louis Dumont (*Homo Hierarchicus*, Chicago, University of Chicago Press, 1965, Appendix), who has rightly remarked that 'Indian anthropology without Indology has no scope at all'. My approach has been to take up the study of Indian *tīrthas* from the historical and cultural end, not in a general way but in the particular context of Prayāga. This shift in methodology and approach may be looked upon as a distinctive feature of the present enterprise.

The present work is an attempt to outline the essential features of the cultural history of Prayāga from varied sources with a view to bringing out that magnetic quality of the Tīrtharāja which has been attracting multitudes from far and near. The greatness of Prayāga, perceptible since the Vedic period, is adumbrated in the Epic-Purāṇic literature, and is attested by epigraphic records, Buddhist and Jaina texts, foreign (Chinese,

Muslim and European) accounts, treatises on *tīrtha*, and vernacular literature which received and developed further this great traditional lore about Prayāga. Archaeological evidences have also been accumulated to a considerable extent. The task of sifting and interpreting this immense material, contained *inter alia* in the numerous and varied texts is not easy. The most ticklish problem faced by the researcher consists of imparting the traditional pronouncements an interpretation intelligible to the modern world but without prejudice to their original import. As such, the researcher is inevitably faced with innumerable odds. The success or failure of the present work is, therefore, to be viewed in the context of these inherent difficulties and predicaments.

Prayāga is called Tīrtharāja on account of its special features, not possessed by other *tīrthas.* Among innumerable rivers and confluences the Gaṅgā-Yamunā-Saṅgama at Prayāga is unique. The Kumbha Melās are also held at Haridvāra, Nāsik and Ujjain, but none of them is comparable to the Kumbha Melā at Prayāga. It is the biggest, the most sacred, the most attractive and the most spoken of and written about melā in the world. The month of Māgha attains special significance only in relation to Prayāga where the sādhus and the Maṭhādhīśas, the peasants and the princes, the naked and the clothed, the young and the old, the rich and the poor, the learned and the ignorant – all congregate to attain the *puṇya* of bathing in the sacred Saṅgama in holy moments of the most auspicious day of the year. Herein lies the greatness of Prayāga, the "King of sacred places" in the three worlds, which is inseparably linked with the cultural and religious heritage of India. The study of the cultural history of such a place helps to understand the character of Indian culture and civilization, which makes it a repository of different kinds of people and traditions fusing them into a vast cultural unity while allowing them to retaining the dynamism and diversity of their own.

The cultural history of Prayāga has not received the scholarly attention it deserves. There are, however, some monographs on Prayāga. Saligram Srivastava, H.P. Sinha, B.N. Pandey and B.N. Tiwari have written *Prayāga Pradīpa* (1937), *Bhārata ko Prayāga kī Dena* (1953), *Allahabad: Retrospect and Prospect* (1955) and *Prayāga Darśana* (1976) respectively, but these scholars pay little attention to the historical perspective of the cultural heritage of Prayāga. They describe rather uncritically. Their works are more of the nature of a popular guide than of serious research. There is no doubt a research work entitled *Pilgrims and Priests as Links between a Sacred Centre and the Hindu Culture Region: Prayāga's Māgha Melā Pilgrimage* by Anita Lee H. Caplan, but as the title suggests it is devoted to a specific topic only. Moreover, this work is an unpublished Ph.D. dissertation (1982) in Geography of the University of Michigan, U.S.A. Some essays and articles on Prayāga by a few modern scholars can hardly claim the status of a thorough research work. A critical study devoted to the sacred complex of the foremost place of pilgrimage and its cultural significance is yet a desideratum. The present work is a humble attempt to remove this gap by seriously and critically ransacking various sources with a view to understanding Prayāga in the context of its sacred complex and traditions.

The cultural profile of Prayāga is so multifaceted that no single work howsoever large can encompass all of them. Therefore, the present work is confined to certain select and significant aspects only. It consists of seven chapters. The first chapter is introductory in nature and deals with the significance of the nomenclature of the place and the importance of Prayāga in the cultural history of India. The second chapter delineates the geographical horizons of Prayāga and discusses the myth of Triveṇī. The third chapter deals with the holy spots under Prayāga. The historicity of Akṣayavaṭa is discussed in the fourth chapter. In the next two chapters the rituals performed by pilgrims and the abandoned practice of suicides at Prayāga have been discussed. The last chapter discusses the origin and historicity of the Māgha Melā and the Kumbha Melā. Each chapter is of topical significance and contains its own conclusion. This dispenses with the need of giving any overall conclusion of the work.

I am aware of the valuable help received from different quarters without which it would not have been possible for me to give the work its present form, which has grown out of a dissertation accepted by the Banaras Hindu University for the degree of Ph.D. I do not find adequate words to express my deep sense of gratitude to late Prof. Lallanji Gopal who not only initiated me into the field of peregrinological studies but also encouraged me continuously to pursue my researches aimed at bringing to light the neglected heritage of Prayāga. It would have been impossible to complete this work without his invaluable guidance, personal kindness and affection which sustained me in moments of difficulty. I can never pay the debt I owe to him.

I express my gratefulness to Prof. Vishuddhanand Pathak and Prof. Om Prakash who have helped me in organizing and structuring the ideas and informations assembled in this work. My thankful obligations are due to Prof. R.L. Singh and Prof. A.K. Narain for their valuable suggestions which benefited the present work immensely. To Prof. S.M. Bhardwaj, Prof. V.N. Mishra, Prof. G.C. Tripathi, Prof. J.S. Negi, Prof. Jacob Ensink and Dr. Miloslav Krása, I owe much by way of their pertinent advice and comments. I am deeply indebted to Prof. Axel Michaels for contributing a foreword to this book, and for his kind words of appreciation. I heartily thank Dr. Rana P.B. Singh for critical suggestions and also for the maps he made for me. Acknowledgments are due to the following individuals and organisations who have provided photographs or given permissions to quote their material: Dr. Miloslav Krása, Sri Neepu Babu, Sri Sanjay Yadav, Sri Kamal Kishor 'Kamal', Goyal Studio and British Museum. I also wish to extend my obligation to all those scholars whose valuable works have been of immense use to me.

I earnestly recall the sweet memories of my revered grandfather, late Pt. K.P. Dubey *alias* Phalahari Baba, from whom I imbibed a genuine love for the Sanskrit learning and who initiated me into the study of Indology. I greatly value the affection and tender care I received from my parents whose blessings have all along been my strength and the guiding star.

Finally, I convey my cordial thanks to the Aryan Books International for taking the responsibility of publishing this book in an excellent and prompt manner.

sa tīrtharājo jayati prayāgaḥ

Allahabad
July 15, 2000

D.P. Dubey

LIST OF ILLUSTRATIONS

FIGURES

PLATES

ABBREVIATIONS

AgP	:	Agni Purāṇa
AR	:	Asiatic Researches
AV	:	Atharvaveda
Ait.Br.	:	Aitareya Brāhmaṇa
AsK	:	Avantisundarīkathā
BP	:	Brahma Purāṇa
BhagP	:	Bhāgavata Purāṇa
BhavP	:	Bhaviṣya Purāṇa
BrhP	:	Brahmāṇḍa Purāṇa
BrvP	:	Brahmavaivarta Purāṇa
BnP	:	Bṛhannāradīya Purāṇa
BrS	:	Bṛhat Saṁhitā
CII	:	Corpus Inscriptionum Indicarum
Ch.Up.	:	Chhāndogya Upaniṣad
DbhP	:	Devī Bhāgavata Purāṇa
DPPN	:	Dictionary of Pāli Proper Names
DTKN	:	Dharmakṛtyopayogitithyādinirṇayaḥ Kumbha-parvanirṃayaśca
DvP	:	Devī Purāṇa
Ep.Ind.	:	Epigraphia Indica
fn	:	Footnote
GP	:	Garuḍa Purāṇa
Gobhila	:	Gobhila Gṛhyasūtra
HP	:	Harivaṁśa Purāṇa
IA	:	Indian Antiquary
JAOS	:	Journal of the American Oriental Society
JASB	:	Journal of the Asiatic Society of Bengal
JRAS	:	Journal of the Royal Asiatic Society
JUPHS	:	Journal of the United Provinces Historical Society

KN	:	Kumbhaparvanirṇayaḥ
KM	:	Kumbhaparva Māhātmya
KP	:	Kūrma Purāṇa
l/ll.	:	line/lines
MP	:	Matsya Purāṇa
Mbh	:	Mahābhārata
Manu	:	Manusmṛti
MarP	:	Mārkaṇḍeya Purāṇa
MR	:	Modern Review
NP	:	Nāradīya Purāṇa
NarP	:	Narasiṁha Purāṇa
p	:	page
pp	:	pages
PdP	:	Padma Purāṇa
PPN	:	Prākṛta Proper Names
q.	:	quoted
Rām.	:	Rāmāyaṇa
SkP	:	Skanda Purāṇa
ŚP	:	Śiva Purāṇa
Śat. Br.	:	Śatapatha Brāhmaṇa
Tait. Sam.	:	Taittirīya Saṁhitā
TC	:	Tīrthacintāmaṇi
TP	:	Tīrthaprakāśa
Trsasti	:	Tṛṣaṣṭiśalākāpuruṣacarita
TS	:	Tristhalīsetu
TSSP	:	Trishalīsetu Sāmānya Praghaṭṭaka
TvK	:	Tīrthavivecanakāṇḍa
VP	:	Varāha Purāṇa
VaP	:	Vāyu Purāṇa
VamP	:	Vāmana Purāṇa
VdP	:	Viṣṇudharmottara Purāṇa
VisP	:	Viṣṇu Purāṇa
VsP	:	Vṛhat Svayambhū Purāṇa
Vol.	:	Volume
YT	:	Yoginītantra
Yājñayāj	:	Yājñavalkyasmṛti

Chapter I

INTRODUCTION

Prayāga or Allahabad (lat. 25°27'N and long. 81°50'E), picturesquely situated at the confluence of the rivers Gaṅgā, Yamunā and the invisible Sarasvatī in the heart of the Gaṅgā plain, is one of the most renowned sacred places of India (Fig. 1). It is known as Tīrtharāja (King of the sacred places) and is believed by the Hindus to be the holiest place in the three worlds existing in space (heaven, earth and the netherworld) and in time (past, present and future). The greatness of Prayāga, perceptible since the Vedic period, is adumbrated in the Epics, the Purāṇas and the treatises on *tīrtha*; and is attested by epigraphic records, foreign (Chinese, Muslim and European) accounts, Buddhist and Jaina texts, and the vernacular literature. It is one of the most frequented places of pilgrimage, where people come especially during the month of Māgha for bathing in the sacred waters of the confluence (Saṅgama) and every twelfth year they come by hundreds of thousands to the largest melā of the world, the Kumbha Melā. Kings and commoners from different parts of the subcontinent are also known to have often visited this place on pilgrimage to commit suicide and to make suitable grants in charity to commemorate the event. Prayāga is one of the three great *tīrthas* of the land, the other two being Kāśī and Gayā. Bharati has rightly observed, "Just as shrines of local, regional or sectarian importance all over India compare their own merit giving capacity to that of Banaras (Kāśī), shrines close to a river or located inside a water expanse compare themselves to Prayāga".[1] The land between the Gaṅgā and the Yamunā is said to be the *mons veneris* of the goddess Earth and Prayāga is regarded as its generative organ.[2] This is a cosmogonic allusion to the place suggesting that Prayāga is the mythical 'Centre' of the creation of the universe. According to John Irwin, "There can exist any number of such 'Centres' without logical contradiction, the Centre (or Navel) of the universe existed wherever man felt himself to be in communication with the divine world".[3]

Prayāga occupies an important place in the annals of Indian civilization,

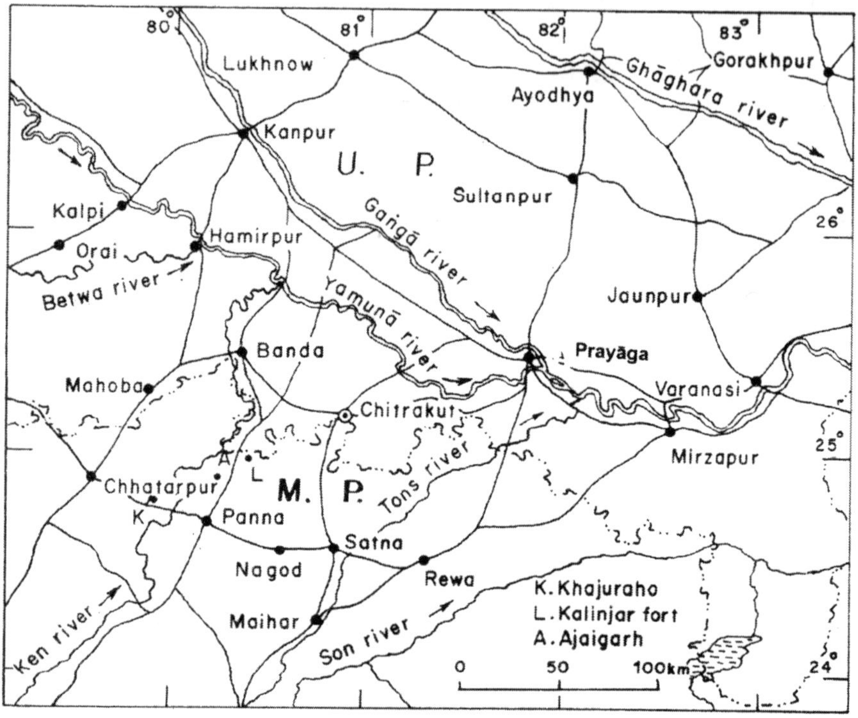

Fig. 1 Prayāga in Regional Setting

serving as a meeting ground of different kinds of peoples and traditions and communicating with every corner of the country. The Gaṅgā-Yamunā Doāb, the region between the two rivers, was regarded as the heart of Āryāvarta, where the Āryan and indigenous world attained its final fusion, later becoming the political epicentre of the great imperial dynasties: Maurya, Gupta, Delhi Sultanate and Mughal. The cultural dominance of the region must have enhanced the fame of Prayāga, which provided its most outstanding feature; the confluence of the rivers at Prayāga came to be regarded as the visible symbol of Madhyadeśa which is depicted in the Varāha cave at Udaigiri around C.E. 400. In tradition, Prayāga formed the eastern boundary of Madhyadeśa.[4] That Prayāga is the eastern point of Madhyadeśa is of spatial significance stressing correspondences between humanity and space in order to make the most out of the various lines of cosmic forces. "The most basic of these forces", observes Brenda Beck, "are fixed in association with the various compass points. The east, for example, is the direction from which many beneficial forces emanate".[5] The front door of a house should open to the east, therefore, to ensure familial well-being. People, when they undergo any of the auspicious life-cycle rituals are careful to sit facing east. The shrines of most of the great gods also face in this direction. The explanation of the importance of the east rests on its association with the rising sun. In fact, east serves as one of the axis of cosmic force; and it again demonstrates that Prayāga is the mythical place where heaven and earth were first separated in *illo tempore*.

Prayāga acquired such great importance that other *tīrthas* are named after it. There are five Prayāgas in the Himālaya, each at the confluence of two rivers: Deva Prayāga at the junction of the Bhāgīrathī and the Alakanandā, Karṇa Prayāga at the confluence of the Alakanandā and the Piṇḍārā, Rudra Prayāga at the confluence of the Alakanandā and the Mandākinī, Nanda Prayāga at the junction of the Alakanandā and the Nandā, and Viṣṇu Prayāga at the junction of the Alakanandā and the Viṣṇu Gaṅgā. Prayāga is also located four miles north-west of Kolhāpur in Mahārāṣṭra where the two tributaries of the Pañcagaṅgā – the Bhogavatī and the Kasārā – meet.[6] This kind of 'transposition of place' indicates that Prayāga has most powerfully collected and refracted the light of India's holy places to become a pan-Indian *tīrtha*.

Prayāga is, in fact, a centre of faith and devotion, where people realize that religion is still an affair of many. It is the sacred place where the miserable, the poor, and those with a firm determination can hope to find liberation.[7] To go to the sin-destroying Prayāga is very meritorious for pious people.[8] All sins are washed off merely by remembrance of that sacred place. Sinners, however, do not repair to this *tīrtha*.[9] It is said that at the very sight of that place or by reciting its name or even by smearing the clay of the place on the body, a man becomes free from sins.[10] The Purāṇas proclaim that it is the sacred space of Prajāpati; those who bathe here go to heaven and those who die here are not born again.[11] All this may suggest the magico-mystical power of the sacred space of Prayāga.

The Epic-Purāṇic texts lay greatest emphasis on the cultivation of high moral and spiritual qualities for securing the full reward of pilgrimage.[12] The *Matysa* and *Padma Purāṇas* say that a wise man, full of devotion and observing celibacy, enjoys the full bloom of his health and attains the benefit of performing the *aśvamedha* sacrifice at every step in his pilgrimage to Prayāga. Such a man gets emancipation from bondage for his manes and posterity for ten generations.[13] The Purāṇas ordain pilgrims not to go to Prayāga in a conveyance. It is said that the pilgrim, who drives to Prayāga on a cart drawn by bulls, makes himself liable to the sufferings in the fearful hell, incurs the terrible wrath of the kine and his *pitṛs* (ancestors) do not accept the libations offered by him at the sacred place. And one who goes there in a conveyance not drawn by bullocks, either because of vanity born of riches or avarice or perplexity, is deprived of all merits of pilgrimage.[14] Therefore, to earn the full merit one is advised to visit Prayāga bare-footed. The significance of these Purānic statements are discussed in the digests.[15] According to the *Tīrthavivecanakānda*, using a conveyance is forbidden only in the case of pilgrimage to Prayāga and not in the case of other *tīrthas*,[16] while the *Tīrthacintāmaṇi* and the *Tīrthaprakāśa* hold that the prohibition expands beyond its immediate context and applies to other *tīrthas* as well.[17] The discussion has been laid to rest in the *Tristhalīsetu* which says that the prohibition refers to both the *tīrtha* in question and those not being explicitly mentioned; it may also be that the statements are placed in the particular context of Prayāga by way of being a supplementary passage which singles out a particular instance.[18] However, Prayāga excels all *tīrthas*. The *Padma Purāṇa* declares, "As the sun is amidst the planets and the moon is amidst the asterisms, so is Prayāga the foremost sacred place in the galaxy of *tīrthas*".[19] The *Matsya Purāṇa* states, "As Brahmā is worshipped in all the beings, so Prayāga is adored by the learned in all the worlds. Prayāga is indeed to be propitiated as the king of all *tīrthas*. Brahmā also thinks of this sacred place everyday, that is why wise men after repairing to Prayāga do not feel inclined to anything else" [20] The same Purāna again says that Brahmā creates the universe, Visnu fosters it and Rudra destroys it at the end of the *kalpa* (aeon). But Prayāga is saved at the time of the dissolution of the universe.[21] Prayāga is, indeed, that great sacred place which fulfils all the desires of the devotees and bestows heaven and salvation upon them.[22]

NOMENCLATURE

Prayāga owes its sanctity to the confluence of the rivers, which emerged as a centre of the Āryan culture in the Vedic period. A *khila* verse of the *Ṛgveda* alludes to this place as 'Sitāsitasaṅgama',[23] *sita* signifying Gaṅgā and *asita* denoting to Yamunā. The *Skanda Purāṇa* refers to this verse as *śruti*.[24] The *Tīrthacintāmaṇi* quotes it as a verse of the *Rgveda*.[25] The *Tristhalīsetu* says that it is a supplementary *śruti* text of the *Āśvalāyana* school.[26] The *Tīrthaprakāśa* also calls it *śruti* and ascribes it to the *Āśvalāyana* school of the *Ṛgveda*.[27] This must have been a comparatively early verse. Scheftelowitz has argued an early date for this particular *khila* verse,[28] and has remarked, "Dieser Vers ist notch Vedisch, Vgl. die Formen *āplutāsah* und *janāsah*" [29]

In the Upaniṣads it is named Prayāga.[30] But the themes of the Upaniṣads referring to Prayāga are alien to the classical ones; they are sectarian in character. Their insistence on *tīrthas* reveals that they were written when the practice of *tīrthayātrā* was well-established. They were possibly written to give a kind of official 'philosophical' approval to the practice of pilgrimage. Moreover, Sharma places these sectarian Upaniṣads between first century C.E. and sixth century C.E., though some of them can be ascribed to as late a period as fifteenth century C.E.[31]

The word 'Prayāga' is derived from *pra√yaj*, the prefix '*pra*' means 'great' and the term '*yāga*' signifies 'sacrifice', and this reminds of the way in which pilgrimage to a sacred place came to be considered the primary substitute for the Vedic sacrificial rites (*yajñas*). The *Mahābhārata* says that since Prajāpati performed a great sacrifice there, it is known as Prayāga.[32] Though composed between 400 B.C. and C.E. 400, it describes real and mythological events that return to the beginnings of Indian civilization. In the later Vedic age sacrifice was the most important religious activity and Prajāpati, the Creator of the universe and the Lord of sacrifices, was the supreme deity. The performance of sacrifice by Prajāpati at this place signifies that during the later Vedic period the Āryan culture spread in the Gaṅga-Yamunā Doāb and the adherents of the Vedic lore performed sacrifices at the junction of the rivers to establish their hold in the region. Prayāga is the middle sacrificial altar (*madhyamā vedi*) of Prajāpati; out of five such *vedis* on the earth, the other four being at Gayā, Kurukṣetra, Virajā and Puṣkara.[33] In the *Padma Purāṇa*. Prajāpati is said to have performed the great sacrifice there in order to gain power for creating the universe at the beginning of the creation.[34] The *Skanda* and *Padma Purāṇas* also supply another etiology which centres on the story of the recovery of Vedas from Śaṅkhāsura; the recovered holy scriptures were presented by the sages (*ṛṣis*) at Prayāga to Viṣṇu who sanctified the place with his own presence as *matsyāvatāra* and to Brahmā who performed the first sacrifice there to show his satisfaction for the findings of the Vedas.[35] It acquired its name because when all the sacrifices were placed on one scale of the balance and Prayāga on the other, the former kicked the beam.[36] According to the *Skanda Purāṇa*, Prayāga was the name given to it by the gods Hari, Hara and others seeing that it is superior to all sacrifices though the latter be enriched with fees and the like.[37] This was the greatest of all sacrifices as is signified by the preposition '*pra*'. The Epic-Purāṇic texts appear to emphasise on the prefix '*pra*', when it is said that Prayāga predominates over all places on account of its supernatural efficacy.[38] The Purāṇas explain '*pra*' in Prayāga as '*prakṛṣṭa*',[39] generally translated as 'excellent', but it may also be taken to mean 'drawn forth' or 'drawn out', alluding to the act of ploughing.[40] This may suggest that the name Prayāga owes its origin to the introduction of plough cultivation in this region with the transplantation of Vedic culture, but is explained in a mythical way in the texts. This is corroborated by the Epic-Purāṇic evidence which personifies Prayāga as the symbol of fertility by saying that "the thighs of the goddess Earth are between the rivers Gaṅgā and Yamunā, and Prayāga is her generative organ".[41] Moreover, ploughing itself is traditionally regarded as a sacrificial ritual.

According to the *Brahma Purāṇa*, it is called Prayāga on account of its eminence and it has the suffix 'rāja' applied to it on account of its being the chief.[42] The *Matsya Purāṇa* affirms, 'On account of its efficacy as compared with all other *tīrthas* it prevails far more'.[43] Tiwari, from the study of some Jaina sources, has opined that prior to the performance of the great sacrifice by Prajāpati, this place was known as Purimatāla or Puṣpabhadrapura.[44] But how this priority has been maintained by him is not clear, as the Epics stand far older than the Jaina literature which were finally codified in the sixth century C.E. Moreover, Purimatāla itself is mentioned as a suburb of Ayodhyā in the Jaina texts[45] and Puṣpabhadrapura is identified with Pāṭaliputra.[46]

Prajāpati is said to have created Prayāga for the combustion of the burden due to the multitude of sins on the earth. He has, in fact, created it out of desire for the benefit of his subjects.[47] Hence, it is called Prajāpatikṣetra.[48] The earliest epigraphic reference to Prayāga as Prajāpatikṣetra occurs in the Ridhpur copperplate inscription of the Nala king Bhavattavarman,[49] assigned to the latter half of the fifth or first half of the sixth century C.E. Inscriptions of the Sena kings, assignable to the first quarter of the thirteenth century C.E., also refer to the performance of sacrifices by the lotus-born Prajāpati on the banks of Triveṇī.[50] It is also called Brahmakṣetra in the *Padma* and *Skanda Purāṇas*.[51]

Prayāga is known as Tīrtharāja,[52] because it is the most sacred in the three worlds and the foremost of all *tīrthas*.[53] It is believed that at Prayāga, whose praises have been sung by *ṛṣis*, there is the presence of gods with Brahmā at their head, Dikpālas (guardians of the quarters), Lokapālas (guardians of the world), Sādhyas (realised souls), Pitṛs (manes), Maharṣis like Sanatkumāra and others, Nāgas, Cakradharas, Garuḍa, Siddhas, Gandharvas, Apsarās, the rivers, the seas and Lord Hari.[54] The Vedas and the *yajñas* are present there in embodied forms and ascetics and sages adore Brahmā there. The gods and the kings adore Prayāga by performing sacrifices there.[55] It is guarded by Indra and the region is protected by Viṣṇu along with other gods. The gods like Brahmā, Viṣṇu, Śiva and great sages and several sacred places are always present there.[56] This holiest of the holy places is, therefore, indeed to be worshipped as the king of all *tīrthas*.[57] This title, proudly asserted to the present day, was acknowledged by Rājā Birbal, who recorded his visit to Prayāga on the Aśokan pillar in C.E. 1575.[58]

The superiority as Tīrtharāja of this place over all other *tīrthas* undoubtedly makes it Prayāgarāja. According to the *Tristhalīsetu*, the word 'Prayāga' is employed in the neuter when connected with such words as *tīrtha* or *kṣetra*; but when employed along with words in the masculine gender such as *tīrtharāja*, it takes the masculine gender.[59] In the Buddhist[60] and Jaina[61] texts the place is mentioned as Payāga, Pāyāga or Payāta, which are evidently the Pāli-Prākṛta renderings of the word 'Prayāga'. The Chinese-pilgrim traveller Hsüan Tsang, who went there to attend the sixth quinquennial assembly of Harṣa in the first half of the seventh century C.E., records it as Po-lo-ya-ka,[62] which is an equivalent of the name Prayāga. Albirūnī refers to it as Piāg,[63] which is also identical to Prayāga. An admonitory formula in old Kanarese language, which usually occurs in the inscriptions of the early medieval period from the Dharwar region, indicates that Prayāga was regarded as one of the three, four, five or seven sacred places of the country.[64] These evidences cut the very root of the belief, maintained in some circles,[65] that the name of the place owed its origin to a brāhmaṇa named Prayāga, who lived during the reign of the Mughal emperor Akbar in the sixteenth century C.E. This belief has no historical foundation and hence should not be taken seriously.

The name Allahabad was given to Prayāga by the Mughal emperor Akbar who visited the confluence of the Gaṅgā and the Yamunā at the close of C.E. 1582. He was so impressed with the strategic importance of the site that he, at a propitious moment, founded a fort and ordered for the lay-out of a city there to which he gave the name of Ilāhābād. This is evidenced by the testimony of the *Muntakhab-ut-Tawārīkh* of Abdul Qādir Badāunī which records that, His Majesty commanded a city and a fort to be built at Piāg (Prayāga) under the name of Ilāhābās, where the waters of the Gaṅgā and the Yamunā unite'.[66] Nizāmmuddīn Ahmad in his *Tabakāt-i-Akbarī* says that "His Majesty commanded a city and a fort to be built at Payāg (Prayāga), at the confluence of the Ganges and Jumna, to which the name of Ilāhābās was given".[67] Abul Faẓl also states that Ilāhābād, anciently called Piyāg (Prayāga), was distinguished by the emperor by the former name.[68] The *Khulāṣat-ut-tawārīkh* (C.E. 1695)[69] and the *Hadīqat-ul-Aqālīm* (C.E. 1776-87)[70] record that "emperor Akbar, having built between the rivers Ganges and Jumna at Prayāga a strong stone fort and excellent mansions, founded a city and named it Illāhābās or Ilāhābād". The *Tīrthamālā* of Saubhāgyavijaya (C.E. 1693) also says that the Mughal emperor Akbar made Prayāga famous by the name of Illāvāsa.[71] Akbar the Great, thus, changed the name of Prayāga to Illāhābās or Ilāhābād, as it is also written on the coins[72] minted there by him and his successors. This does not seem to be a new name coined by Akbar. It is probable that in the Epic and Purāṇic times this sacred place was also famous as Ilāvāsa after the celebrated king Ila, the founder of Pratiṣṭhāna,[73] which is still an important sub-*tīrtha* under Prayāga. In course of time this name receded into the background, but remained popular in the learned circle. When Akbar founded the new city in C.E. 1583, he revived this Hindu name of antiquity by giving it an Islamic colour. He adopted this name as the official designation of the new city, which is still in force. From the time of Akbar onwards, the place came to be known by its new name i.e. Ilāhābās or Ilāhābād which subsequently became Allahabad in the time of emperor Shāhjahān.[74] It has, however, been suggested that the place came to be called as Alāhābād after Ālhā, one of the celebrated Banāfar twin-brothers of the Hindu story.[75] This legendary view, not corroborated by any historical evidence, seems nothing but a mere conjecture, and, therefore, must be rejected for the sake of history. Incidentally, it was also called Faqīrābād, i.e., "Beggars' Town" during the eighteenth-nineteenth centuries, partly on account of poverty, and partly on account of the great resort of faqīrs and pilgrims.[76] The Muslim historians of the late medieval period refer to the existence of twelve *dāirās* and eighteen *sarāis* at Allahabad. Due to the abundance of these *sarāis* (inns) and *dāirās* (hermitages of faqīrs), this place possibly came to be designated as such in the past. There is still a Mohallah of the same name near Kutchehery in the modern city.

The name Prayāga is, however, still used among the Hindus, but denotes the scene of religious worship rather than city. It has, to some extent, been popularised by the adoption of the name for the station on the Allahabad–Lucknow railway line in the early years of the twentieth century C.E.

Prayāga, from the Vedic period, is one of the chief places of pilgrimages in the country, and in this respect is equal if not superior to Vārāṇasī, Mathurā and Haridvāra. It has remained the great centre of Hindu culture and civilization, and has been the confluence of many ideas and cultures. It claims to be Tīrtharāja or foremost of holy spots, and has been able to maintain its ancient celebrity and distinction uninterruptedly. The original name Vārāṇasī has been revived as the official name of Banaras in Free India. Even the original name Karṇāṭaka has been restored to the state of Mysore. But no such change has been made in the name of Allahabad. The acceptance of the original name Prayāga as the official name of Allahabad will be a fitting tribute that Free India can pay to the greatness and glory of Tīrtharāja.

REFERENCES

1. Bharati, Agehananda, 'Pilgrimage Sites and Indian Civilization', in *Chapters in Indian Civilization*, Vol. I, p.107.
2. *Mbh*, III.83.71 = *TP*, 321; *KP*,I.35.11; *AgP*, 111.4; *VsP*, 7.386; *PdP*, III.39.71b-72a, 43.19b-20a, 47.6; *MP*, 105.19, 109.6 = *TvK*, 142, 151 = *TC*,24 = *TS*, 6 = *TP*, 324-25.
3. John Irwin, 'The Ancient Pillar-cult at Prayāga (Allahabad) : Its Pre-Aśokan Origins', *JRAS*, 1983, p.254.
4. *Manu*, II.21; *AsK*, p.194; Sircar, D.C., *Studies in the Geography of Ancient and Medieval India*, pp.21-22.
5. Beck, E.F. Brenda, 'The Symbolic Merger of Body, Space and Cosmos in Hindu Tamil Nadu', *Contributions to Indian Sociology* (NS), Vol. 10(2), 1976, p.214.
6. *CII*, Vol. VI, p.209.
7. *MP*, 104.2.
8. *MP*, 102.25; *PdP*, III.40.40.
9. *PdP*, III.41.11-12a; *VsP*, 7.384; *MP*, 103.10 = *TvK*, 137=*TP*, 323; *TS* (*SkP*), 12.
10. *Mbh*, III.83.75 = *TvK*, 152 = *TP*, 322; *AgP*, 111.6b-7a; *KP*, I.34.27 = *TS*, 14; *VsP*, 7.384-85; *PdP*, III.39.76, 41.12b-13a, 43.21; *MP*, 103.11, 105.20 = *TvK*, 137, 142 = *TS*, 6 = *TP*, 323, 329.
11. *KP*, I.34.20 = *TS*, 28; *MP*, 103.5, 110.14 = *TS*, 7; *SkP*, IV. 7.47.
12. *Mbh*, III.80.30-33; *SkP*, IV.6.3; *VaP*, 77.125, 127 = *TvK*, 5-6; *BP*, 25.4-6; Kane, *History of Dharmaśāstra*, Vol. IV, pp.562-564.
13. *MP*, 107.3-5 = *TvK*, 147 = *TP*, 345; *PdP*, III.45.2-4 = *TC*, 50.
14. *MP*, 105.4-5, 7 = *TvK*, 141 = *TS*, 14; *PdP*, III.43.4-5. 7; *VsP*, 7.386; *KP*, I.35.2-3, 5.
15. Kane, *op.cit.*, Vol. IV, pp.576-577.
16. *TvK*, 11.
17. *TC*, 8; *TP*, 45.
18. *TSSP*, 118.3-4.
19. *PdP*, VI.24.3-4a.
20. *MP*, 108.13b-16 = TS, 6; *PdP*, III.46.13b-16.
21. *MP*, 110.3-4.
22. *SkP*, IV.22.59 = TS, 12.
23. सितासिते सरिते यत्र संगथे तत्राप्लुतासो दिवमुत्पतन्ति ।
    ये वै तन्वं वि सृजन्ति धीरास्ते जनासो अमृतत्वं भजन्ते ॥
    Ṛgveda, *khila*, 22.1.
24. *SkP*, IV.7.54.
25. *TC*, 47.
26. *TS*, 3.
27. *TP*, 321, 342.
28. Scheftelowitz, J., *Die Apokryphen des Ṛgveda* (*Khilāni*), p.169.
29. *Ibid.*, p.171.

30. कुरुक्षेत्रं कुचस्थाने प्रयागं हृत्सरोरुहे ।
Jābāladarśanopaniṣad, 4.49a.
प्रयागं कामिकं तीर्थमविमुक्तं तु नैष्ठिकम् ।
Śivopaniṣad, 6.192a.
31. Sharma, T.R., *Studies in the Sectarian Upaniṣads*, pp.30-33.
32. यत्रायजत भूतात्मा पूर्वमेव पितामहः ।
प्रयागमिति विख्यातं तस्माद् भरतसत्तम ॥
Mbh, III.85.14=*TS*, 8=*TP*, 322.
33. *VamP*, 23.19-20.
34. *PdP*, VI.128.263b-264a.
35. *SkP*, II.13 (4). 38-48; *PdP*, VI.91.6-16.
36. *SkP*, IV.7.59=*TS*, 11.
37. *SkP*, IV.22.61=*TS*, 13.
38. *Mbh*, III.83.74=*TP*, 322; *MP*, 109.10b-11a=*TvK*, 151=*TC*, 24=*TS*, 7=*TP*, 325; *PdP*, III.39.75, 47.10b-11a; *NP*, II.63.57.
39. प्रकृष्टं सर्वयागेभ्यः प्रयागमिति गीयते ।
यज्वनां पुनरावृत्तिर्न प्रयागार्द्रवर्ष्मणाम् ॥
SkP, IV. 7.49=*TS*, 11, 13.
प्रकृष्टत्वात्प्रयागोऽसौ प्राधान्याद्राजशब्दवान् ।
BP q. in *TS*, 13=*TP*, 327.
40. Upadhyaya, G.P., 'The Origins and Functions of Tīrthas–Some Epic and Purāṇic Testimonies', *Indian History Congress Proceedings*, Calicut, 47th session, 1976, p.127.
41. *Mbh*, III.83.71=*TP*, 321; *KP*, I.35.11; *AgP*, 111.4;
VsP, 7.386; *PdP*, III.39.71b-72a, 43.19b-20a, 47.6;
MP. 105.19, 109.6=*TvK*, 142, 151=*TC*, 24=*TS*, 6=*TP*, 324-25.
42. *BP q.* in *TS*, 13=*TP*, 327.
43. *MP*, 109.10b-11a=*TvK*, 151=*TC*, 24=*TS*, 7=*TP*, 325.
44. Tiwari, B.N., *Prayāga Darśana*, p.25.
45. *Triṣaṣṭiśalākāpuruṣacarita*, I.3.389-512; *Kalpasūtra*, 7.212; *Harivaṁśa Purāṇa* of Jinasenācārya, 9.205-6; *Āvaśyakacūrṇī*, I. 181; *Vipākasūtra*, 15; *Ādipurāṇa* of Jinasenācārya, I. 20.218-219; Yadav, J., *Jaina Dharma kī Aitihāsika Rūparekhā*, p.18.
46. Jain, J.C., *Life in Ancient India as Described in the Jaina Canons*, p.324.
47. *NP*, II.63.21b-22a; *PdP*, VI.126.31=*TC*, 20=*TP*, 331; *TS* (*MP*), 7.
48. *MP*, 103.4, 110.14=*TvK*, 136=*TC*, 47=*TS*, 7, 15=*TP*, 323, 327, 342; *AgP*, 111.5; *NP*, II.63.130,b; *PdP*, III.41.5; *SkP*, IV.7.47; *KP*, I.34.20=*TS*, 28.
49. भगवतः प्रजापतेः प्रसादसिद्धक्षेत्रे गङ्गायमुनयोस्संवेद्ये प्रयागस्थितैः ।
Ep. Ind., Vol. XIX, p.102, ll.4-5.
50. तीरोत्सङ्गे त्रिवेण्याः कमलभवमखारम्भनिर्व्याजपूते येन --- ।
Mandanapada copperplate of Viśvarūpasena, *Ep. Ind.*, Vol. XXXIII, p.322, verse 12; Edilpur copperplate of Keśavasena, *Corpus of Bengal Inscriptions*,

p.335, verse 13; The Calcutta Sahitya Parisad copperplate of Viśvarūpasena, *Corpus of Bengal Inscriptions*, p.324, verse 14.

51. *PdP*, VI.91.16; *SkP*, II.13(4).49.
52. *SkP*, IV.7.67, 22.72; *PdP*, VI.24.31, 81.33, 128.231; *MP*, 108.15-16.

    Such a designation, although used for many holy places like Haridvāra (*PdP*, VI.231.41), Kapālamocana-tīrtha (*PdP*, VI.132.6), Utkalakṣetra (BP, 42.45, 44.46), etc. is commonly applied to Prayāga.
53. *Mbh*, III.83.74; *MP*, 109.10b-11a; *PdP*, III.39.75, 47.10b-11a, VI.24.3b-4a; *NP*, II.63.57; *BnP*, I.6.5; *BP* q. in *TS*, 8; *BP*, 59.21; *YT*, II.6.168.
54. *Mbh* III.83.65-68=*TS*, 8=*TP*, 321; *MP*, 105.15-18=*TvK*, 142; *PdP*, III.39.66-69, 43.15b-19a.
55. *Mbh*, III.83.73=*TP*, 321; *MP*, 109.9-10=*TvK*, 151=*TC*, 24=*TS*, 6=*TP*, 325; *PdP*, III.39.73-74, 47.9-10.
56. *MP*, 103.5b-6a, 8-9=*TvK*, 137=*TS*, 4-5=*TP*, 323; *PdP*, III.41.6, 9-10; *KP*, I.34.24-25=*TS*, 9; *VsP*, 7.384; *AgP*, 111.1-2.
57. *MP*, 108.15; *PdP*, III.46.15.
58. *CII*, Vol. I: *Inscriptions of Aśoka*, p.39.
59. अत्रोभयथा पुराणे प्रयोगादुभयलिङ्गः प्रयागशब्दः ।

    तत्र तीर्थक्षेत्रादिशब्दसामानाधिकरण्ये क्लीबता ।

    तीर्थराजादिशब्दसामानाधिकरण्येपुंलिङ्गतेति वृद्धाः ।

    TS,13; Kane, *op.cit.*, Vol. IV, p.598.
60. *Vinayapiṭaka*, Vol. III, p.11; *Majjhimanikāya*, Vol. I, p.39; *Mahāvaṁśa*, XXXI. 6; *Dīghanikāya*, II.7.2.8; *Papañcasūdanī*, Vol. I, p.226; *Jātaka*, VI. 198.3; *DPPN*, Vol. II, p. 146.
61. *Āvaśyakacūrṇī*, Vol. II, p.179; *Niśīthacūrṇī*, Vol. III, p.193; *Karakaṇḍacariu*, VI.6.5,7; *PPN*, Vol. I, p.400.
62. Watters, *On Yuan Chwang's Travels in India*, Vol. I, p.361.
63. Sachau, *Albirūnī's India*, Vol. I, p.200.
64. Pathak, V.S., 'Prayāga in Inscriptions', *JUPHS*, Vol. VI (II), p.31.
65. Cunningham, A., *Ancient Geography of India*, Vol. I, p.329.
66. *Muntakhab-ut-Tawārīkh*, Vol. I, p.243.
67. Elliot and Dowson, *The History of India as told by Its own Historians*, Vol. 5, p.437; *Tabaqāt-i-Akbarī*, Vol. II, p.577.
68. *Āin-i-Akbarī*, Vol. III, p.335; *Akbaranāmā*, Vol. III, pp.124, 616.
69. *Khulāṣat-ut-Tawārīkh*, folio 37a.
70. *Hadīqat-ul-Aqālīm*, folio 214a.
71. *Prācīna Tīrthamālāsaṅgraha*, p.77.
72. *Āin-i-Akbarī*,Vol. I, p.32; Srivastava, Shaligrama, *Prayāga Pradīpa*, pp.33-34.
73. *Rām*, VII.81.22-23; *PdP*, I.8.124; *BhagP*, IX.1.42; *DbhP*, I.13.1-2; *HP*, 26.47-48.
74. *Khulāṣat-ut-Tawārīkh*, folio 37a; *Hadīqat-ul-Aqālīm*, folio 57a; *Akbaranāmā*, Vol. III, p.616fn.
75. Nevill, H.R., *Allahabad District Gazetteer*, p.196.
76. Leopold von Orlich, *Travels in India*, Vol. II, p.119.

Chapter II

SACRED GEOGRAPHY

The importance of Prayāga, also called Tīrtharāja for its eminence, derives from the fact that for Indian people the confluence of two rivers or of a river with the ocean has a special meaning. As rivers are considered holy entities, the meeting-point of two streams adds the sacredness of the first river to that of the second one. Prayāga excels all these meeting-points because it stands at the confluence of the two most sacred Indian rivers: the Gaṅgā and the Yamunā.

The sacred complex of Prayāga is often divided into three parts – Veṇī or Triveṇī, Prajāpatikṣetra, and Prayāga-maṇḍala – each preceding one being smaller and holier than each subsequent one (Fig. 2). This śāstric division, when put to test, has still not lost its relevance in the sacred geography of Prayāga. Prayāga-maṇḍala is said to be five *yojanas* in extent.[1] Some scholars take the 'five *yojanas*' to be equal to forty miles treating one *yojana* as equal to eight miles symbolizing the circumference of Prayāga-maṇḍala.[2] In fact, it corresponds with the diameter of the *maṇḍala*. And one *yojana* of the Purāṇic sacred geography represents one *krośa* only;[3] a *krośa* being a unit of measurement equivalent to 2.26 miles.[4] Hence, the circuit of Prayāga-maṇḍala would be about eleven and a half miles or eighteen kilometers in diameter. The geographical centre of this *maṇḍala* according to the medieval digests, is the Brahmayūpa (the sacrificial post of Prajāpati)[5] which may be identified with the Aśokan pillar standing in the vicinity of the confluence of the rivers in the sacred complex. According to the *Tristhalīsetu* and the *Tīrthaprakāśa*, Prayāga-maṇḍala is measured as follows:

> Taking Brahmayūpa as the peg, stretch a string of two and a half *yojanas* (i.e. 5.65 miles) long, move that string in all directions so as to form a circle. The sacred space is what is inside the arc.[6]

The word *maṇḍala* means 'circle' and 'centre'. According to Olsson, 'It signifies a diagram which symbolizes the thought and actions of Tantric

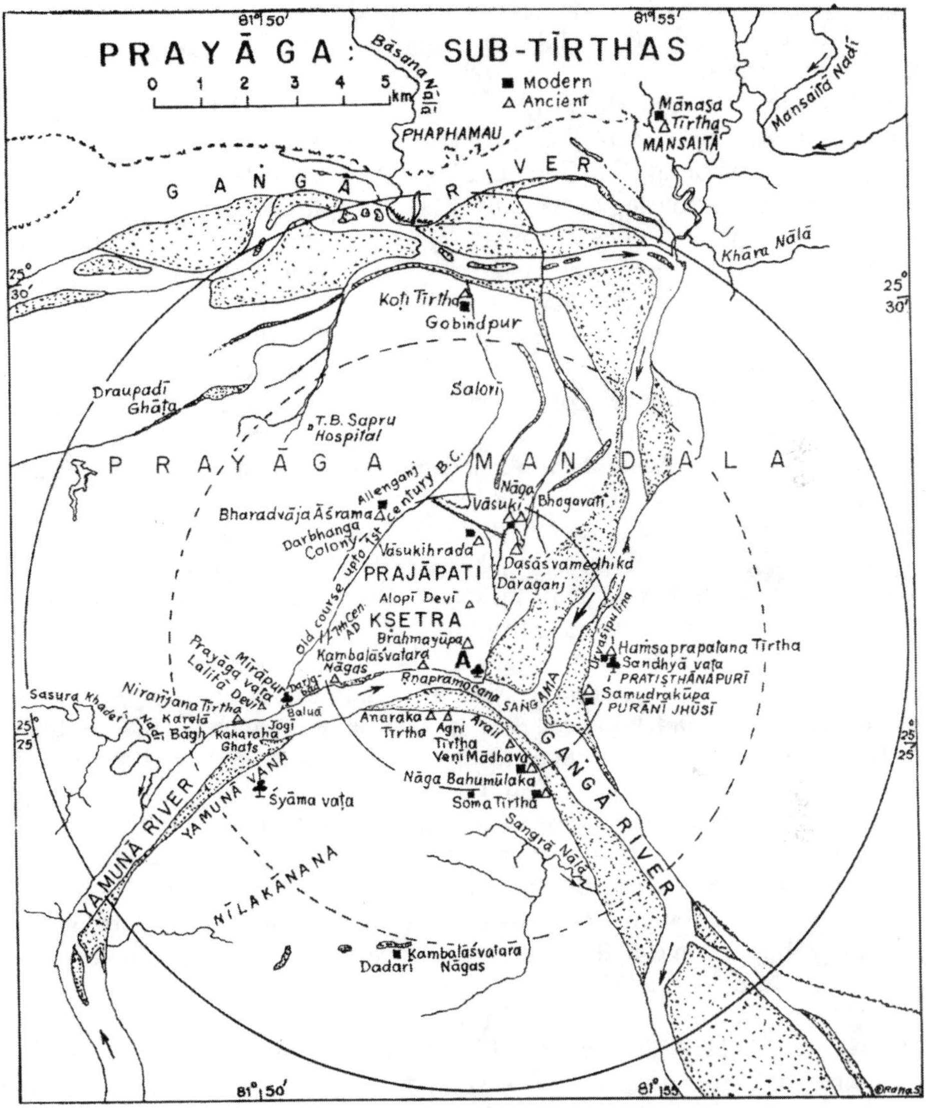

Fig. 2 Demarkated sacredscape and sub-*tīrthas*

Hinduism and Buddhism. It is basically a representation of the universe in which an encircled consecrated area is treated as a receptacle for the gods and a collection point of universal forces'.[7] In fact, "the *maṇḍala* is a cosmogonic symbol which represents creation and dissolution, form and emptiness, social wholes and individual parts".[8]

Vidyāpati, who calls it Mahā Prayāga,[9] sets its boundaries as extending from Ābālacandra in the west to Pratiṣṭhānapura in the east, another peripheral locality either in the north or in the south being Nīlakaṇṭhapura.[10] Pratiṣṭhānapura is modern Jhūsī. Ābālacandra may be identified with the village Ālumcanda by the Gaṅgā, 18 km to the west of Prayāga. But it is now quite embarrassing to spot out Nīlakaṇṭhapura in modern topographic setting. He, however, does not treat *yajanas* identical to *krośa*; the area of Mahā Prayāga is five *yojanas* and that of Prayāga is five *krośas*.[11] But in locating the big village Karelā (*Karelākhya-mahāgrāma*), distanced one and a half *yojana* in the south and Malakā village (*Malakākhya-grāma*), one *yojana* away in the north from Prayāga,[12] he is a bit disconcerted. The distances mentioned by him do not correspond to realities. The actual distance of Karelā (Karelābāgh locality near Kakarahāghāṭa) from the old confluence is 3 km and that of Malakā (Malāka Harahar across the Gaṅgā) is 9 km.

Prayāga is also called Prajāpatikṣetra. It extends from Pratiṣṭhāna in the east to Kambalāśvatara Nāgas in the west and Vāsuki-hrada in the north to Nāga Bahumūlaka in the south.[13] The *Tristhalīsetu* and the *Tīrthaprakāśa* say that 'taking all these as four cardinal points draw a circle; Prayāga-kṣetra is that what is inside it'.[14]

It is notable that the sacred landscape was demarcated, differentiated, and objectified into something spatially distinct. It shows order and emanates power, and two fences (Fig. 2), though formless, encircle it for the same reason "that a station generating electricity is fenced in to warn and shield unwary men".[15] The enclosures demarcating Prayāga and Prayāga-maṇḍala delimit areas of concentrated divine powers. The circles serve to warn profane man of the danger to which he would be exposed if he is to enter without purificatory rites, as Tuan[16] leads us to believe. That is why religious-minded people approach it in fear and trembling because "they believe it to be the habitation of supernatural powers that far exceed human grasp".[17]

Veṇī or Saṅgama is the confluence of the rivers Gaṅgā and Yamunā at Prayāga (Pl. 1a, b). The physical landscape of Prayāga is dominated by the Gaṅgā and the Yamunā and Prayāga derives much of its sanctimonious importance from their confluence, the confluences of rivers being regarded sacred from the *Ṛgvedic* period.[18] It gives to Prayāga the most attractive natural character which is not found at any other place in the world. There are many rivers in India and in the world, which meet each other at different places but their confluences are not treated in as high a measure as the confluence of the Gaṅgā and the Yamunā at Prayāga. In Indian literature and mind, it is thought to be unparalleled. Some scholars[19] have questioned the existence of the confluence at Prayāga in the hoary past. They, mostly on the basis of literary testimonies, have tried to prove that the Gaṅgā and the Yamunā united together near Rājāpur (birthplace of the famous Hindi poet-saint Tulasīdāsa) on the Yamunā in the Bāndā district during the first millennium B.C. and the confluence has, since then, been gradually shifting[20] downstream so as to occupy the present site at Prayāga. Other scholars, however, have endeavoured to show that the confluence of the two rivers has always taken place at Prayāga. They rule out the possibility of the shifting confluence involving material changes in the courses of the two rivers. Therefore, it is necessary to examine the question whether the change in the courses of the two rivers has shifted the confluence to the present site from any other place or it has always remained at Prayāga from the prehistoric times.

That Saṅgama took place near Rājāpur, about 85 km upstream the Yamunā from Prayāga, is impossible on two grounds. Firstly, archaeological excavations conducted at Śriṅgaverapura, situated at a distance of 40 km from Prayāga, have established its existence in about 1000 B.C. Rāma with his party is said to have crossed the Gaṅgā at this place and to have proceeded towards the hermitage of *ṛṣi* Bharadvāja, located near the confluence of the Gaṅgā and the Yamunā at Prayāga. A mere glance at the map showing the locations of Śriṅgaverapura and Rājāpur would reveal the impossibility of the turning of the Gaṅgā towards Rājāpur, when it has once reached Śriṅgaverapura. Secondly, according to Wadia and Chhibber, the courses of many of the rivers of the plains have, of course, undergone great alterations. They have cited many examples to show that the westering of the river courses is a very pronounced phenomenon for which several causes have been suggested.[21] The westerly drift of the river channels has been ascribed to two main causes: (a) the rotation of the earth from west to east, and (b) the sideward tilting of the whole plain due to the upthrust going on in the Himālayan ranges. The westering of the tributary streams of the Gaṅgā seems to involve an upstream shift of the confluences also. The westward drift of the river courses and the upstream shift of the confluences are thus established facts of geology. There is the lone instance of the eastering in the case of the river Tistā, once a confluent of the Gaṅgā, now flowing into the river Brahmaputra.[22] The possibility of the confluence of the rivers Gaṅgā and Yamunā, once being near Rājāpur at a distance of 85 km from Prayāga, is thus ruled out on grounds of the ancient geography and the current views regarding the changes in the river courses, for that supposition would involve the eastering of the river courses and a downstream shift of the confluence. According to Saran, from Hussainganj to Prayāga the Gaṅgā has definitely moved west as there is an extensive flood plain in the east with signs of old beds, horseshoe lakes and deserted channels. The extensive mound of Tushārāma, a *vihāra* (ancient Buddhist monastery) in the district of Pratāpgarh stands on the northern bank of an old bed of the Gaṅgā below which the flood waters of the river still find their way in rains. Similarly, the Yamunā also appears to have moved south-west, because the soil found to the north of it is dark and friable resembling the mar of the Bundelkhand region.[23] This fact is also borne out by the presence of the outcrops of hard rocks to the north of the Yamunā at Pabhosā, 60 km to the south-west of Prayāga.

As with the westering of the two rivers is tied up the question of the upstream shift of the confluence, this problem is also to be examined. It should be noted, however, that while both the rivers might have migrated westward, the confluence does not appear to have shifted much owing to the hard headlands over which Jhūsī in the east and Jogīghāṭa on the Yamunā in the west are located. Bhikhari Sewanand had rightly remarked, "Since the combined stream is pushed up north from Prayāga by a projection of the Deccan massif, the confluence here is wedged in within an angle and its movement one way or the other appears impossible. It might have been here even in the time of Rāma".[24] A survey of the banks of the Gaṅgā from Belī to Dārāganj would show that here the course of Gaṅgā lies between the Mehadaurī and Jhūsī uplands. This means that the Gaṅgā has never been able to shift far from Prayāga. The antiquity of the confluence at Prayāga has also been proved on the archaeological grounds. The excavations at Bhīṭā on the Yamunā and Bharadvāja Āśrama on the Gaṅgā and excavations at Jhūsī overlooking the confluence have yielded the early Northern Black Polished Wares datable to the eighth-seventh centuries B.C. and the pre-NB horizon datable to the fourteenth century B.C. has been encountered at the latter site. The mounds at these sites came into being when at least one river terrace had already been formed. It would mean that the two rivers were already flowing near Prayāga in the first millennium B.C. and even earlier. This, however, does not suggest that the confluence has always remained fixed near the fort of the Mughal emperor Akbar. Before the bunds were raised by Akbar during the closing quarter of the sixteenth century C.E. for protecting the city from the flood fury of the rivers, the confluence actually used to shift between Jhūsī and Jogīghāṭa. In the summer it generally took place near Jhūsī, and in the rainy season it lay quite close to Jogīghāṭa somewhere in the Baluāghāṭa-Dariābād area. Even today, it shifts every year between the fort and the mound of Jhūsī, sometimes occurring close to the fort and sometimes near Jhūsī. Apart from this minor shift in its site, the confluence of the two rivers has never moved far from this place; and Prayāga has never been devoid of the scenic grandeur of the meeting-point of the Gaṅgā and the Yamunā.

Water is one of the greatest gifts of nature and it has been highly extolled as the originator of life in the Indian tradition. The *Bṛhadāraṇyakopaniṣad* speaks of the origin of truth from water; truth that originated Brahma; Brahma who is the originator of Prajāpati; and Prajāpati who is the father of all Beings.[25] The great water-bodies like the Gaṅgā and the Yamunā have, therefore, naturally been glorified. These two rivers are highly esteemed rivers of India. Traversing through the very heartland of the country, they represent the best of the natural phenomena. Their fall from the snow-clad Himālaya, their bursting into the open plains, their meeting at Prayāga, and the gradual march of the conjoint stream towards the sea are interspersed by such natural beauties that have attracted poets to sing their praises, the saints and seers to adore their banks, the ordinary people to take dips in them and feel purified, and many more souls to treat them as their very mothers. The rivers serve as easy means of irrigation and make the fertile plains of Northern India a rich agricultural country. It was on the banks of these rivers that flourishing seats of civilization have developed from very early times. The large navigable rivers served in olden times as means of communication also, and thus became media for the development of inland and foreign trade. The economic prosperity that they give has thus been abundant. It is, therefore, no wonder that they occupy an immortal place in the thought and culture of the Indian people.

The wonderful sight offered by the mixing of the two rivers – the white coloured Gaṅgā and the blue flowing Yamunā – has often been sung by poets. Kālidāsa (fourth or fifth century C.E.) describes the beauteous tumult of waves and ripples at Saṅgama in the *Raghuvaṁśa*: "Look here, the stream of the Gaṅgā mixed up with the waves of the Yamunā, looks at one place like the string of pearls interspersed with the lustre-imparting sapphires and, at other place, like a garland of white lotuses intertwined with the blue ones".[26] Subandhu (sixth century C.E.) likens the shores of Prayāga in the guise of the junction of the Gaṅgā and the Yamunā with Vāsavadattā's pearl necklace and line of down.[27] Bāṇabhaṭṭa (first half of the seventh century C.E.) fancies that the confluence of the holy rivers came of its own accord for anointing Harṣavardhana as king. To him the blending of the bright light of pearls and of the rays of dark-green emerald in his top-knot presented the appearance of the braidlike stream of the Gaṅgā and the Yamunā at Prayāga.[28] Daṇḍin (latter half of the seventh century C.E.) refers to the surpassing beauty of the famous confluence of the Gaṅgā and the Yamunā at Prayāga as a place of pilgrimage.[29] Dāmodaragupta (last quarter of the eighth and early ninth century C.E.) imagines that the drops of sweat, naturally white because of residing on the body of a fair damsel but mixed with collyrium-tinted tears, when falling on the edge of her bosoms, bear resemblance to the confluence of the waters of the Gaṅgā and the Yamunā at Prayāga.[30] Murāri (tenth century C.E.) is also attracted to the astonishing beauty of the confluence at Prayāga. He says, "The two rivers, flowing through the *antaravedi* which is the original home of the brāhmaṇas, proceed to meet each other as if they bathe the earth with the liquid of the fragrant aloewood and sandal. The Gaṅgā is white because it has lived in the laps of its father, the snowy Himālaya and the Yamunā is black because of the scorching heat of its father, the Sun".[31] In the *Naiṣadhacarita* of Śrīharṣa (twelfth century C.E.) the limpid waters of the Gaṅgā mixed with the dark waters of the Yamunā are compared to the battlefield where the pure fame of the king comes in contact with the dark disgrace of his defeated enemies.[32] The description of the confluence as given by Tulasīdāsa (C.E. 1532-1624) is no less inspiring. In a priceless piece of the nature poetry, he says: "Beautiful is the meeting of the white and dark waters of the two rivers Gaṅgā and Yamunā. Tulasī's heart leaps with joy at the sight of the waves; it looks as if strong groups of calves of the divine cow are grazing green grass".[33] In fact, the view the waters of the two rivers present to the visitors is bewildering. In the winter, the Yamunā looks blue and the Gaṅgā appears white. The waters of the Yamunā present a reddish hue, while those of the Gaṅgā the muddy grey in the rainy season.

The confluence of the two rivers at Prayāga is popularly called Veṇī. The purport of several Purāṇic passages[34] is that it signifies the meeting-point of the Gaṅgā and the Yamunā there. Epigraphic records also support this interpretation.[35] Even the *Tristhalīsetu* says that the Veṇī denotes to the junction of the Sita (white) and Asita (black) rivers at Prayāga. It is located at the meeting-point of the northern bank of the Yamunā and the western bank of the Gaṅgā and is to the east of the (Akṣaya-) vaṭa.[36] In the *Vividhatīrthakalpa* and the *Rāmacaritamānasa* also Veṇī stands for the junction of the Gaṅgā and the Yamunā.[37] According to the Purāṇas, it is twenty bows (120 feet) in length.[38] Bathing at the meeting-point of two rivers is believed to be much more meritorious than at just any point in the course of a river. The confluence seems more than to double the effect of bath. The confluence of the Gaṅgā and the Yamunā at Prayāga is by far the most renowned. The miraculous power of waters at the Saṅgama is attested by scientific investigations carried on there by S.S. Nehru, an eminent scientist, some years ago. He measured the radioactivity of the Gaṅgā and Yamunā waters separately at a respectable distance from the confluence, and also at the junction of the two rivers. He was amazed to notice that the radioactivity at the confluence was much greater than the sum total of the two figures about the two rivers.[39] To complete such a power, according to the tradition, deep beneath the two streams the Sarasvatī mingles its waters with the dark ones of the Yamunā and the clear ones of the Gaṅgā. At one place in the *Skanda* and *Padma Purāṇas*, Veṇī appears to denote the triple floods at Prayāga.[40]

It is generally believed that three rivers viz., Gaṅgā, Yamunā and Sarasvatī (underground between the two), meet at Prayāga, giving the confluence the name Triveṇī. The three together are the triple blessings found nowhere else on the earth. Mystic significance is attached to it. The confluence of the three rivers is compared with Oṁkāra, the mystic *mantra* which comprehends the whole universe, and the three parts of the syllable *Om* (A, U, M) are respectively said to be the Sarasvatī, the Yamunā, and the Gaṅgā.[41] Triveṇī is also the name of a *cakra* in yogic practices. This is the microcosmic counterpart of the confluence at Prayāga; in the human body the three rivers, Gaṅgā, Yamunā and Sarasvatī, are represented by the three main canals, *suṣumnā*, *iḍā*, and *piṅgalā* respectively.[42] The united flood of the Veṇī is represented by the delightful tale of the deeds of Hari and Hara at Prayāga. Faith in Rāma is the river Gaṅgā, contemplation on Brahmā is the Sarasvatī and purificatory ritual is the Yamunā.[43] Kesavadāsa (C.E. 1556-1618) describes the scenic beauty of the confluence in glowing terms. According to him, the grains of fine sand there shine as though heavenly gods with tiny bodies were serving Triveṇī. The flames of the lighted lamps in the evening, reflected in the water, seem like many goddesses bathing there. Gaṅgā's splendour gives pleasure, the Yamunā joins it, and between them the Sarasvatī is like a lovely woman whose body anointed with saffron shines forth beneath a thin black *sāṛī*. He pays the highest encomium on it: "The Triveṇī is like a bridge over the ocean of worldly existence. It has brought all splendour under its sway and shines with the light of the three gods – Brahmā, Viṣṇu and Maheśa. It cures men of the three diseases caused by wind, bile and phlegm and saves them from death. The Triveṇī is pure like the three Vedas. It drives the three sins to the netherworld. The people of the three worlds pay homage to it in all the three ages, because it is the banner of the famed god Vāmana (Viṣṇu). The Triveṇī is charming as the peak of the earth; it is like a road to heaven; or the watery form of the eternal Lord. It is the source of all splendour and bliss. It seems to me a wonderfully chaste and performed object, which by the mere touch washes off countless sins of creatures".[44]

The word Triveṇī occurs in the *Padma* and *Brahma Purāṇas*[45] where it denotes the triple floods at Prayāga; but in the *Rāmacaritamānasa*[46] it also stands for the junction of the Gaṅgā and the Yamunā. It is referred to in the Sena inscriptions (*tīrotsaṅge Triveṇyāḥ*)[47] of the first quarter of the thirteenth century C.E., but it is doubtful whether it denotes to the triple floods. The *Hadīqat-ul-Aqālīma* and the *Tīrthamālās* of Haṁsasoma, Jayavijaya, Saubhāgyavijaya and Śīlavijaya of the sixteenth-seventeenth centuries C.E. mention the presence of the river Sarasvatī at the confluence of the Gaṅgā and the Yamunā.[48] The *Padma* and *Nāradīya Purāṇas* speak of the *vidarbhaṇa* (piercing) of the confluence of the Gaṅgā and the Yamunā by the Sarasvatī at Prayāga. While describing the river Sarasvatī there, they remark that it was created by Brahmā for the purpose of attaining Brahmaloka.[49] If we scrutinise *vidarbhaṇa*, the term would no doubt imply the existence of the Sarasvatī in root form. This meaning is more clearly brought out by another description of the Sarasvatī in Prayāga which points to the existence of the river in an invisible form there.[50]

But the most natural question which arises in this context is whether there was any form of this river in Prayāga or it was purely mythical and conceptual. The apocryphal verse of the *Ṛgveda* refers to the confluence of the rivers Gaṅgā and Yamunā only.[51] The Epics,[52] classical Sanskrit texts already mentioned above, epigraphic records,[53] the Chinese and Muslim works mention the junction of only two rivers at Prayāga. It is only in a few Purāṇic passages and the vernacular literature that the river Sarasvatī in its concealed form is said to join the Gaṅgā and the Yamunā at Prayāga, otherwise they also generally refer to the confluence of the two rivers only. Bhāsa (second century C.E.) has derided the very thought of the presence of a third stream between the Gaṅgā and the Yamunā through the mouth of Bharata: "O Kaikeyī ! you do not appear well standing between mother Kausalyā and mother Sumitrā, like a polluted river let in between the Gaṅgā and the Yamunā".[54] The idea does not appear until the later Purāṇas and is a mythological projection of the ancient river Sarasvatī, on the banks of which the Vedic culture developed. That association of the river Sarasvatī with the confluence became entrenched in the mythology of Prayāga earlier than the fourteenth century C.E. is proved by its mention by Vidyāpati,[55] the famous poet of Mithilā, who lived between C.E. 1368 and C.E. 1475.

The Sarasvatī played an important role in the physical and religious structures of the Āryan life during the Vedic times. It was regarded as the foremost of the rivers in the *Ṛgveda*.[56] The Purāṇic parallel of this reference can be clearly perceived in the *Vāmana Purāṇa* showing how this river had the potency of tearing asunder thousands of hillocks and possibly for this apparent reason, it was called *mahānadī* or greatest of the rivers.[57] Arising from the Śivālika hills in the east, it flowed towards the west and joined the bay of Combay on the west coast in the Vedic period.[58] But in the time of the *Brāhmaṇas* it disappeared in the sands at Vinaśana near

Sūratgarh in northern Rājasthan.[59] The Sarasvatī never flowed in the south-eastern direction followed by the Gaṅgā and the Yamunā. Vinaśana is the western limit of Madhyadeśa and Prayāga represents the eastern point of this geographical entity. Thus, the question of the Sarasvatī flowing towards Prayāga and joining the Gaṅgā and the Yamunā there does not arise. The very idea of the change in its course does not appear feasible. Had it been so it would have formed an angle of 30°-50° towards the south-east from Vinaśana caused by some great tectonic obstructions in its way. But neither geology nor archaeology nor literature nor any tradition speaks of that natural obstruction. From the prehistoric times to the later Vedic period when it dried up, we do not find any evidence to this effect. Therefore, the meeting of the Vedic river Sarasvatī with the Gaṅgā and the Yamunā at Prayāga can not be accepted as a geographical reality. It is only a historical myth.

It is only on account of a deep sense of respect, purity and religiosity associated with the river Sarasvatī that this river was projected to Prayāga, the land of *yajñas* and *tapas*. The itinerant sacrificial sessions were performed and the Vedas were revealed on the banks of the Sarasvatī. Though the river disappeared at Vinaśana during the later Vedic age, its grandeur and sight remained ever fresh in the minds of the authors of the Purāṇas. The river was so important in the Vedic rituals and sacrifices that the neo-Vedic orthodoxy, realizing that the Vedic river could not be physically transferred to Prayāga, fancied that it was there though only in an invisible form. "This myth", suggests V.N. Mishra, "would appear to enshrine the folk memory of a period when the Sarasvatī and the Yamunā did actually converge above ground. Sometime in the Late Harappan times, the Yamunā shifted its course leaving the Sarasvatī in possession of a dry channel, and helped create the myth of the river having gone underground to join the Yamunā together with the Gaṅgā at Prayāga".[60]

The Purāṇic references to the river Sarasvatī revolve round the Vedic tradition. The Purāṇic motive seems to have been the preservation of the Vedic account of the Sarasvatī in the mode it was handed down to it by the Vedic sages. Without the water of the river Sarasvatī, the upholders of the Vedic religion could not accept the sacredness of a place in the same way as the Gaṅgā is regarded as the real purifier and is deemed to be present in all the holy water-bodies in the Purāṇic tradition. Thus, the river Sarasvatī is associated with several *tīrthas* whose association with this river is not mentioned in the Vedic literature. The *Padma Purāṇa* describes how the Sarasvatī reached Puṣkara in an invisible (*antardhāna*) form. It is stated that one who bathes in the Sarasvatī at Puṣkara goes to the Brahmaloka where he enjoys happiness in the company of Brahmā.[61] The Sarasvatī is referred to in Prabhāsa.[62] But in order to distinguish it from the Vedic Sarasvatī, it is called Pratyak Sarasvatī,[63] It rises in the Arbuda (Ābū) mountain and flows through the Arbudāraṇya.[64] In the *Matsya Purāṇa* it is called Arbuda-Sarasvatī and is said to be sacred for *śrāddha* performance.[65] It may be noted that three small rivers – Kapilā, Sarasvatī and Hiraṇyā – join each other near Prabhāsa and fall into the sea. Their confluence is also known as Triveṇī, though actually the Kapilā joins the Sarasvatī which flows into the Hiraṇyā falling into the ocean. It is also mentioned as one of the five rivers under Vārāṇasī. It is said that five rivers, Kiraṇā, Dhūtapāpā, Sarasvatī, Gaṅgā and Yamunā meet at Pañcanada-tīrtha (Pañcagaṅgāghāṭa) in Vārāṇasī.[66] Actually there is only the Gaṅgā river at the ghāṭa; the existence of other four streams is a matter of faith. The *Skanda Purāṇa*[67] gives interesting stories regarding the names of these rivers. The *Nāradīya Purāṇa*[68] speaks of the creation of the Sarasvatī river by Brahmā at Gayā. But the *Vāyu Purāṇa*[69] refers to a Sarasvatī-kuṇḍa created by the goddess Sarasvatī and Prācī Sarasvatī as a holy *tīrtha* there. According to the *Nāradīya Purāṇa*,[70] the Sarasvatī together with a group of one hundred *tīrthas* is present under the Narmadā river. The presence of Sarasvatī is also referred to in the sacred zone of Mathurā.[71] Entwistle has remarked, "What the texts and local devotees wishfully refer to as the Sarasvatī is really no more than a stream serving as a drain that becomes increasingly filthy as it nears the Yamunā, though the amount of water does increase for a while during the monsoon. It begins to the west of Mathurā and flows through the area that is designated Ambikāvana.... Only later Gauḍīya sources include it in their enumeration of the bathing places".[72]

In fact, the account of the Vedic Sarasvatī river as floating in tradition was preserved by the Purāṇic authors by conceiving its presence at several *tīrthas* either in the form of a water-body or in an invisible form. Its sacredness was also transferred to other rivers of the country and the term Sarasvatī became a synonym of river (*nadī*). For instance, the *Vāmana Purāṇa*[73] speaks of the fourfold character of the Sarasvatī. Its course towards the north is called the Sindhu (river Indus), while to the east, south and west it is called the Gaṅgā, the Narmadā and the Yamunā respectively. In the *Mahābhārata*[74] it is said that the world is encompassed by seven Sarasvatīs which are Suprabhā in Puṣkara, Kāñcanākṣī in the Naimiṣa forest, Viśālā in Gayā, Manohradā in Uttarakosala, Suveṇu in Ṛṣabhadvīpa, Oghavatī in Kurukṣetra, and Vimalodakā in Gaṅgādvāra.

So far as the literary references to the Sarasvatī in Prayāga are concerned, its river form is out of question. The association of Prayāga with the performance of sacrifices led to the natural corollary of associating the river Sarasvatī with it. S.N. Roy, however, explains away the presence of the river Sarasvatī in Prayāga in the form of the *kuṇḍas* (pools), "the word Sarasvatī means one which consists of *saras* (ponds)". According to him, 'There are references in the Purāṇas to the three or five *kuṇḍas* at Prayāga and these could have been the most probable form of the river Sarasvatī in Prayāga'.[75] But a direct or indirect allusion to their association with the Sarasvatī is not found in the Purāṇas, digests and other texts. Moreover, the Epic-Purāṇic literature clearly associates these *kuṇḍas* with the river Gaṅgā, through the middle of which it flows there.[76] Of course, the *Mahābhārata*[77] and the *Padma Purāṇa*[78] mention the Sarasvatī as one of the seven streams of the Gaṅgā. But it has been rightly identified with a tributary of the Alakanandā (a branch of the Gaṅgā) in the Garhwāl Himālayan ranges by N.L. Dey.[79] Therefore, the view of S.N. Roy remains a good conjecture having no convincing evidence in its support.

Some other interpretations may also be given. The holy character of Prayāga is attributed to the sacrifice of Prajāpati. Sarasvatī, the goddess of learning in the Epic-Purāṇic literature, is regarded as the consort of Prajāpati. This may have been another reason for conceiving Sarasvatī present in Prayāga. The Sasurakhaderī (Ambā),[80] a rivulet which joins the Yamunā at a small distance from the confluence near Kakarahāghāṭa, could have been misunderstood to be the Vedic river Sarasvatī by the people. Even the confluence of the Gaṅgā and the Yamunā alone may be called as Triveṇī. The three currents visible to the eyes there are the current of the Gaṅgā from the left, the current of the Yamunā from the right and the conjoint stream of the two in the front, which give the title Triveṇī to the confluence. It is just like the meeting-point of the two roads which in popular parlance is known as a crossing of the three (*tripatha*) meaning thereby that the two roads coming from the two sides, joining each other and going to the third direction. How far this interpretation is correct may be a matter of argument.

The earliest reference to the confluence of the rivers Gaṅgā and Yamunā occurs in a paralipomena verse of the *Ṛgveda*. Prayāga is mentioned first in the Epics and the concept of Prayāga-maṇḍala is first noticed in the Purāṇas. Thus, the sacred complex beginning with the Saṅgama gradually extended to the surrounding areas. This shows how a single sacred site in course of time develops into a sacred zone. Such extension of the sacred topography is also found at other *tīrthas*, such as in Kāśī where four civic units – Antargṛha, Avimukta, Vārāṇasī and Kāśī – with definite geographical boundaries are mentioned in the Purāṇic texts.[81] The creation of new holy spots on the periphery of the sacred place by the *tīrtha*-controllers (Paṇḍās and Purohitas) to lure the pilgrims for lavish endowments from time to time possibly necessitated it. It may also have been due to the "positive technique in the process of 'land taking' or land settlement by the pioneers" of the *tīrtha*.[82]

It is significant that the sacred complex is divided into three parts and not into four in keeping with the quarternary principle. The tripartite division seems to reflect the Sāṅkhya theory of the three *guṇas* (qualities), viz. *sattva*, *rajas* and *tamas*. The supreme Brahma is also divided into these three qualities consisting of Viṣṇu, Brahmā and Śiva; and it may be said that this is the basic principle that led to the tripartite division of the sacred complex of Prayāga, which is also called Brahmakṣetra in the *Padma* and *Skanda Purāṇas*.[83] The Purāṇas refer to the close association of Prayāga with the prominent gods of the Hindu Trinity. Once again we notice the emphasis on the number three when the third river Sarasvatī in the concealed form was conceived to meet the Gaṅgā and the Yamunā there, thus giving the confluence the name Triveṇī. This idea of trinity continues to dominate later Hinduism, the highest magnitude of which is met with in Prayāga.

REFERENCES

1. पञ्चयोजनविस्तीर्णं प्रयागस्य तु मण्डलम् ।
   MP, 107.9a, 110.8a = *TvK*, 147, 151=*TS*, 7, 15, 50=*TP*, 328, 345; *PdP*, III.45.8a=*TC*, 23, 50; *NP*, II.63.44a, 162a.
2. Roy, U.N., *Studies in Ancient Indian History and Culture*, Vol. I, p.179.
3. यद्वा क्रोशशब्दोऽत्र योजनपरस्तेन मण्डलक्षेत्रमेवानेनोक्तं भवति । *TS, 16.*
   अत्र योजनं क्रोशः । *TS*, 101.
   योजनं क्रोश इति प्राञ्चः ।। *TP*, 176.
4. Vishwakarma, Ishwar, S., 'Dūrion kī Māpa: Yojana, Li and Farsakh', *Bharatiya Itihasa Sankalana Samiti Patrika*, Vol. 3, 1985, p.233.
5. प्रयागस्तु ब्रह्मयूपोपलक्षितः प्रदेशः ।
   TC, 23; *TP*, 328.
6. अत्र ब्रह्मयूपं मध्ये शङ्कुं प्रकल्प्य सार्धयोजनद्वयपरिमितया रज्ज्वा
   वर्तुलक्षेत्रे निष्पादिते पञ्चयोजनं मण्डलं ज्ञेयम् । *TS*, 15.
   ब्रह्मयूपमवधीकृत्य सार्धयोजनद्वयमिते सूत्रे चतुर्दिक्षु भ्रामिते
   वर्तुलं प्रयागमण्डलं ज्ञेयम् ।। *TP*, 328.
7. Olsson, Gunnar, *Birds in Egg/Eggs in Bird*, p.19e.
8. *Ibid.*, p.20e.
9. *Bhūparikramaṇam*, III.8, 21.
10. आबालचन्द्रादारभ्य प्रतिष्ठानपुरावधि ।
    नीलकण्ठपुरं यावत् पञ्चयोजनसम्मतम् ।।
    Ibid., III. 4.

11. *Ibid.*, III. 4-5.
12. *Ibid.*, III. 9, 19.
13. *Mbh*, III. 83.72=*TP*, 321; *NP*, II.63.54b-55a, 129b-130; *AgP*, 111.5; *PdP*, III.39.72b-73a, 41.4-5, 47.8; *MP*, 103.3-4=*TvK*, 136=*TC*, 47=*TS*, 15=*TP*, 323, 327, 342.
14. प्रतिष्ठानशब्देन तत्कूपो लक्ष्यते ततश्च प्राच्यां कूपोऽवधिः। उत्तरतो वासुकिह्रदः । पश्चिमे कम्बलाश्वतरौ ।
    दक्षिणे बहुमूलकः । एवं दिगवधिषूक्तेषु तेभ्यश्चतुरस्रसाधनप्रकारेण कोणेषु
    साधितेषु चतुरस्रं यत्संपद्यते तत्प्रयागक्षेत्रमिति संपिण्डितार्थः ।
    TS, 15.
    गङ्गापूर्वतः सामुद्रकूपः, दक्षिणे बहुमूलकः, पश्चिमे कम्बलाश्वतरौ,
    उत्तरस्यां वासुकिह्रद इति दिशामवधयः । अनेन क्रमेण कोणसूत्रं साधयित्वा
    चतुरस्रं प्रयागक्षेत्रं ज्ञातव्यमिति वदन्ति । *TP*, 327.
15. Tuan, Yi-Fu, 'Sacred space: Exploration of an idea', in *Dimensions of Human Geography*, p.92.
16. *Ibid.*, p.85.
17. *Ibid.*, p.98.
18. *Ṛgveda*, VIII. 6.28; *Vājasaneyī Saṁhitā*, 26.15.
19. Katju, K.N., 'Where was Bharadvāja Āshrama?', *The A.B. Patrika*, August 19, 1945; Mittal, C.P., 'Why Bharadvāja Āshram Shifted?', *The A.B. Patrika*, Sept. 2, 1945; Ghosh, N.N., 'Sanctity of Present Bharadvāja Āshram', *The A.B. Patrika*, Sept. 2, 1945.
20. Bhikhari, Sewanand, 'Rāma's Journey to Chitrakūṭa', *The A.B. Patrika*, Sept. 16, 1945; Shastri, R.M., 'Full Light on the Real Site of the Bharadvāja Āshram', *Journal of the G.N. Jha Research Institute*, Vol. III, 1945, p.159; Saran, B., 'Geomorphology of the Saṅgam Region', *JUPHS*, Vol. II(2), 1945, pp.46-53.
21. Wadia, D.N., *Geology of India*, pp.389-390; Chhibber, H., *Physical Basis of Geography of India*, p.56.
22. Wadia, D.N., *op.cit.*, p.390.
23. Saran, B., *op.cit.*, p.51.
24. Bhikhari, Sewanand, *op.cit.*
25. *Bṛhadāraṇyakopaniṣad*, 5.5.1.
26. *Raghuvaṁśa*, XIII.54.
27. हारलतारोमराजिव्याजगङ्गायमुनासंगमप्रयागतटाभ्याम् ।
    Vāsavadattā, p.44.
28. शिखण्डाभरणभुवा मुक्ताफलालोकेन मरकतमणिकिरणकलापेन
    चान्योन्यसंवलनवृजिनेन प्रयागप्रवाहवेणिकावारिणेवागत्य स्वयमभिषिच्यमानम्--- ।
    Harṣacarita, Ucchavāsa II, p.34.
29. *AsK*, pp.59, 92, 194.
30. वाससितस्वेदजलं कज्जलमलिनाश्रुवारिणा मिश्रम् ।
    कुचतटपतितं तस्याः प्रयागसम्भेदसलिलमनुकुरुते ॥
    Kuṭṭanīmatam, 297.

31. *Anargharāghava*, VII, 125.
32. *Naiṣadhacarita*, XII.12.
33. सोहै सितासित को मिलिबो, तुलसी हुलसै हिय हेरि हलोरे ।
    मानों हरे तृन चारु चरैं, वगरे सुर धेनु के धौल कलोरे ।।
    Kavitāvalī, VII. 144.
34. *NP*, II.63.6, 7, 11; *PdP*, VI.81.38, 126.41, 43, 52, 56, 72, 128.65, 68, 242, 265.
35. श्रीमत्प्रयागे मन्वन्तरादौ वेण्यां स्नात्वा देवश्रीगङ्गादित्यसन्निधौ ।
    The Kamauli copperplate of Jayacandra (C.E. 1172),
    Ep.Ind., Vol. IV, p.122, l.22; वेण्यां स्नात्वा भगवन्तं देवदेवं ।
    The Benares copperplate of Karṇadeva (C.E. 1042),
    Ep.Ind., Vol. II, p.244, l.40.
36. वेण्या एव च सितासितमिति संज्ञान्तरम् । इदमेव क्षेत्रमवधिभिरुपलक्ष्योक्तम्–कालिन्द्या उत्तरे कूले भागीरथ्याश्च दक्षिणे ।
    वटश्च पूर्वदिग्भागे स्नातः किमनुशोचसि । *TS*, 16.
37. *Vividhatīrthakalpa*, p.85; *Rāmacaritamānasa*, VI. 119.5-8.
38. धनुर्विंशतिविस्तीर्णे सितनीलाम्बुसङ्गमे ।
    NP, II.63.90a; *PdP*, VI. 127.163a=*TS*, 16, 32=*TP*, 328, 335.
    TC, 29 ascribes it to the *MP*.
39. Sukul, K.N., *Varanasi Down the Ages*, p.197.
40. *SkP*, IV.7.65=*TS*, 12; *PdP*, VI.23.33.
41. ओमित्येकाक्षरं ब्रह्म परब्रह्माभिदायकम् ।
    तदेव वेणी विज्ञेया सर्वसौख्यप्रदायिनी ।।
    अकारः शारदा प्रोक्ता प्रद्युम्नस्तत्र जायते ।
    उकारो यमुना प्रोक्ताऽनिरुद्धस्तज्जलात्मकः ।।
    मकारो जाह्नवी गङ्गा तत्र संकर्षणो हरिः ।
    एवं त्रिवेणी विख्याता वेदवीजं प्रकीर्तिता ।। *TS* (*BP*), 8.
42. Kooij, K.R. van, *Worship of the Goddess according to the Kālikā Purāṇa*, p.20., fn. 4.
43. *Rāmacaritamānasa*, I.1.7-10.
44. *Rāmacandrikā*, I.32-33.
45. *PdP*, VI. 23.32, 36; *BP* q. in *TS*, 8.
46. *Rāmacaritamānasa*, II.203.3-4.
47. The Madanapada copperplate of Viśvarūpasen, *Ep. Ind.*, Vol. XXXIII, p.322, verse 12; The Calcutta Sahitya Parisad copperplate of Viśvarūpasen, *Corpus of Bengal Inscriptions*, p.324, verse 14; The Edilpur copperplate of Keśavasen, *Corpus of Bengal Inscriptions*, p.335, verse 13.
48. *Hadīqat-ul-Aqālīma*, folio 56; *Prācina Tīrthamālāsaṅgraha*, pp.15, 24, 77, 108.
49. सितासिता तु या धारा सरस्वत्या विदर्भिता ।
    तं मार्गं ब्रह्मलोकस्य सृष्टिकर्ता ससर्ज वै ।।
    PdP, VI.126.35=*TC*, 20=*TS*, 7=*TP*, 331; *NP*, II.63.23b-24a.

50. गङ्गायमुनयोर्मध्ये यत्र गुप्ता सरस्वती ।
    प्रयागः स तु विज्ञेयः सर्वपापप्रणाशनम् ॥
    SkP, V.ii.71.62.
51. *Ṛgveda*, *khila*, 22.1.
52. *Mbh*, III.83.70, 80, 85.13, 93.6, XIII.26.34; *Rām*, II.54.2, 55.4.
53. The Mainamati copperplate of Laḍahcandradeva, *Pakistan Archaeology*, No.3, pp.39-40, ll.31-32; The Baroda copperplate of Karka II, *Indian Antiquary*, Vol. XII, p.159, l.23; The Cintra Praśasti of the reign of Sāraṅgadeva, *Ep.Ind.*, Vol. I, p.287, verse 26; The Mau Chandell Stone Inscription of Madanavarmā, *Ep. Ind.*, Vol. I, p.201, verse 40; The Ridhpur copperplate of Bhavadatta-varman, *Ep. Ind.*, Vol. XIX, p.102, ll.4-5; The Khajuraho Inscription of Dhaṅgadeva, *Ep. Ind.*, Vol. I, p.146, verse 55.
54. मम मातुश्च मातुश्च मध्यस्था त्वं न शोभसे ।
    गङ्गायमुनयोर्मध्ये कुनदीव प्रवेशिता ॥
    Pratimānāṭakam, III.17.
55. तीर्थराजमहाक्षेत्रं नदीत्रयसमन्वितम् ।
    सितासितारुणा राजन् वेणीरूपेण संस्थिता ॥
    Bhūparikramaṇam, II.3.
56. *Ṛgveda*, II. 41.16.
57. *VamP*, 32.1-4; Kane, *History of Dharmaśāstra*, Vol. IV, p.556, fn.
58. एकाचेतत् सरस्वती नदीनां शुचिर्यती गिरिभ्य आ समुद्रात् ।
    Ṛgveda, VII.95.2a.
59. *Tāṇḍya Brāhmaṇa*, 25.10.1; *Pañcaviṁśa Brāhmaṇa*, 25.10.1,16; *Mbh*, III.82.111, IX.36.1, 37.4; Kane, *History of Dharmaśāstra*, Vol. IV, p.557.
60. Mishra, V.N., 'Climate, A Factor in the Rise and Fall of the Indus Civilization—Evidence from Rajasthan and Beyond', in *An Archaeological Tour along the Ghaggar-Hakra River*, pp.148-115.
61. *PdP*, V.18.202-203.
62. *NP*, II.70.39-40; *SkP*, VII.i.185.1-6.
63. *BhagP*, XI.30.10.
64. *PdP*, VI.134.2-7.
65. *MP*, 21.38.
66. *SkP*, IV.59. 115-117; *NP*, II.51. 15-16.
67. *SkP*, IV.59. 101-114.
68. *NP*, II.44.15.
69. *VaP*, II.46. 62, 50.29.
70. *NP*, II.77.6.
71. *NP*, II.79.42; *VP*, 159.48, 173.13, 174.53, 64.
72. Entwistle, A.W., *Braj : Centre of Krishna Pilgrimage*, p.326.
73. *VamP*, 42.7-8.
74. *Mbh*, IX. 37.12-28; Kane, *op.cit.*, Vol. IV, p.686.
75. Roy, S.N., 'Some aspects of the river Sarasvatī as gleaned from the Purāṇas', in *Historical and Cultural Studies in the Purāṇas*, pp.310-311.

76. *Mbh*, III. 83.69=*TP*, 321; *PdP*, III. 39.69b-70a, 41.13b-14a, 47.4; *VsP*, 7.384; *NP*, II. 63.45, 50b-51a; *AgP*, 111.2b-3a; *KP*, I. 34.28; *MP*, 103.12, 109.4=*TvK*, 137, 151=*TC*, 23-24=*TS*, 6, 15=*TP*, 323-325.
77. *Mbh*, VI.7.44-45.
78. *PdP*, III.33.68.
79. Dey, N.L., *The Geographical Dictionary of Ancient and Medieval India*, p.181.
80. The Sasurakhaderī river may be identified with the river Ambā in Vatsabhūmi (tract of land between the Gaṅgā and the Yamunā), to which princess Ambā, the eldest daughter of the king of Kāśī, carried off by Bhīṣma to be married to Vicitravīrya but released, was changed after death with only half her body in consequence of her ascetic merit, while with the other half she remained a maiden as before. The river is described as filled only during the rainy seasons, abounding with crocodiles, crooked in her course, and destitute of easy access to her water. *Cf. Mbh*, V.187.34-40, 188.17-18.
81. EcK, Diana L., *Banaras : City of Light*, pp.350-355.
82. Agrawala, V.S., *Matsya Purāṇa – A Study*, p.115.
83. *PdP*, VI.91.16; *SkP*, II.13 (4). 49.

Chapter III

SUB-*TĪRTHAS*

In a major *tīrtha* are enshrined several important and cognate *tīrthas*, which may be called its *upatīrthas*; for instance, the *Varāha Purāṇa* enumerates many holy spots in the sacred complex of Mathurā, the *Vāyu Purāṇa* in Gayā and the *Kāśīkhaṇḍa* of the *Skanda Purāṇa* in Vārāṇasī. Prayāga is famous as the king of sacred places. Therefore, all *tīrthas*, cities, streams, mountains, gods, and sages dwell here, desiring their own liberation as well as their attendance being always registered in the kingly court. Prayāga is, thus, dense with holy spots. Prayāga is said to contain so many holy spots that *ṛṣi* Mārkaṇḍeya declared his inability to enumerate them in total.[1] This statement suggests that various objects and spots, viz. shrines, trees, confluence of the Gaṅgā and the Yamunā, etc. existing in this sacred place were perceived as *tīrthas*. The sub-*tīrthas* that fall under Prayāga are not separate units which happen to be in the same geographical complex, but are parts of a whole, i.e. Prayāga which is supported and vivified by the two most holy rivers. These sub-*tīrthas* also commanded veneration of pilgrims who visited Prayāga. The main idea in enumerating the sub-*tīrthas* is that the pilgrims should plastically become aware that at Prayāga they are in a most sacred space, and after visiting such a place they need not go to any other *tīrtha*. The cluster of the holy spots at Prayāga is the spatial extension of the sacred ecumene, which served the cause of socio-religious harmony and integration at various levels, local and national, of the cultural personality of India.

Most of the texts consulted describe a few out of the hundred thousands of holy spots at Prayāga, with the result that the disagreement about their number and names in the texts is bewildering. While the *Mahābhārata* supplies a list of six sub-*tīrthas*, the *Kūrma Purāṇa* refers to the sanctity of eleven, the *Agni Purāṇa* of twelve and the *Nāradīya Purāṇa* of twenty-one holy spots. The *Matsya Purāṇa* and the *Padma Purāṇa* contain the names of twenty-five sub-*tīrthas*. The number of holy spots at Prayāga range from twenty-one to thirty five in the treatises on pilgrimage. Thus, the number of sub-*tīrthas* under Prayāga shot up from six in the *Mahābhārata* to more than twenty in the Purāṇas and the treatises. This gradual proliferation of sub-*tīrthas* at Prayāga is to be viewed in the light of the fact that the number of sacred places in India itself swelled from a few hundreds in the post-Vedic period to about four thousand by the medieval times.[2] The number of sub-*tīrthas* at Prayāga appears to be very insignificant when compared with that of Vārāṇasī where around three hundred and fifty sub-*tīrthas* exist. The multiplication of *tīrthas* in a single place, adding power to power, is well-known in Hindu sacred geography.

In this chapter, an attempt has been made to identify all the sub-*tīrthas* of Prayāga on the basis of materials found mainly in the Epics, Purāṇas, and the treatises on *tīrtha*. The purpose is also to show the extent to which the different traditions of Hindu civilization are reflected in the sacred geography of Prayāga.

The holy spots at Prayāga are generally located by the literary sources near the banks of the rivers in the sacred zone. But the texts are often vague about their situation in most cases. It is a very tedious task, sometimes even a fruitless effort, to find out the exact location of all the holy spots of antiquity. We have, however, made endeavours to locate the sub-*tīrthas* with the help of available meagre data as far as possible. Many of them are still regarded sacred by modern pilgrims. Therefore, an attempt has been made to solve many of the doubts and difficulties about their identifications by means of actual journeys to them and investigations on the spot. The sub-*tīrthas* at Prayāga (Fig. 2) referred to in the texts are arranged here in an alphabetical order. However, Akṣayavaṭa and Saṅgama are hereby being excluded, for they have been dealt with separately due to their complex nature.

1. *Agni-tīrtha* : The Purāṇas[3] locate it on the southern bank of the Yamunā. It may be identified with the present Agni-tīrtha at Arail which is visited by the pilgrims on the second day during the ten-day *bahirvedi parikramā* (outer circumambulation) of Prayāga. People who bathe here are held out a promise of stay in heaven; and death at this *tīrtha* is said to liberate one from the cycle of rebirth.[4]

2. *Anaraka-tīrtha* : It is to the west of Agni-tīrtha on the southern bank of Yamunā and is sacred to god Dharmarāja. The *Kūrma Purāṇa*[5] refers to it as Anaraka-tīrtha; but the *Matsya*[6] and *Nāradīya*[7] *Purāṇas* mention it as Naraka-tīrtha. It is named Vāsaraka-tīrtha and Haravara-tīrtha in the *Agni Purāṇa*[8] and the *Padma Purāṇa*,[9] respectively. The *Tīrthavivecanakāṇḍa*[10] calls it as Naraka-tīrtha. Kane[11] proposes to read Anaraka-tīrtha and holds that other names are misreadings because several *tīrthas* called Anaraka are known at other sacred places also. It is said that people go to heaven by

Pl. 1a. Saṅgama with the wall of Akbar's fort in the background

Pl. 1b. Saṅgama viewed from the river

Pl. 2. Bharadvājeśvara Temple

Pl. 3a. Nāga Vāsuki Temple

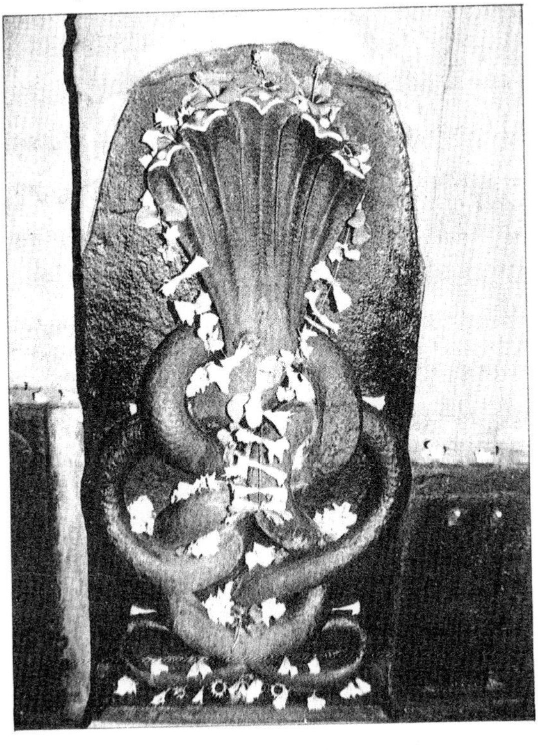

Pl. 3b. Icon of Nāga Vāsuki

Pl. 4. Daśāśvamedheśvara Temple

Pl. 5. General view of the mound of Jhūsī

Pl. 6. Samudrakūpa

Pl. 7. Temple of Someśvaranātha

Pl. 8. Diminishing Vāsuki-pond

Pl. 9. New Akṣayavaṭa inside the fort

Pl. 10. Ritual shaving — an indispensable part of the pilgrimage

Pl. 11. Pilgrims bathing at Saṅgama

Pl. 12. Sadhus at Kumbha Mela

Pl. 13. Suicide by jumping from the Banyan tree (Prayāgapaṭṭa of c. 10th century C.E.)

Pl. 14a. A procession of Nāgās arriving at Saṅgama for the ritual bath, Ardha Kumbha Melā, 1948

Pl. 14b. A procession of sādhus heading towards Saṅgama for the ritual bath, Kumbha Melā, 1977

Pl. 15a. Bathing crowd in the Kumbha Melā, 1954

Pl. 15b. Bathing crowd in the Kumbha Melā, 1989

Pl. 16a. A scene of bodies trampled in the Kumbha stampede, 1954

Pl. 16b. Instinct of self-preservation in the panicky situation of Kumbha stampede, 1954

bathing at this holy spot and those who die here are not born again.[12] It is further stated that one, who virtuously bathes and propitiates god Dharmarāja here on the fourteenth day of the dark fortnight, is undoubtedly freed from the gravest of sins.[13]

3. *Bharadvāja Āśrama* : The *Rāmāyaṇa*[14] locates it near the confluence of the rivers Gaṅgā and Yamunā. It is identified with the present site of the Bharadvāja Āśrama near Anand Bhavan, the former house of the Nehru family, in Colonelganj locality. The cliff near the *āśrama* clearly suggests that at one time the river Gaṅgā was flowing nearby, though now it is a couple of kilometres away. In fact, if the two mud bunds that separate this area from the Gaṅgā are removed, the waters of the river would start re-washing the ancient bank at Bharadvāja Āśrama.

The *Rāmāyaṇa* furnishes an elaborate description of this hermitage. It was visited by Rāma, together with Lakṣamaṇa and Sītā, during his exile.[15] Bharata also came to this hermitage with his retinue while in search of Rāma.[16] The *āśrama* site was but a small cleared spot with the forest all round,[17] though the land coming under its jurisdiction was about a *krośa* in extent.[18]

It was a reputed centre of education in ancient India. The final redaction of the *Narasiṁha Purāṇa* took place here. The *Śiva Purāṇa* and the *Padma Purāṇa* were also recited during the religious discourses held here.[19] Tulasīdāsa has eulogised the *āśrama* in the opening couplets of his *magnum opus*. It was in all likelihood here that he became conversant with the Rāma-story during his stay in the month of Māgha, so beautifully alluded to with the help of Bharadvāja-Yājñavalkya dialogue in the *Rāmacaritamānasa*. A temple enshrining Bharadvājeśvara-liṅga, mentioned in the *Śiva Purāṇa*,[20] still exists at the site (Pl. 2).

The excavations at Bharadvāja Āśrama during 1977-79 revealed the occupation of the two widely separated periods. Sherds of the Black-slipped and Northern Black Polished Wares were found intermixed in a matrix of sandy loam. In a part of the site some post-holes were noticed. There also occurred a few charcoal bits and lumps of clay with reed-impressions, but there were no regular floors or house remains.[21] This kind of evidence suggests that the site may really have been that of an *āśrama* with a few odd huts here and there. The only other occupation met with in the Bharadvāja Āśrama was that of the Gupta period, assignable to *circa* fourth-sixth centuries C.E., as evidenced by the typical pottery and terracotta seals and sealings and brick structure.[22] The nature of the remains shows that the earliest time when the site could have existed was that of the early phase of the Northern Black Polished Ware which was around the beginning of the seventh century B.C. It should be noted that early NBP is the lowest common denominator at all the Rāmāyaṇic sites and so according to Lal and Dikshit[23] it represents the time of the *Rāmāyaṇa* episode. The site was evidently deserted in *circa* sixth century B.C. and was re-occupied only during the fourth-fifth centuries C.E. The desertion of the Bharadvāja Āśrama is also alluded in the *Mahābhārata*[24] which says that the Kālakeya *daityas* (demons) slew a full score of brāhmaṇas of subdued souls in the retreat of Bharadvāja.

4. *Bhogavatī* : It is located to the north of Vāsukihrada.[25] The *Tīrthacintāmaṇi*[26] reads : *'bhogavatī nadī snāne'*, indicating that Bhogavatī-tīrtha was situated on the very bank of the Gaṅgā. The *Agni Purāṇa*[27] says :*'Vāsukerbhogavatyatra'*; and hence, Kane[28] rightly identifies it with Vāsuki-tīrtha. It forms one of the points of the sacrificial altar of Prajāpati at Prayāga.[29] Bhogavatī is regarded as the general name for the Nāga-capital in the netherworld and the mythological serpent Vāsuki is extolled as the lord presiding over it.[30] The *Mahābhārata*[31] and the *Padma Purāṇa*[32] clearly describe it as an excellent *tīrtha* dedicated to the serpent Vāsuki, and state that one, who performs ablutions here, obtains the merit of an *aśvamedha* sacrifice. The temple of Nāga Vāsuki (Pl. 3a, b) on the bank of the Gaṅgā in the Buxi Mohullah possibly represents the ancient site of Bhogavatī. An Indian scholar, writing in 1873, reports that 'the temple is beautifully situated amidst a grove of trees, overlooking the Gaṅgā, which flows just under it. It is a massive building on an elevated terrace, looked quite new having been repaired but a hundred years ago. The stone ghāṭa under it was constructed by the millionaire of the adjoining locality of Dārāganj. About a foot and a half high and carved out of a black stone set in the front wall of the cella, the image of Nāga Vāsuki hovers as if enraged'.[33] A large fair is held here on the *nāgapañcamī* day every year. To the pilgrim, the merit of bathing at the sacred confluence of the Gaṅgā and the Yamunā is not complete until he visits the temple of the king of serpents.

5. *Daśāśvamedhika* : The *Mahābhārata*[34] and the Purāṇas[35] locate it near the Bhogavatī-tīrtha on the bank of the river Gaṅgā. The *Agni Purāṇa*[36] mentions this *tīrtha* as Aśvamedha. It may be identified with a ghāṭa of this name on the right bank of the Gaṅgā in the Dārāganj locality. The *Brahma Purāṇa* as quoted in the *Tristhalīsetu*[37] says that there lies an auspicious Brahmakuṇḍa on the western bank of the Gaṅgā where Lord Brahmā performed ten *aśvamedha* sacrifices, and hence the site came to be known as Daśāśvamedhika. According to Sinha,[38] it was so called because the Bhāraśiva Nāgas, took their ceremonial baths here in the Gaṅgā at the end of the ten *aśvamedha* sacrifices. But Jayaswal[39] and Upadhyaya[40] are of opinion that the Bhāraśiva Nāgas, who were one of

the Hindu revivalist dynasties in the second century C.E., had their lustral bath in the Gaṅgā at Vārāṇasī on the completion of their ten *aśvamedhas*, on account of which the famous Daśāśvamedhaghāṭa at Vārāṇasī was so named. Roy,[41] however, associates this holy spot with the Gupta king Samudragupta who is credited with the performance of many *aśvamedha* sacrifices in a Vākāṭaka record. The Prayāga-*Praśasti* of Samudragupta is silent about it. A line in the inscription, however, indicates his intention of performing a sacrifice and that intention was later fulfilled is clear from his coins and the inscriptions of his successors.[42] Prayāga might have appealed to the emperor as the proper place for the *aśvamedha* sacrifice, as tradition records many sacrifices at this place. Whatever the source of its name, this *tīrtha* has long been said to confer the lavish benefit of the performance of the *aśvamedha* sacrifice upon the devotee who bathes here; he is also assured to become a very rich, handsome, wise, generous, and virtuous man in his next brith.[43] Even a mere sight of this holy spot is capable of reducing to ashes crores of great sins in the same way as the entire heap of cotton is burnt by the fire in no time.[44] According to the *Śiva Purāṇa*, Brahmeśvara-liṅga was formerly installed at the holy spot of Daśāśvamedha at Prayāga by Brahmā. It is the bestower of the fourfold aims of life.[45] A renovated temple called Daśāśvamedheśvara (Pl. 4) still commands veneration.

6. *Haṁsaprapatana* : The *Mahābhārata*[46] and the Purāṇas[47] refer to this holy spot. The *Tīrthavivecanakāṇḍa*[48] mentions it as Haṁsapratapana. It is situated to the north of Pratiṣṭhāna and to the east of the Bhāgīrathī.[49] According to Roy,[50] the site of this *tīrtha* is now represented by the eastern sandy bank of the river Gaṅgā. But Agrawala[51] has rightly identified it with the expansive swampy area overgrown with weeds towards the north of Jhūsī on the eastern bank of the Gaṅgā. He observes that the name Haṁsaprapatana is meaningful signifying the place where the migratory swans alight on their way from and back to their abode in the Himālaya during the months of October–November. The area north of Jhūsī and on the eastern bank of the Gaṅgā offers a natural attractive ground for the winter-home of these birds; and, therefore, this is truly called Haṁsaprapatana.[52] He also remarks that "there is still a Haṁsakūpa at Jhūsī to mark the Haṁsaprapatana-tirtha".[53] It may be noted here that the *Tīrthacintāmaṇi*[54] reads: "*tataḥ Pratiṣṭhānāduttarasmin Gaṅgāpūrvataḥ Haṁsaprapatanam nāma kuṇḍam tatra snāne*". The Haṁsaprapatana-kuṇḍa can be associated with the Haṁsakūpa, because the meaning of both the words is quite identical, i.e. a pool or well associated with the swans. It is said that bathing at this spot enables one to acquire a reward of the performance of an *aśvamedha* sacrifice and the residence in heaven as long

as the sun and the moon shine in the firmament.[55] The same merit is promised even by the very remembrance of this holy spot.[56]

7. *Kambalāśvatara Nāgas* : The site of the Kambalāśvatara Nāgas forms the western boundary of the Prajāpatikṣetra.[57] The *Kūrma*[58] and *Padma*[59] *Purāṇas* locate it on the southern bank of the Yamunā, but the *Matsya*[60] and *Nāradīya*[61] *Purāṇas* vaguely place it on the spacious bank of the Yamunā. The *Tīrthavivecanakāṇḍa*[62] reads '*dakṣiṇe yamunātaṭe*' but notes '*vipule yamunātaṭe*' and '*Gaṅgāyamunayostaṭe*' as its *variants* in P and B, respectively. An old *gāthā* in the *Bhūridatta-Jātaka* refers to Kambala and Assatara (Aśvatara) as residing in the Nāga-world near the Yamunā, who were ordered by their king Dhataraṭṭha to summon all the Nāgas and gherao Vārāṇasī for avenging the insult caused to him by the king of Kāśī.[63] The site seems to have been represented by two separate shrines dedicated to the serpents named Kambala and Aśvatara, who are regarded as legendary Nāga chieftains in the religious literature of ancient India. It is now associated with one of the same name on the banks of the shallow pool called Sainī in the village Dadarī in Naini industrial area. But it is difficult to identify the site of these two Nāga shrines with this place; for, it is said to represent the western boundary of the Prajāpatikṣetra whereas the present one lies in the southern direction. The *Tīrthacintāmaṇi*[64] interprets '*Kambalāśvatarau nāgau vipule Yamunātaṭe*' as '*Yamunāyāḥ uttarakūle Kambalāśvatarasamīpe Prayāgapaścime*'. This clearly shows that the site of the Kambalāśvatara Nāgas was situated on the northern bank of the Yamunā somewhere possibly near Baluāghāṭa. It is said that he, who bathes in and drinks the water of the Yamunā at this holy spot, is freed of all his sins; and by paying a visit to the nearby shrine of Lord Śiva, he liberates from bondage his ten previous and ten subsequent generations.[65] He is also assured to derive the merits of the performance of an *aśvamedha* sacrifice and enjoyment of the bliss in heaven till the time of dissolution if he sprinkles the holy waters over his body on this spot.[66]

8. *Koṭi-tīrtha* : The Purāṇas mention this *tīrtha*. It is identified with the present Śivakuṭī on the right bank of the Gaṅgā. It is said that he, who breathes his last at this holy spot, is honoured in heaven for a period of ten million years[67] and after the exhaustion of his religious virtues he is reborn as a handsome person in the most wealthy family.[68]

9. *Pratiṣṭhāna* : Some Purāṇas[69] locate it on the north bank of the Gaṅgā, but some[70] on the north bank of the Yamunā. Other Purāṇas,[71] however, place it on the east side of the Gaṅgā. The ruins of ancient Pratiṣṭhāna are now represented by the high mounds of Jhūsī (Pl. 5) on the eastern bank of the Gaṅgā overlooking the confluence. The remains are spread over an area of about four square miles but a large portion of the site appears

to have been eroded by the Gaṅgā during the course of centuries.

Pratiṣṭhāna was the most important locality of Prayāga. It was founded by king Ila[72] and was the capital of Purūravas and other kings of the Lunar dynasty.[73] Kālidāsa lays the scene of his drama *Vikramorvaśīyam* in Pratiṣṭhāna. He has given an imaginary account of the palace of Purūravas, which was the crest jewel of Pratiṣṭhāna and the splendour of which was reflected in the waters of the Gaṅgā-Yamunā-saṅgama.[74] A mass of mythological narrations centres around Pratiṣṭhāna. It contains the places of pilgrimage called Haṁsaprapatana and Urvaśīpulina on its northern side and Samudrakūpa in its heart. It was also known as Samudrakūpa because of a well of this name there.[75]

An inscription of Trilocanapāla, the Pratīhāra king, was discovered from the site in 1830. This copperplate grant dated C.E. 1027 mentions six thousand brāhmaṇa donees of various *gotras* and *pravaras* belonging to Pratiṣṭhāna.[76] The same place appears to be meant by Śrīśapratiṣṭhāna in the grant of king Govindacandra of the Gāhaḍavāla dynasty which was issued in C.E. 1126.[77] This shows that the place had its political importance and was famous as Pratiṣṭhāna down to the twelfth century C.E.

It cannot be said definitely how the name Pratiṣṭhāna changed into Jhūsī. There is a curious legend about the name of Jhūsī. Tradition has it that the place was once being ruled by Harbonga, an imbecile and foolish king, in whose reign chaos prevailed everywhere. When the cup of his inequity was full there was an upheaval of the earth and the capital Pratiṣṭhāna was turned upside down due to the curse of the sage Gorakhanātha and his teacher (*guru*) Matsyendranātha. There was conflagration which completed the destruction of the city and the ruins went by the name of Jhūsī, a 'burnt town'[78] from the Hindi root *jhulasanā*. It is also said that the town was destroyed in an earthquake in C.E. 1359 as a result of the invocations of the saint Saiyid Alī Murtazā.[79] These traditions and the etymological meaning of the name Jhūsī possibly indicate to the destruction and burning of the site by the Muslim invaders in the thirteenth century C.E. The traditions relating to the scattering of brāhmaṇa and kṣatriya clans abandoning their homes in Jhūsī and emigrating to distant places[80] during the medieval period lend colour to this theory. Perhaps part of the reason for such beliefs was the strangely scattered, turbulent look of the deposits of bricks and stones that could clearly be seen sticking out of the much eroded sides of the high mound at Jhūsī. Interestingly, there is some evidence of a burned layer in parts of the mound, but no real indication revealed in the recently conducted excavations that the city had either been burned or otherwise destroyed during early medieval period – so much for the romantic tales.

In spite of the rich traditional accounts associated with Pratiṣṭhāna, it appears very strange to note that the city so close to Prayāga escaped the attention of the Chinese travellers Fa-hien and Hsüan Tsang. The site also did not attract the attention of archaeologists for quite a long time. Alexander Cunningham extensively toured the Allahabad region, but for unknown reasons he did not visit Jhūsī. Its importance was first pointed out by Sir Mortimer Wheeler, who in the course of a statement on future archaeological planning in India, suggested, "The survey should begin at Allahabad where, at the confluence, the great mound of Jhūsī offers an inspiring start, and should be continued steadily upwards into the foothills of the Himālaya, including a strip some five miles broad on each side of the present course of the river (Gaṅgā)".[81] The stress laid by Wheeler on Jhūsī as a landmark in the upper Gaṅgā valley shows that he was aware of its archaeological wealth. This impression was confirmed when in 1960 P.K. Khasnavis noticed here traces of a moat and a defence wall.[82] Several rare and valuable coins, terracottas, ivory and bone objects, seals and sealings, sculptures and NBP Ware sherds have been collected from this site and are preserved in the Allahabad Museum. Their study has revealed that the ancient city entombed beneath the high mound existed from *circa* sixth century B.C. to about thirteenth century C.E.

The recent excavations carried out at the great mound of Jhūsī under the auspices of the department of Ancient History, Culture and Archaeology, University of Allahabad, from 1995 to 1998, have revealed five cultural phases ranging from chalcolithic to early medieval period. The earliest culture represented at the site is marked by the pre-NBP Ware deposit which composed of potsherds, burnt clay lumps, ash, animal bones, floor levels, post-holes and hearths. The ceramic assemblage, manufactured on wheel, is represented by Black-slipped Ware, Black-and-Red Ware and Red Ware. Early layers of this deposit have yielded iron objects. Some pottery types and other antiquities of this deposit compare favourably well with their counterparts at different chalcolithic sites of eastern Uttar Pradesh, Bihar and northern Vindhyas. The NBP Ware phase has yielded pottery, iron and copper objects, beads fashioned on semi-precious stones, terracotta objects, charred grains and bone objects. Pits, hearths and post-holes along with burnt clay lumps were encountered at the early phase. From the mid-NBP Ware phase onwards brick bats and brick structures were available. A burnt horizon related to this phase has been noticed at a considerable length beyond the exposed trench, suggesting thereby that during this period the site witnessed a conflagration on a massive scale. A few uninscribed cast copper coins were obtained from the same horizon. The Śuṅga – Kuṣāṇa phase has revealed pottery, beads fashioned on semi-precious stones and terracotta, bone objects and a few terracotta figurines. Burnt brick walls, rooms with brick flooring, hearths, etc. were encountered at. A few sealings with legends in the Kuṣāṇa Brāhmī script were also obtained from this phase. The Gupta period at the site is characterised by the typical Gupta pottery, terracotta figurines, carved bricks, beads fashioned on semi-precious stones and terracotta, iron and copper objects. Remains of a few houses with brick flooring were exposed. A few sealings with legend were also obtained from this phase. The culture of the last phase is marked by early medieval pottery including Glazed Ware, terracotta, iron and copper objects, animal bones, etc. A few miniature stone sculptures representing various Hindu deities were also obtained. The discovery of stone chips on a large scale indicates that sculptural or architectural activity possibly related to some temple had taken place at the site during early medieval period.

From the pre-NBP Ware period to the Gupta period there is continuous settlement at the site. However, there appears to be a cultural gap between the end of Gupta period and the beginning of early medieval period. There is every likelihood that the site may show up no gap at all when exposed extensively. This possibility is based on the strategic location of the site itself which, by virtue of the same reason, would have never been abandoned after having been occupied once. Recently some radio carbon dates have become available for different cultural periods. Two radio carbon dates[83] from the pre-NBP Ware phase have pushed back the antiquity of occupation at the site to the middle of the second millennium B.C. Obviously, the area that has so far been excavated provides nothing but a hint that there is a lot left to be found. Comprehensive and careful explorations and excavations of the mounds of Jhūsī are urgently needed for filling the gaps in our knowledge regarding various phases of its history and also for unveiling the glorious past of Prayāga.

10.*Mānasa-tīrtha* : This *tīrtha* is referred to in the Purāṇas. It is located on the northern bank of the Gaṅgā.[84] It may be identified with the one situated at Mansaitā village where the stream named Mansaitā joins the Gaṅgā. It is said that he, who observes a fast for three nights here, gets all his desires fulfilled.[85] The merits acquired by the gifting away of cow, land and gold are attainable by the mere remembrance of this *tīrtha*.[86] This holy spot is also believed to be the destroyer of egoistic notion.[87]

11.*Nāga Bahumūlaka* : It marks the southern limit of Prajāpatikṣetra.[88] Its exact location is difficult to ascertain on the basis of available data. This *tīrtha* might have been situated at Arail, which is to the south of the confluence. The name, however, suggests that the site was represented by a shrine dedicated to the serpent-worship; Bahumūlaka being born to

Kaśyapa Prajāpati from his wife Kadrū, the mother of serpents.[89]

12.*Nirañjana-tīrtha* : It stands on the northern bank of the Yamunā and is sacred to Āditya.[90] There is one Nirañjana-tīrtha to be visited during the *antarvedi parikramā* (inner circumambulation) of Prayāga; so this one of the texts may be identified with it. The *Tīrthavivecanakāṇḍa*[91] and the *Tristhalīsetu*[92] read : *'tīrtham Nirujakam nāma'* and the former notes *'Nirudakam'* as its *variant* in P. The *Padma Purāṇa*[93] says *'tīrtham tu Varajam nāma'*. Gods with Indra are believed to perform here *sandhyā* (devotional prayers) thrice a day and the wise people are said to reside in this *tīrtha*.[94]

13.*Ṛṇapramocana-tīrtha* : The *Kūrma*,[95] *Matsya*[96] and *Padma*[97] *Purāṇas* mention this holy spot as Ṛṇapramacona, but the *Nāradīya Purāṇa*[98] and the *Tīrthaprakāśa*[99] refer to it as Ṛṇamocanaka and Ṛṇamocana, respectively. It is on the northern bank of the Yamunā and to the south of Prayāga.[100] It can be identified with the one which is to the west of the fort at a distance of half a kilometre. A person, who spends a night and takes a holy dip in the Yamunā there, is liberated from all his debts for ever, attains the Svargaloka or Sūryaloka, and becomes immortal.[101] The word 'all debts' possibly refers to the three religious debts an *ārya* owes to gods, ancestors, and seers.

14.*Samudrakūpa* : The *Mahābhārata* is silent about Samudrakūpa. Its earliest reference is to be found in the Purāṇas,[102] which locate it on the eastern bank of the Gaṅgā at Pratiṣṭhāna. The *Matsya Purāṇa*[103] and the *Padma Purāṇa*[104] refer to this well as Sāmudrakūpa and say that it is also known as Pratiṣṭhāna. The *Kūrma Purāṇa*[105] mentions it as Sarva-Sāmudrakūpa. Agrawala[106] is of opinion that the name Sarvasāmudra is the same as Saptasāmudra, because the well is believed to represent the seven oceans. The Samudrakūpa (Pl. 6) is a large well which exists on a high mound on the left bank of the Gaṅgā in Jhūsī overlooking the confluence. According to a local tradition, the well oozes out from the sea by a subterranean conduit; and, therefore, it is named as such. It is interesting to note that this was filled with earth almost to the brim when Bābā Sudarśana Dāsa, an enlightened and public-spirited Vaiṣṇava saint of Ayodhyā, re-excavated it in C.E. 1885.[107] According to another view,[108] the well is so called because it was sunk by emperor Samudragupta of the Gupta dynasty. Agrawala[109] has suggested that it was considered to be the representative of the seven seas during the Gupta period. Businessmen, who returned from their successful voyages across the seas, used to perform religious rites there. The relatives of the business-magnates in their absence also performed the worship of the Sea-god there for their safe journey. Thus, Samudrakūpa was of cultural significance. He also informs that such wells existed at all the five great centres, viz. Mathurā, Ujjayinī,

Prayāga, Vārāṇasī, and Pāṭaliputra, of the Gupta civilization. According to Irwin,[110] "This is no ordinary well providing water for the functional needs of a small community: its massive proportions leave no doubt that it had always been a cult spot, still obligatory for pilgrims to worship when they come to the Māgha Melā". It is said that he, who dwells there for three nights, observing sexual purity, and keeping himself dispassionate, is freed from all his sins, and gets the merit of the performance of an *aśvamedha* sacrifice.[111] A devotee is also advised to bathe and offer oblations of water to the manes and gods with full mental control at this holy spot.[112]

15.*Sandhyāvaṭa* : There is a Banyan tree named Sandhyāvaṭa near the eastern gate of Haṁsa-tīrtha at a short distance to the north of Samudrakūpa, which is visited on the ninth day during the *bahirvedi parikramā* of Prayāga. This may be taken to mark the site of ancient Sandhyāvaṭa. An observance of continence and a fast there enables one to attain the Brahmaloka.[113] It is also said that a celibate, who keeps a fast endowed with deep and abstract meditation at this gratifying spot, achieves the *brahma-jñāna*.[114]

16.*Soma-tīrtha* : The temple of Someśvaranātha (Pl. 7) near the village Devarakha on the southern bank of the conjoint stream of the Gaṅgā and the Yamunā possibly represents this *tīrtha*. The *Matsya Purāṇa*[115] glorifies it as a dispeller of great sins and says that he, who bathes there, gets the deliverance of hundreds of his ancestors. The *Śiva Purāṇa* says that the *darśana* of Someśvara wards off all adversities.[116] The *Brahma Purāṇa* as quoted in the *Tristhalīsetu*[117] states that a person, who worships the Supreme Being after taking a bath there, is emancipated from rebirth. According to a local tradition, the Moon-god became free from diseases by performing penance and worshipping Lord Śiva there.[118]

17.*Urvaśīpulina* : The *Matsya Purāṇa*[119] reads Urvaśīramaṇa for Urvaśīpulina. According to Roy,[120] this holy spot is now represented by the sandy tract on the eastern bank of the Gaṅgā, facing the mound of Jhūsī. Agrawala[121] identifies it with the vast stretch of white sandy area to the east of Jhūsī. This sub-*tīrtha*, sacred to the celestial nymph, is generally mentioned in the texts after Haṁsaprapatana and is said to be whitish due to the presence of flocks of swans there.[122] Urvaśī, as the name indicates, is the symbol of universal energy that takes her birth from the Primeval flood.[123] Hence, this holy spot may be associated with the vast beautiful stretch of land on the eastern bank of the Gaṅgā near the Haṁsaprapatana-tīrtha. There is still a Urvaśī-kuṇḍa in the shallow valley clothed with various kinds of trees and plants near the Bābā Dayārāma Āśrama at Jhūsī. The tradition associates this site with the famous legendary romance between Purūravas and Urvaśī. Agrawala[124] is of the view that this is the site where king Purūravas had his palace gardens outside the city of Pratiṣṭhāna. The place-name appears to be explained when it is said that by a suicide or water-offering to the manes there, one would see Urvaśī daily in heaven and after his return therefrom he would get hundred Urvaśī-like girls in this world.[125] A promise is also held out that he, who perpetually wears white raiments or sits on the mat of *kuśa* grass and takes his meals only once a day preserving sexual purity at this *tīrtha* for a month continuously, becomes a king and gets one hundred gold bedecked maidens. He rules over a vast territory whose boundaries extend up to the ocean. He constantly remains as a donor endowed with wealth and food grains; and after enjoying enormous pleasures, he again retires to this *tīrtha.*[126] It should be noted that the rewards promised for suicide and penance at Urvaśīpulina are sex pleasure and secular objects like becoming a king. This is in conformity with the nomenclature of the *tīrtha* where Purūravas and Urvaśī had enjoyed themselves.

18. *Vāsuki-hrada* : It represents northern boundary of Prajāpatikṣetra.[127] It was a significant pool of water consecrated to the mythical serpent Vāsuki and was situated near the Gaṅgā. Agrawala[128] identifies its site with the present Nāga Vāsuki temple. Roy[129] says that "a part of the site of the ancient Vāsuki-hrada is now represented by the modern Nāga Vāsuki temple. The sandy tract to the north-east of this temple, which torms the bed of this river (Gaṅgā) in the rainy season, at one time represented the major part of the Vāsuki pond". The site of the pool should, however, be identified with the deep low lying area by the southern side of the Buxi bund, which is at a very short distance towards the south-west of Nāga Vāsuki temple. Singh[130] takes it to be a shallow pond, which seems to be remnant of the ancient Vāsuki-hrada. It appears that due to the change in the course of the Gaṅgā, this pool of water went below the surface of its stream; and thus its entity is lost. The modern land hunger created by rapid growth of urbanisation has swallowed almost the whole of the pond (Pl. 8); it will vanish altogether in a couple of years.

Over and above these holy spots, Prayāga is said to abound in countless sub-*tīrthas*, out of which Vikira, Brahmakuṇḍa, Cakra-tīrtha, Lakṣamī-tīrtha, Kāśyapa-tīrtha, Pāpamocana-tīrtha, Kāpila-tīrtha, Sudhārasa-tīrtha, etc. may be mentioned. Since these are mentioned in the *Tristhalīsetu*[131] only and are neither referred to in the Purāṇas nor in the *Tīrthavivecana-kāṇḍa*, the *Tīrthacintāmaṇi*, and the *Tīrthaprakāśa*, it may be suggested that they came into existence in the sixteenth century when the *Tristhalīsetu* was composed but had not become popular by the time of the composition of the *Tīrthaprakāśa* in the next century. It should be mentioned that most of the local *tīrthas* in Prayāga are found at several sacred places of the country also. For example Daśāśvamedhika[132] is found, besides Prayāga, at

Vārāṇasī, Mathurā, Kurukṣetra, Gayā, Avantī, etc.; and Koṭi-tīrtha[133] is also enumerated as an auspicious spot in Kāśī, Puṣkara, Kurukṣetra, Haridvāra, etc. Some holy spots under Prayāga such as Haṁsaprapatana, Nirañjana-tīrtha, Vāsuki-hrada, Nāga Bahumūlaka, Bhogavatī, Sandhyāvaṭa are, however, not met with elsewhere. It is said that thirty crores, sometimes sixty crores and ten thousand sacred places such as Naimiṣa, Puṣkara, Go-tīrtha, Sindhusāgara, Gayā, Dhenuka, and Gaṅgāsāgara, and several holy hills and streams are always present there,[134] though in abstract and gross forms. The presence of all *tīrthas* of the earth in Prayāga is more than a matter of literary eulogy; many are part of the sacred geography of Prayāga, altogether contributing to its glory. These sub-*tīrthas* exhibit a certain locational significance which is related to certain sectarian and ritualistic considerations. The map (Fig. 2) clarifies that most of the holy spots are placed at the circumferential sites of Prayāga/Prajāpatikṣetra. It is comparable to Turner's remark that peripheral location is a geographical emblem of anti-structure, pilgrimage being a movement from structure to anti-structure.[135] Prayāga is, thus, the epitome of the holy land. It is also spatially transposed at other sacred places in the country. For instance, it is located at two places in Kāśī. The first is Prayāgaghāṭa where it is symbolized in the form of Mādhava;[136] the second place in Kāśī is represented by Prayāgeśa-liṅga.[137] It is also present as Prayāgeśvara-liṅga in Ujjayinī,[138] and as Prayāga at the Prayāgaghāṭa on the Yamunā in Mathurā.[139] Prayāga is, thus, the paradigm of sacred place, to which other places subscribe in their claims to sanctity. Spatial transposition is, indeed, a fascinating fact of India's sacred topography; this notion further reflects towards fusion and fission of Indian culture in terms of space, time and sanctimony.

The Epics and most of the Purāṇas and treatises on pilgrimage have carefully been consulted and analyzed accordingly; the exhaustive references to all the texts referring particular sub-*tīrtha* are given in Table 1. The table helps to understand the process of growth and elaboration of holy spots in a place of pilgrimage. The foregoing discussion when viewed in the light of the table and the map shows how a single sacred place in course of time develops into a sacred zone. It also brings out the expansion of the scope of a sacred place, ranging from the local area to the wide region and, ultimately, to the entire Hindu universe.

The sacred geography of most of the holy sites in India is related with water symbolism comparable to the theological interpretation of the origin of the universe affiliated to the cosmic flood. In India its highest magnitude has been transposed at Prayāga. It is, therefore, many sites in India are replicated in the form of Prayāga throughout India. This idea clearly

TABLE 1: PRAYĀGA : REFERENCES OF SUB-*TĪRTHAS* IN ANCIENT TEXTS

Sub-tīrtha	Mahā-bhārata	Rāmā-yaṇa	Agni Purāṇa	Kūrma Purāṇa	Matsya Purāṇa	Padma Purāṇa	Nāradīya Purāṇa	Tīrtha-vivecana-kāṇḍa	Tīrtha-cintā-maṇi	Tristha-līsetu	Tīrtha-prakāśa
	1	2	3	4	5	6	7	8	9	10	11
1. Agni	—	—	—	I.37.4	107.27	III.45.27	II.63.164	149	51	56	—
2. Ana-raka	—	—	111.4	I.37.4	107.27	III.45.27	II.63.164	149	51	56	—
3. Bhara dvāja Āśrama	—	II.54.7-36 II.90-91 VI.124.1-2	—	—	—	—	—	—	—	—	—
4. Bhoga-vatī	III.83.72,81	—	111.5,10	—	105.46	III.39.73,82	II.63.54,97	145,151, 153	24,30,41	6,7,56,57	321,325, 340
					109.8	III.43.46					
						III.47.8					
5. Brahma-kuṇḍa	—	—	—	—	—	—	—	—	—	58	—
6. Caitraka	—	—	—	—	109.2	—	—	—	—	—	—
7. Cakra	—	—	—	—	—	—	—	—	—	59	—
8. Daśāśva-medhika	III.83.82	—	111.14	Aśvamedha —	105.46	III.39.83 Daśāśva-medhaka III.43.47	II.63.97	145,153	30,40	56,58 Aśvamedha 57	340
9. Dhenuka	—	—	—	—	—	—	II.63.48	150	23	6	324
10. Gaṅgā-sāgara	—	—	—	—	109.2	III.47.2	II.63.48	150	23	6	324

Sub-tīrtha	Mahā-bhārata 1	Rāmā-yaṇa 2	Agni Purāṇa 3	Kūrma Purāṇa 4	Matsya Purāṇa 5	Padma Purāṇa 6	Nāradīya Purāṇa 7	Tīrtha-vivecana-kāṇḍa 8	Tīrtha-cintā-maṇi 9	Tristha-līsetu 10	Tīrtha-prakāśa 11
11. Gaṅgā-Yamunā-saṅgama	III.83,76 — —	II.54.2,6 II.55.4	111.7, 13	I.35.12, 15 I.36.6	106.12	III.39.81 III.43.14, 22 III.44.8-9 VI.i127. 145	II.63.18, 21,42 66,90	143,146, 152,153	22,24, 25,26, 29,39	8,10, 16,29, 30,48	322,328 334,335, 346
Veṇī	—	—	—	—	—	VI.i.23.33 VI.i.81.38 VI.i.126.41 VI.i.128.65	II.63.6,7,11	—	18,37	8,12,15, 22,32,60	328,330
Triveṇī	—	—	—	—	—	VI.i.23.32, 36	—	—	—8	—	
12. Go	—	—	—	—	109.2	III.47.1	II.63.48	150	23	6	324
13. Gayā	—	—	—	—	109.2	III.47.2	II.63.48	150	23	6	324
14. Haṁsa-prapatana	III.83.82	—	111.10	I.35.23	105.32	III.39.83 III.43.33	II.63.95	143,153	pratapana 30,41	56 Haṁsāyatana 57	339
15. Kamb-alāśva-tara Nāgas	III.83.72	—	111.5	I.35.18	103.3 105.27 109.8	III.39.72 III.41.4 III.43.28 III.47.8	II.63.54, 91	136,143, 151	24,29, 38,40,47	6,7,15, 55	321,323, 325,327, 338,342
16. Kāpila	—	—	—	—	—	—	—	—	—	59	—
17. Kāśyapa	—	—	—	—	—	—	—	—	—	59	—
18. Koṭi	—	—	111.14	I.35.28	105.44	III.43.44	II.63.151	144	49	50,57	340,344
19. Kuru-kṣetra	—	—	—	—	—	III.47.2	—	—	—	—	—
20. Lakṣamī	—	—	—	—	—	—	—	—	—	59	—

Sub-tīrtha	Mahābhārata 1	Rāmāyaṇa 2	Agni Purāṇa 3	Kūrma Purāṇa 4	Matsya Purāṇa 5	Padma Purāṇa 6	Nāradīya Purāṇa 7	Tīrtha-vivecana-kāṇḍa 8	Tīrtha-cintāmaṇi 9	Tristhalīsetu 10	Tīrtha-prakāśa 11
21. Mānasa	—	—	111.14	—	106.2	III.44.2	—	145	—	57	340
22. Nāga Bahumūlaka	—	—	—	—	103.3	III.41.4	II.63.130	136	47	15	323,327, 342
23. Naimiṣa	—	—	—	—	109.8	III.47.1	II.63.48	150	23	6	324
24. Nirañjana	—	—	—	—	107.29	II.45.29	—	149	—	57	—
25. Pāpamocana	—	—	—	—	—	—	—	—	—	59	—
26. Pratiṣṭhāna	III.83.72 III.85.14	VII.90. 22-24	111.5 273.9	I.35.21	103.3 105.30	III.39.72 III.41.4 III.43.31	II.63.93, 129	136,151	30,41,47 -nagara 23	15,56	321,337 342 -nagara 325
Samadhiṣṭhāna	—	—	—	—	109.8	III.47.8	II.63.54	—	24	6,7	—
27. Puṣkara	—	—	—	—	109.1	III.41.1	II.63.48	150	23	6	324
28. Ṛṇapramocana	—	—	—	I.36.14	106.20	III.44.22	II.63.100	147	-mocanaka 30 38	56	328,341
29. Sāmudrakūpa	—	—	—	Sarva- I.35.21	105.30	III.43.31	Kūpa II.63.93	143	30,41	Sarva- 56	327,338
30. Sandhyāvaṭa	—	—	111.13	I.35.27	105.43	vaṭa III.43.43	—	144	—	25,56,57	339
31. Śaṅkha	—	—	—	—	—	—	—	—	—	58	—
32. Sindhusāgara	—	—	—	—	109.1	III.47.1	II.63.48	150	23	6	324
33. Soma	—	—	—	—	108.2	—	—	—	—	60	—
34. Sudhārasa	—	—	—	—	—	—	—	—	—	60	—
35. Urvaśīpulina	—	—	111.13	I.35.25	-ramaṇa 105.34	III.43.35	II.63.142	144	48	49,57	—

Sub-tīrtha	Mahā-bhārata 1	Rāmā-yaṇa 2	Agni Purāṇa 3	Kūrma Purāṇa 4	Matsya Purāṇa 5	Padma Purāṇa 6	Nāradīya Purāṇa 7	Tīrtha-vivecana-kāṇḍa 8	Tīrtha-cintā-maṇi 9	Tristha-līsetu 10	Tīrtha-prakāśa 11
36. Vaṭamūla	—	—	111.13	I.35.18 I.37.9 Nyagrodha I.34.25	105.11 Vaṭa 103.9 110.9	III.43.11, 13 Vaṭa III.41.6 III.48.10 VI.i.81.38 Ādivaṭa VI.i.23.31 Śyāmavaṭa VI.i.23.27 Akṣayavaṭa VI.i.24.7-8.	II.63.139 — —	142 Vaṭa 137,151 —	48 — —	5,48, 49 Vaṭa 5,7,16, 60 Prayāga-vaṭa 53 11,60	343,344 Vaṭa 323,326 348 325
37. Vāsuki-hrada	—	—	—	—	103.3	II.41.4	II.63.129	136	47	15	342
38. Vikira	—	—	—	—	—	—	—	—	—	58	—

indicates the concept of integration of Indian landscape in terms of attachment to the place, people and philosophy, This metaphysical personality of Prayaga is one of the reasons to accept it as Tīrtharāja. The sub-*tīrthas* in Prayāga further enhance that characteristics which might be taken to work further. The symbiosis between visible (the Gaṅgā and the Yamunā) and invisible (the Sarasvatī) reflects the unity between the self and the infinite. Similar interpretations may be given for other sacred places of the world but the uniqueness of Prayāga is unparalleled.

REFERENCES

1. *MP*, 103.6; *PdP*, III.41.6a-7.
2. Kane, *History of Dharmaśāstra*, Vol. IV, pp.730-825.
3. *KP*, I.37.4a; *MP*, 107.27a=*TvK*, 149=*TS*, 56; *PdP*, III.45.17a=*TC*, 51; *NP*, II.63.164a.
4. *KP*, I.37.4c; *MP*, 107.28a=*TvK*, 149=*TS*, 56; *PdP*, III. 45.28a=*TC*, 51; *NP*, II.63.165a.
5. *KP*, I.37.46.
6. *MP*, 107.27b=*TS*, 56.
7. *NP*, II.63.164b.
8. *AgP*, 111.14b.
9. *PdP*, III.45.27b=*TC*, 51.
10. *TvK* (*MP*), 149.
11. Kane, *op.cit.*, Vol. IV, p.615, fn. 1399.
12. *KP*, I.37.4c; *MP*, 107.28a=*TvK*, 149=*TS*, 56; *PdP*, III. 45.28a=*TC*, 51; *NP*, II.63.165a.
13. *KP*, I.37.5; *TS* (*MP*), 56.
14. *Rām*, II.58.8.
15. *Rām*, II.54.9-12, VI.124.1-2.
16. *Rām*, II.89-92.
17. *Rām*, II.54.7.
18. *Rām*, II.90.1.
19. Bonazzoli, G., 'Places of Purāṇic Recitation according to the Purāṇas', *Purāṇa*, Vol. XXXIII (1), p.49.
20. *ŚP*, IV.2.14.
21. *Indian Archaeology – A Review* 1978-79, p.56.
22. *Ibid.*
23. Lal, B.B. and Dikshit, K.N., 'Śriṅgaverapura : A key-site for the proto-history and early history of the Central Gaṅgā Valley', *Purātattva*, Vol. X, p.6.
24. *Mbh*, III.100.5.
25. *MP*, 105.46a=*TvK*, 145=*TC*, 30, 40=*TS*, 56=*TP*, 340; *PdP*, III.43.46b.
26. *TC*, 41.
27. *AgP*, 111.10a, *TS* (*Ādi P.*), 57.

28. Kane, *op.cit.*, Vol. IV, p.739.
29. *Mbh*, III.83.72b=*TP*, 321; *AgP*, 111.5b=*TS*, 7; *MP*, 109.8b=*TvK*, 151=*TC*, 24=*TS*, 6=*TP*, 325; *PdP*, III. 39.73a, 47.8b; *NP*, II.63.55a.
30. Bajapai, K.D. (ed.), *The Geographical Encyclopaedia of Ancient and Medieval India*, Vol. I, p.68.
31. *Mbh*, III.83.81=*TvK*, 153.
32. *PdP*, III.39.82.
33. Kashinath, 'Serpent worship', *Indian Antiquary*, Vol. 2, 1873, p.124.
34. *Mbh*, III.83.82b=*TvK*, 153.
35. *MP*, 105.46=*TvK*, 145=*TC*, 30=*TS*, 56=*TP*, 340; *PdP*, III.39.83b, 43.46b-47a; *NP*, II.63.97.
36. *AgP*, 111.14a; *Ādi P. q.* in *TS*, 57.
37. *TS* (*BP*), 58.
38. Sinha, H.P., *Bhārata ko Prayāga kī Dena*, Vol. I, p.28.
39. Jayaswal, K.P., *History of India, 150 C.E. to 350 C.E.*, p.57.
40. Upadhyaya, B.S., *Gupta Kāla kā Sānskritika Itihāsa*, p.55.
41. Roy, U.N., *Studies in Ancient Indian History and Culture*, Vol. I, p.215.
42. Gupta, P.L., *The Imperial Guptas*, Vol. I, p.281.
43. *MP*, 105.47=*TvK*, 145=*TC*, 30, 40=*TS*, 56-57=*TP*, 340; *PdP*, III.43.47b-48a; NP, II.63.98.
44. *TS* (*BP*), 58.
45. *ŚP*, IV, 2.13.
46. *Mbh*, III.83.82a=*TvK*, 153.
47. *AgP*, 111.10a; *KP*, I.35.23-24; *MP*, 105.32-33=*TvK*, 143; *PdP*, III.39.83a, 43.33-34; *NP*, II.63.95-96.
48. *TvK*, 143, 153.
49. *Mbh*, III.83.82a=*TvK*, 153; *KP*, I.35.23; *NP*, II.63.95; *PdP*, III.39.83a, 43.33; *MP*, 105.32=*TvK*, 143=*TC*, 30, 41=*TS*, 56=*TP*, 339.
50. Roy, U.N., *op.cit.*, Vol. I, p.219.
51. Agrawala, V.S., *Matsya Purāṇa – A Study*, p.182.
52. *Ibid.*, p.183.
53. *Ibid.*
54. *TC*, 41.
55. *MP*, 105.33=*TvK*, 144=*TC*, 30=*TS*, =*TP*, 339; *PdP*, III.43.34; *NP*, II.63.96.
56. *KP*, I.35.24.
57. *Mbh*, III. 83.72; *MP*, 103.3b-4a=*TvK*, 136=*TC*, 47=*TS*, 15=*TP*, 323, 327; *NP*, II.63.129b-130; *PdP*, III.41.4-5a.
58. *KP*, I.35.18a.
59. *PdP*, III.43.28a; *TS* (*MP*), 55; *TP* (*MP*), 338.
60. *MP*, 105.27a=*TC*, 29.
61. *NP*, II.63.91a.
62. *TvK* (*MP*), 143.
63. *Jātaka*, Vol. VI, p.165.
64. *TC*, 40.

65. *KP*, I.35.18b-19; *PdP*, III.43.28b-29; *NP*, II.63.91b-92; *MP*, 105.27b-28=*TvK*, 143=*TC*, 29, 40=*TS*, 55=*TP*, 338.
66. *KP*, I.35.20; *PdP*, III.43.30; *MP*, 105.29=*TvK*, 143=*TC*, 29=*TS*, 55=*TP*, 338.
67. *KP*, I.35.28; *PdP*, III.43.44b-45a; *NP*, II.63.151b-152a; *MP*, 105.44=*TvK*, 144-145=*TC*, 49=*TS*, 50=*TP*, 340, 344.
68. *PdP*, III.43.45b-46a; *NP*, II.63.152b-153a; *MP*, 105.45=*TvK*, 145=*TC*, 49=*TS*, 50 =*TP*, 340.
69. *BP*, 8.10; *HP*, I.26.49.
70. *VaP*, II.2.47.
71. *KP*, I.35.21; *PdP*, III.43.31; *MP*, 105.30=*TC*, 30=*TS*, 56=*TP*, 327.
72. *Rām*, VII.90.22-23.
73. *Mbh*, I.81-90; *BP*, 8-9; *HP*, I.26-27.
74. *Vikramorvaśīyam*, II.45.
75. MP, 105.30b=*TC*, 30=*TS*, 56=*TP*, 327; *PdP*, III.43.31b;
गङ्गापूर्वकूले प्रतिष्ठानं नाम नगरं तत्रैव सामुद्रो नाम कूपः स एव प्रतिष्ठानशब्देनात्र लक्ष्यते. *TC*, 41; *TP*, 327; प्रतिष्ठानशब्देन तत्कूपो लक्ष्यते. *TS*, 15.
76. *Indian Antiquary*, Vol. XVIII, p.35.
77. *JASB*, Vol. XXVII, p.243.
78. *Modern Review*, Vol. VIII (5), 1910, pp.659-660.
79. Srivastava, Shaligrama, *Prayāga Pradīpa*, p.272.
80. *Ibid.*, p.273.
81. Wheeler, R.E.M., 'Archaeological Fieldwork in India: Planning Ahead', *Ancient India*, No. 5, p.10.

82. *Indian Archaeology—A Review* 1961-62, p.52.
83. JHS/16 PRL 2081 1325 2700 ± 90 2700 ± 90 830 B.C.
JHS/18 PRL 2083 1520 3200 ± 90 3290 ± 90 1340 B.C.
84. *PdP*, II.44.2a; *MP*, 106.2a=*TvK*, 145=*TS*, 57=*TP*, 340.
85. *PdP*, III.44.2b; *MP*, 106.2b=*TvK*, 145=*TS*, 57=*TP*, 340.
86. *PdP*, III.44.3; *MP*, 106.3=*TvK*, 145=*TS*, 57=*TP*, 340.
87. *AgP*, 111.14b=*TS*, 57.
88. *PdP*, III.41.4b; *NP*, II.63.130a; *MP*, 103.3b=*TvK*, 136=*TC*, 47=*TS*, 15=*TP*, 323.
89. Mani, Vettam, *Purāṇic Encyclopaedia*, p.98.
90. *PdP*, III.45.29; *MP*, 107.29=*TvK*, 149=*TS*, 57.
91. *TvK*, 149.
92. *TS*, 57.
93. *PdP*, III.45.29b.
94. *PdP*, III.45.29b-30; *MP*, 107.29b-30=*TvK*, 149-150=*TS*, 57.
95. *KP*, I.36.14b.
96. *MP*, 106.20b=*TvK*, 147=*TS*, 56.
97. *PdP*, III.44.21a.
98. *NP*, II.63.100b; *TC* (*MP*), 30.
99. *TP* (*MP*), 328, 341.

100. *KP*, I.36.14a; *PdP*, III.44.20b; *MP*, 106.20a=*TvK*, 147=*TC*, 30=*TS*, 56=*TP*, 328, 341; *NP*,II.63.100a (reads पायतेश्चोत्तरे कूले for यामुने चोत्तरे कूले).
101. *KP*, I.36.15; *PdP*, III.44.21b-22; *NP*, II.63.101; *MP*, 106.21=*TvK*, 147=*TC*, 31=*TS*, 56=*TP*, 341.
102. *KP*, I.35.21; *PdP*, III.43.31; *NP*, II.63.93a; *MP*, 105.30=*TvK*, 143=*TC*, 30, 41=*TS*, 56=*TP*, 338.
103. *MP*, 105.30b=*TvK*, 143=*TC*, 4=*TP*, 338.
104. *PdP*, III.43.31b.
105. *KP*, I.35.21b.
106. Agrawala, V.S., 'The Seven-Sea-Gift in the Matsya Purāṇa', *Purāṇa*, Vol. I(2), p.209.
107. Srivastava, Shaligrama, *op.cit.*, p.281.
108. Roy, U.N., *op.cit.*, Vol. I, p.217; *Modern Review*, Vol. VIII (5), 1910, p.657.
109. Agrawala, V.S., *op.cit.*, p.182.
110. Irwin, John C., 'The Ancient Pillar-cult at Prayāga (Allahabad) : Its Pre-Aśokan Origins', *JRAS*, 1983, pp.258-259.
111. *KP*, I.35.22; *PdP*, III.43.32; *NP*, II.63.94; *MP*, 105.31=*TvK*, 143=*TC*, 30=*TS*, 56=*TP*, 339.
112. *NP*, II.63.93.
113. *KP*, I.35.27; *MP*, 105.43=*TvK*, 144=*TS*, 56=*TP*, 340.
114. *PdP*, III.43.43b-44a.
115. *MP*, 108.2.
116. *ŚP*, IV.2.14.
117. *TS*, 60.
118. *Prayāga Māhātmya Śatādhyāyī*, 87.2-6.
119. *MP*, 105.34a.
120. Roy, U.N., *op.cit.*, Vol. I, p, 217.
121. Agrawala, V.S., *op.cit.*, p.183.
122. *KP*, I.35.25a; *PdP*, III.43.35a; *NP*, II.63.142b; *MP*, 105.34a=*TvK*, 144=*TC*, 48=*TS*, 49=*TP*, 339.
123. Agrawala, V.S., *op.cit.*, p.132.
124. *Ibid.*,p.183.
125. *KP*, I.35.25b-26; *PdP*, III.43.35b-39; NP, II.63.143-148a; *MP*, 105.34b-39=*TvK*, 144=*TC*, 48-49=*TS*, 49-50=*TP*, 339.
126. *NP*, II.63.148b-151a; *PdP*, III.43.40-42; *MP*. 105.40-42=*TvK*, 144=*TC*, 39=*TP*, 339.
127. *PdP*, III.41.4a; *NP*, II.63.129b; *MP*, 103.3a=*TvK*, 136=*TC*, 47=*TS*, 15=*TP*, 323, 327.
128. Agrawala, V.S., *op.cit.*, p.181.
129. Roy, U.N., *op.cit.*, Vol. I, pp.213-214.
130. Singh, Ujagir, *Allahabad—A Study in Urban Geography*, p.3, Fig.7.
131. *TS* (*BP*), 58-59.
132. Nambiar, K.D., *Nārada Purāṇa – A Critical Study*, p.374; Kantawala, S.G., *Cultural History from the Matsya Purāṇa*, p.319; Kane, *op.cit.*, Vol. IV, p. 745.

133. Nambiar, K.D. *op.cit.*, pp.404-405; Kane, *op.cit.*, Vol. IV, p.770.
134. *Mbh*, III.83.79=*TvK*, 152-153; =*KP*, I.37.6; NP, II.63.48-50a; *AgP*, 111.9; *PdP*, III.39.80, 43.24, 47.1b-3; *MP*, 109.1b-3=*TvK*, 143, 150-151=*TC*, 23-24=*TS*, 6=*TP*, 324.
135. Turner, Victor, 'The Centre out there: Pilgrim's goal', *History of Religions*, Vol. 12 (3), pp.212-213.
136. *SkP*, IV.61.29-31.
137. *SkP*, IV.61.35-36.
138. *SkP*, V.ii.58.41.
139. *NP*, II.79.76; *VP*, 150.39.

Chapter IV

HISTORICITY OF AKṢAYAVAṬA

One of the most important pilgrimage sites in Prayāga is the famous Banyan tree (Ficus Indica), popularly known as Akṣayavaṭa. This tree commanded the adoration of the people from early times and is still an object of worship. Presently, however, there is no trace of it and it appears in the form of a bifurcated log in one corner of the Pātālapurī temple inside the local fort. There is a heated controversy among scholars about its identity. The main problem is as to where the original Banyan tree (*Vaṭa-vrikṣa*) existed. Some scholars hold that the pilgrims coming to the Pātālapurī temple are shown the relics of the traditional Banyan tree.[1] Others assert that it is a forged piece of wood being worshipped at the spot where the tree did not exist.[2] To reach a definite conclusion, we have to examine thoroughly all possible literary and epigraphical references. The question of the historicity and antiquity of the worship of this tree and of the Banyan tree in general is to be discussed in all its ramifications.

Tree-worship is one of the oldest and most widely current form of worship. It has continued from the Harappan period through the long vistas of the Vedic and post-Vedic ages to this day. According to William Crooke, "The worship of trees originated in the pre-animistic state and rapidly grew in the period of animism when the tree began to be treated as occupied by an indwelling spirit. The two stages often overlap and devotion to the tree represents the worship of the spirit abiding in it".[3]

The veneration of Banyan tree is widely prevalent.[4] It is one of the most majestic and beautiful trees. In India it has been held sacred since the Vedic times. The *Ṛgveda* does not mention it, but it is referred to twice in the *Atharvaveda*[5] as the haunt of Apsarās (celestial nymphs). According to the *Śatapatha Brāhmaṇa*, this tree is termed nyagrodha due to its downward (*nyak-rodha*) growth. It has the characteristic of bending its branches down to the ground and developing new secondary trunks. So, a single tree, in course of time, forms a large grove. Moreover, it never grows straight but slightly inclines to one side.[6] Divine origin has been attributed to it for making this tree[7] a substitute of the soma plant which did not grow in the plains of Northern India. The airy descending roots of nyagrodha are as reddish as the top of the soma plant, hence they became the substitutes of the real soma. It has been enjoined in the *Aitareya Brāhmaṇa* that a kṣatriya should not drink the juice prepared of the soma plant. He may, however, take the same extracted from the airy descending roots of the nyagrodha tree, together with the fruits of the udumbara, aśvattha and plakṣa trees.[8] The drinking of this juice by a kṣatriya has been justified on the ground that among human beings the kṣatriya occupies the same place as the nyagrodha does among the trees.[9] The *Chāndogya Upaniṣad* draws an analogy between the growing of the seed of nyagrodha into a big tree and the manifestation of the universe from Brahman who is even smaller in size than the former.[10] The *Taittirīya Saṁhitā* says that the sacrificial wood (*idhma*) should be of the nyagrodha, udumbara, aśvattha, and plakṣa trees as they are the abodes of Gandharvas and Apsarās.[11] The *Gobhila Gṛhyasūtra* contains a verse mentioning that the nyagrodha tree belongs to god Varuṇa.[12] In the Epics the sacred trees like pippala, vaṭa, śamī, etc. are termed as *caitya-vṛkṣas* or *sthala-vṛkṣas*. It is said that not even the leaf of a *caitya-vṛkṣa* (the tree that has a platform around it) may be destroyed, for it is the resort of Devas, Yakṣas, Nāgas, Apsarās, and Bhūtas.[13]

Originally trees were worshipped in their tree form but later on their worship was intended to appease the tree-deity. It was believed that the tree-god could appear in a visible form and grant request. When Sujātā's maid servant Pūrṇā saw Gautama seated under a Banyan tree she thought that the tree-deity had become visible in a human form. She informed Sujātā and the latter came to the tree with a bowl full of rice and milk which Gautama accepted.[14] According to the *Mahāvāṇija-Jātaka*, some merchants went out in search of treasures and reached a big Banyan tree of the nature of a *kalpavṛkṣa*. It produced from its eastern branches streams of water, from southern branches food and drinks, from western branches fair damsels, and from northern branches all desired objects.[15] In the *Dummedha-Jātaka*, devoted people are mentioned as offering sacrifice to the Banyan tree with the entrails, blood and flesh of the victims—goats, cocks, pigs, and other living creatures—and praying to the Vaṭa-Yakṣiṇī to grant them sons and daughters, honour and wealth.[16] There is evidence in the *Mahābhārata* and Purāṇas, revealing a connection of the Vaṭa-tree with Viṣṇu,[17] Śiva,[18] Kāla[19] and Brahmā.[20] This tree appears in the story of Sāvitrī as a symbol of life.[21] It has specific mention in the exploits of Garuḍa in bringing nectar.[22] It is difficult to say whether the worship of this tree was of non-Āryan origin. It has been suggested that this tree, in its most respectful form, was popular with the Nāgas who worshipped it with all devotion.[23] That this tree figures very prominently in some famous tales about the serpents may indicate its non-Āryan associations. The banyan worship was, however, incorporated by the Āryans in their religious system in a slightly modified form and the tree came to be worshipped as a cult object by them since the later Vedic period.

We have seen the significance of the Banyan tree in the religious life of the people from the later Vedic times. Thus, a Banyan tree, in a sacred place, becomes a venerable object of worship. Many Vaṭa-trees have been regarded holy because of their situation at different sacred places, e.g., the Viṣṇupada hill at Gayā,[24] Go-tīrtha to the north of the Vindhya,[25] the bank of the Narmadā where Pulastya performed penance,[26] Puruṣottamakṣetra,[27] Puṣkara,[28] and Prayāga, etc.

The Vedic literature does not mention any Banyan tree at Prayāga. A reference to a Banyan tree at Prayāga occurs for the first time in the *Rāmāyaṇa*. When Rāma, along with Sītā and Lakṣmaṇa, was leaving for Citrakūṭa, the sage Bharadvāja explained the route from Prayāga to Citrakūṭa. They were to go to the confluence of the Gaṅgā and the Yamunā, and then taking a turn to the right, walk a little distance on the bank of the Yamunā upstream to the west.[29] They would find a much frequented passage, which was worn out on account of being too old, where they should construct a small float to cross the Yamunā.[30] They would reach a Banyan tree, known as Śyāmanyagrodha,[31] standing on the other side of the Yamunā. Bharadvāja advised Sītā to worship it with joined palms and then they were to decide whether to stay there or to leave for onward journey.[32] There was a forest named Nīlakānana at a distance of a *krośa* from that tree through which the route, trodden several times by Bharadvāja, went straight to Citrakūṭa.[33]

Rāma did exactly as he was directed. He, along with Sītā and Lakṣmaṇa, crossed the river and reached the Śyāmanyagrodha.[34] As advised by Bharadvāja, Sītā bowed to and circumambulated the tree, prayed to it to fulfil the vows of her husband, and to enable her to see her mothers-in-law Kausalyā and Sumitrā again.[35]

This Śyāmanyagrodha seems to be the earliest Banyan tree at Prayāga. It was extensive in its growth and its boughs were green. It was surrounded by innumerable other trees of the Yamunā-vana and was resorted to by the Siddhas.[36] That the tree was revered as auspicious is beyond doubt. The reference indicates the prevalence of Vaṭa-worship in Prayāga in the *Rāmāyaṇa* age. But the tree is not called Akṣayavaṭa and later practices of giving extreme physical torture to oneself or committing suicide by jumping from its top were not associated with it. Its situation in the jungle (*vana*) on the southern bank of the Yamunā apparently faced the much frequented but an old ghāṭa[37] on the other side of the river.

The *Mahābhārata*, which describes the holy spots of Prayāga in the *Tīrthayātrā* section of the Āraṇyakaparvan, does not refer to any Banyan tree there, though it eulogizes the *Akṣayavaṭa* at Gayā in the *Āraṇyakaparvan*[38] and the *Anuśāsanaparvan*.[39] However, the *Āraṇyakaparvan*, while narrating the story of the dissolution of the universe as witnessed by the sage Mārkaṇḍeya, refers to the Divine Child resting on the extended branch of a huge nyagrodha tree in the midst of the Great Deluge. It says that the whole world was overwhelmed and the whole creation was submerged. Mārkaṇḍeya found himself alone walking on the waters of the ocean. Extremely distressed and feeling lonely and forlorn he kept on swimming to find some refuge for rest. All of a sudden he sighted in the midst of the Deluge a huge nyagrodha tree and a little child resting comfortably on a gorgeous couch on one of its branches.[40] Mārkaṇḍeya was given shelter inside the mouth of that child.[41] He roamed in amazement through the boundless interior of the child for hundreds of years. Bewildered he sincerely prayed to that God. The child opened its mouth and Mārkaṇḍeya came out to see the same wonderful sight of the child resting on the branch of the nyagrodha.[42] Inside the stomach of the Divine Child, Mārkaṇḍeya saw the whole world with its kingdoms, cities and rivers. The first river that he saw was the Gaṅgā.[43] According to P.K. Gode, this reference to the river Gaṅgā shows that the great nyagrodha tree may perhaps be taken to exist on the bank of the Gaṅgā at Prayāga.[44] But the speculation is without any support. The site of this tree is not specified in the *Mahābhārata*. This narrative occurs in the Purāṇas.[45] But they are also silent about the specific location of this tree.[46] A reference to the location of the tree was not required in the episode because the *Mahābhārata* aimed at showing the identity between Nārāyaṇa and Vāsudeva,[47] whereas the Purāṇas wanted to bring out the identity of Nārāyaṇa with Bhagavān Puruṣottama[48] and some other objects and to sing the greatness of Nārāyaṇa.

Thus, in the *Mahābhārata* there is no mention of any Banyan tree at Prayāga. The silence of the *Tīrthayātrā* section of the *Āraṇyakaparvan* of the *Mahābhārata* about a Banyan tree there is not without significance. Possibly it suggests that the Banyan tree referred to in the *Rāmāyaṇa* became extinct long before the composition of the *Tīrthayātrā* section of the *Āraṇyakaparvan* of the *Mahābhārata*. The excavations conducted at the *Rāmāyaṇa* sites show that if the Epic episode has any historicity it can be placed at the earliest during the early phase of the NBP Ware, which was around the beginning of the seventh century B.C.[49] It is generally believed that the *Rāmāyaṇa* had its literary formation between the fourth century B.C. and the second century C.E.,[50] and the *Ayodhyākāṇḍa*, wherein the relevant references occur and which belongs to the original body of the Epic, appears to have been composed by Vālmīki by utilising the traditional story coming down orally from earlier times in the fourth or third century B.C. The *Mahābhārata* is supposed to have assumed its present form between the fourth century B.C. and the fourth century C.E.,[51] and the *Tīrthayātrā* section of its *Āraṇyakaparvan* was composed possibly between the first century B.C. and the first century C.E.[52] Thus, we can suggest that the *Śyāmanyagrodha* was in existence on the southern bank of the Yamunā from circa tenth century B.C. to the sencond century B.C. or sometime later but had perished by the beginning of the Christian era.

The Banyan tree of the *Rāmāyaṇa*-fame is, however, mentioned in some ancient Sanskrit texts. Thus, Kālidāsa (c. 4th-5th century C.E.) in his *Raghuvaṁśa* refers to the Śyāmavaṭa on the southern bank of the Yamunā at Prayāga. Rāma, while travelling from Laṅkā to Ayodhyā, says to Sītā, "This is the same Banyan tree, known by the name of Śyāma, that was entreated by you formerly. Covered with fruits it resembles the heap of emeralds intermixed with rubies".[53] In the *Uttararāmacarita* of Bhavabhūti (c. eighth century C.E.), Lakṣmaṇa while describing the scenes on the canvas portraying Rāma's career and exploits, says, "This is the Banyan tree, Śyāma by name, on the bank of the Kālindī, by the side of the road leading to Citrakūṭa, pointed out to us by the sage Bharadvāja".[54] The poet Murāri Miśra (9th or 10th century C.E. according to some, but c. C.E. 1050-1153 according to others) in his drama *Anargharāghava* has also referred to the same tree.[55]

The above references to the Śyāmavaṭa on the southern bank of the Yamunā at Prayāga indicate that the memories of the Banyan tree of the *Rāmāyaṇa* survived up to the early medieval times. This, however, does not necessarily establish the survival of that tree up to the early medieval period. The Purāṇas and other works do not take notice of it. The *Amarakośa*, a work of the Gupta period, does not mention Śyāma as the name of Prayāga-vaṭa.[56] These literary references to the Banyan tree called Śyāma were possibly modelled after the description of that tree in the Vālmīki's *Rāmāyaṇa*. The classical Sanskrit poets were simply following the traditional version of Rama-story. It was not material to them if the tree, referred to in the *Rāmāyaṇa*, did not exist in their own times. They likewise did not mention the Banyan tree on the Gaṅgā near the confluence which is highly eulogized in the Purāṇas, digests on *tīrtha* and other texts and epigraphic records of the early medieval period. Possibly because of their theme taken from the *Rāmāyaṇa* such a reference was not relevant.

The Purāṇas eulogise a Banyan tree at Prayāga by describing it as an enternal one and extol the merit of committing suicide there. This tree stood near the confluence of the Gaṅgā and the Yamunā at Prayāga.[57] Since it grew near the confluence it came to be regarded as being especially sacred. This tree possibly sprang up in the second or third century C.E., for most of the Purāṇas are said to have been composed during the Gupta period. Our suggestion is supported by the Nagardhana copperplate (C.E. 573) of Svāmirāja, which records that while staying under the charming Banyan tree in the Gaṅgā at Prayāga Svāmirāja donated the village named Aṅkollikā to some brāhmaṇas.[58] In the seventh century C.E. the Chinese pilgrim Hsüan Tsang noticed "a great wide-spreading umbrageous tree" at Prayāga, which was said to be the abode of a man-eating demon.[59] According to him, it was in front of a celebrated Deva-temple in the town.[60] This was undoubtedly a Banyan tree which had gained considerable religious popularity by that time, for the practice of committing suicide by jumping down from it is recorded by him.[61] To the east of the town was the spot where the two rivers joined and to the west of this point was a level plain about 10 or 15 li wide covered with white sands.[62] As the tree was in the town, it must have been at a distance of at least two miles to the west of the confluence. The tree mentioned in the Nagardhana copperplate is possibly referred to here. Though in the sixth century C.E. it stood on the very bank of the river, in the next century settlements came up in that area. This could have been possible due to change in the course of the Gaṅgā to the eastern side. This is not unlikely considering the frequent changes in the course of the Gaṅgā from time to time.

In the medieval sources, we come across several references to the sacred Banyan tree at Prayāga. Albirūnī (C.E. 1030) refers to the 'Tree of Prayāga' as if, in his own mind, town and tree were synonymous, the latter giving fame to the former. He says that it was a peculiar kind of tree as its branches sent forth two types of twigs, some directed upward, and others directed downward like roots but without leaves. He locates the tree at the junction of the two rivers and records the practice of committing suicide by jumping from it into the Gaṅgā.[63] Mahmūd Gardīzī (middle of the eleventh century C.E.) speaks of a huge tree named 'batu' (*vaṭa*) on the bank of the river Gaṅgā near the confluence, where suicide was committed.[64] The Maināmāṭī copperplate of king Laḍahacandra (C.E. 1000-1020) mentions the Banyan tree near the confluence.[65] We learn from Kalacuri inscriptions of the eleventh-twelfth centuries C.E. that king Gāṅgeyadeva along with his one hundred wives obtained release from this world at the foot of the famous Vaṭa-tree at Prayāga.[66] Fazlullāh Rashīd-ud-dīn Abdul Khair (C.E. 1247-1317) in his *Jāmi-ut-Tawārīkh* states that the tree of Prayāga was situated at the confluence of the Yamunā and the

Gaṅgā and the latter flowed under it. People mounted the tree and jumped into the river to end their lives.[67] Abdul Qādir Badāunī, who belonged to the sixteenth century, says that some infidels "entered hell by casting themselves down into the deep river from the top of a high tree" at Prayāga.[68] From the description of Tulasīdāsa also it appears that the Vaṭa-tree was near the site of the confluence and stood close to the bank of the Gaṅgā.[69] Thus, all accounts agree that it was at or near the confluence.

On the basis of the above references, we cannot identify the Vaṭa-tree described in the early medieval and medieval sources with that referred to by the Chinese pilgrim.[70] In the time of Hsüan Tsang a sandy plain, 10 or 15 li wide, lay between the town and the place where the rivers met, and the tree in front of a Deva-temple in the town was possibly at least two miles from the confluence. But the Muslim writers speak of the tree on the very bank of the Gaṅgā near the confluence enabling people to cast themselves into its waters and they do not mention any temple near it. It appears that during the long period between the time of Hsüan Tsang and that of Gardīzī and Albirūnī, the Gaṅgā carried away the whole of the sandy plain, encroached upon the town to such an extent as to wash away the temple and the Vaṭa-tree seen by the Chinese traveller. A little later, the river took a new course by changing its direction to the east and the confluence shifted from its original position to the place where emperor Akbar laid the foundation of the fort in C.E. 1583. A new sapling had appeared on the Gaṅgā near the new confluence, growing into a full-fledged tree by the tenth century C.E. Traditional religious practices had come to be associated with it by this time. The Purāṇas do not mention this event and refer to the Vaṭa-tree at the confluence wheresoever it occurred. The locus of the Banyan tree, thus, shifted towards the east due to the change in the position of the confluence sometime during the eighth or ninth century C.E.

The above analysis strikes at the very root of the suggested identification of the Deva-temple mentioned by the Chinese pilgrim with the present Pātālapurī temple in the fort. In the light of the account given by Hṣüan Tsang it may be surmised that the entire area occupied by the fort was under the bed of the Gaṅgā in the seventh century C.E. Hence, Cunningham's suggestion that the area occupied by Akbar's fort represented the site of the town in the time of Hsüan Tsang[71] may not hold good.

The Banyan tree referred to in the medieval sources stood in the open near the confluence from about the ninth century C.E. onwards. But when in the last quarter of the sixteenth century Akbar constructed the fort the tree fell within its four walls. The tree possibly had started pining away as early as the thirteenth century. Rashīd-ud-dīn mentions the withering of one of its two boughs, the suicide being committed from the green one.[72] According to the *Vividhatīrthakalpa*, a Śvetāmbara Jaina work, composed by Jinaprabha Sūri between V.S. 1364 and 1389, the Vaṭa-tree at Prayāga sprouted forth again and again despite being chopped off by the Turks.[73] This is further corroborated by the account of William Finch, a European traveller, who visited the spot in C.E. 1611 in the time of emperor Jahāngīr. He informed that in the 'Moholl' (palace) compound of the fort there was a 'figge tree'. Indians called it "the tree of Life" and believed it to be indestructible. The Paṭhān kings and the ancestors of emperor Jahāngīr had earlier tried – and failed – to destroy the tree. Jahāngīr also made efforts to destroy it by "stocking it up and sifting the very earth under it to gather forth the sprigs". But when the tree made to send forth new shoots from the pit open to the sky, he let it alone with a view to cherish its remains.[74] The *Khulāṣat-ut-Tawārīkh*, a work composed between C.E. 1693 and 1695, also says that within the fort there was a very old tree, called the Akhay Bar, i.e. the imperishable Banyan tree. By the command of emperor Jahāngīr, it was cut down and a cauldron of iron was firmly placed over the stump. But the tree grew again and shook off the obstruction.[75] According to Saubhāgyavijaya, a Jaina saint of the seventeenth century, the tree-spot was obliterated during the reign of Aurangzeb.[76] Thus, the destruction wrought to the Banyan tree by Muslim rulers, especially emperor Jahāngīr, must have proved fatal to it. It may have completely dried up towards the close of Jahāngīr's reign. Joannes De Laet[77] and M.De Thevenot,[78] while describing the fort in C.E. 1628-29 and C.E. 1666-67 respectively, do not mention the worship of any Banyan tree there. The *Prayāga Māhātmya Śatādhyāyī*, a work of the eighteenth century,[79] describes the Vaṭamūla (roots of the Banyan tree) as being five *yojanas* large and gives it hyperbolic attributes.[80] It does not refer to the practice of suicide there. This would suggest that in the eighteenth century the Vaṭa-tree did not exist but the tradition about it was preserved which, in course of time, had been enlarged and transformed into a myth.[81]

The foregoing discussion shows that the celebrated Banyan tree completely withered up during the first quarter of the seventeenth century. It seems that access to it was also denied to the general public, most likely from the time of Jahāngīr. It was deemed not safe to allow pilgrims to visit the site as it had become a part of the Mughal harem. Therefore, a new worship practice, albeit a false one, was started; a log of the Banyan tree was kept in the Pātālapurī temple for satisfying the religious urge of the people. The exact date of the start of the worship of the stump in the temple is, however, not known. It has been mentioned first by Joseph Tieffenthaler, a Jesuit missionary, who happened to be at Allahabad in C.E.

1766-77. While describing the Pātālapurī temple in the fort he wrote in his *Description Historique et Geographique del' Inde*, "However great be the respect which the gentiles have for these idols (in the Pātālapurī temple), they revere more particularly a tree, which in the Indian language, they call Akebar. This tree rises up from the grotto itself, its trunk is similar in thickness to that of the olive tree and divides itself into two equal branches. It is bare, lacking leaves, but nevertheless green and full of sap. If it is cut by a sword, a milk comes out of it. In order that this tree, so strangely sacred for the Hindus, does not dry up, they continually supply its roots with water; people having sweet-smelling flowers on its trunk. Yet it cannot grow further, nor can rise beyond the roof covered with stones. On the four sides around this tree are seen many quadrangular pillars arranged"[82] (Fig. 3).

In this passage there is a reference to the dead forked tree which is found today in the Pātālapurī temple[83] and is worshipped by the public as the relic of the traditional Banyan tree. However, the above account indicates that the Banyan tree worship in the Pātālapurī temple had been in vogue much before C.E. 1765. This is also confirmed by a *sanad* granted by emperor Shāh-i-Ālam II to Ayodhyā Nātha Jogī in Hizri year 1173 (=C.E. 1766), which refers to the donee as the priest of 'Pātālapurī Achaibaṭ'.[84] The existence of the Pātālapurī temple inside the fort was noticed by William Finch (C.E. 1611), Joannes De Laet (C.E. 1628-29), and Thevenot (C.E. 1666-67). However, they do not allude to the banyan worship therein. Thus, it seems that the banyan worship in the Pātālapurī temple was started by some priests sometime between C.E. 1667 and C.E. 1765, the period between the visits of Thevenot and Tieffenthaler. This goes against the suggestion of some scholars that the Pātālapurī temple represents the site of the traditional Banyan tree.[85] It should be noted that the tree existed in the palace area of the fort and a richly paved courtyard in which the Mughal emperor kept his *darbar* intervened between the palace complex and the site of the Pātālapurī temple. This is clearly brought out from the description of the fort by William Finch. He says:

> You enter thorow two faire gates into a faire court, in which stands a pillar of stone (Aśokan pillar) fiftie cubits above ground.... Passing this court you enter a lesse; beyond that a larger, where the king sits on high for his dersane to behold elephants and other beasts to fight. Right under him within a vault are many Pagodas (Pātālapurī temple).... Out of this court is another richly paved where the king keeps his darbar; beyond it another, whence you enter into the mohole, longe, divided into sixteene severall lodgings for sixteene great women with slaves and attendants. In the middest of all the king's lodgings of three stories, each containing sixteene rooms; .... In the midst of the lowest stories is a curious tank

Fig. 3 The everlasting fig-tree (Akṣayavaṭa) as it appears in the *patālpūri*, Allahabad Fort

(Kāmyakūpa). In his moholl is a tree which the Indians call the tree of life (being a wilde Indian fiege tree)[86] (Fig. 4).

The shifting of the venue of the tree-worship from the palace compound to the Pātālapurī temple is recorded by Fanny Parks who lived in Allahabad from C.E. 1827 to C.E. 1845. She writes, "This tree grows in or is enclosed within the walls of the fort, in such a manner that you cannot see it from any place. They take you into a room, which was formerly one of a hammam, or steam bath. This room is called Achibut Chamber, and there with the eyes of faith, the pilgrims behold the ever-lasting tree; which they believe has been there from beginning of time, and will remain there to all eternity. They showed me a crack in the roof, and said, 'Did you not see the branch of the tree has cracked the roof in three places?' I certainly saw three cracks, but whether from a tree or ivy I cannot say; not even a leaf was visible. The door of this chamber has been blocked up, on account of a native in the Collector's office wishing to put up his idol there; the man is a worshipper of Pārisnāth, the god of the heretical Hindoos. No orthodox Hindoo will worship in a temple where there is an image of Pārisnāth; and as this man had raised an altar in the Achibut Chamber, and wished to place his idol thereon, it caused a great commotion; to quell which, the Commandant of the fort bricked up the door, and has never allowed the people entrance since that time".[87] She further records, "When the Achibut Chamber was blocked up, the Brahmans set up the stump of a ber tree in the Patala Pooree, and declared that it was a branch of the real Achibut, that had penetrated through walls. They certainly have established it firmly in that situation, making good the proverbs. Its roots have already reached to Patal (the infernal regions). The morning I visited the Patal Pooree, I saw this stump, which must have been freshly worshipped, as the earth at its base was covered with oil, ghee, boiled rice, and flowers. The passage itself, and the chamber also, were oily, dark, very hot, and slippery. We saw it by lamp-light, the Chiragh (lamp) was carried by a portly Brahman, who has charge of the place,...The resident Hindoos of Prag, who know the trick the Brahmans have played, do not Pooja the false Achibut".[88]

Fanny Parks's account is based on her visit to the respective sites inside the fort in C.E. 1831. She had made her residence on the bank of the Yamunā near the fort and her husband was a high official who became the Collector of Allahabad in C.E. 1836. Therefore, we may accept her account as true, though with certain reservations. Her account proves that the original site of the Banyan tree was not in the Pātālapurī temple but somewhere else inside the fort. The attempt of Jaina devotee to put up an idol of Pārśvanātha in the Akṣayavaṭa chamber and its opposition by

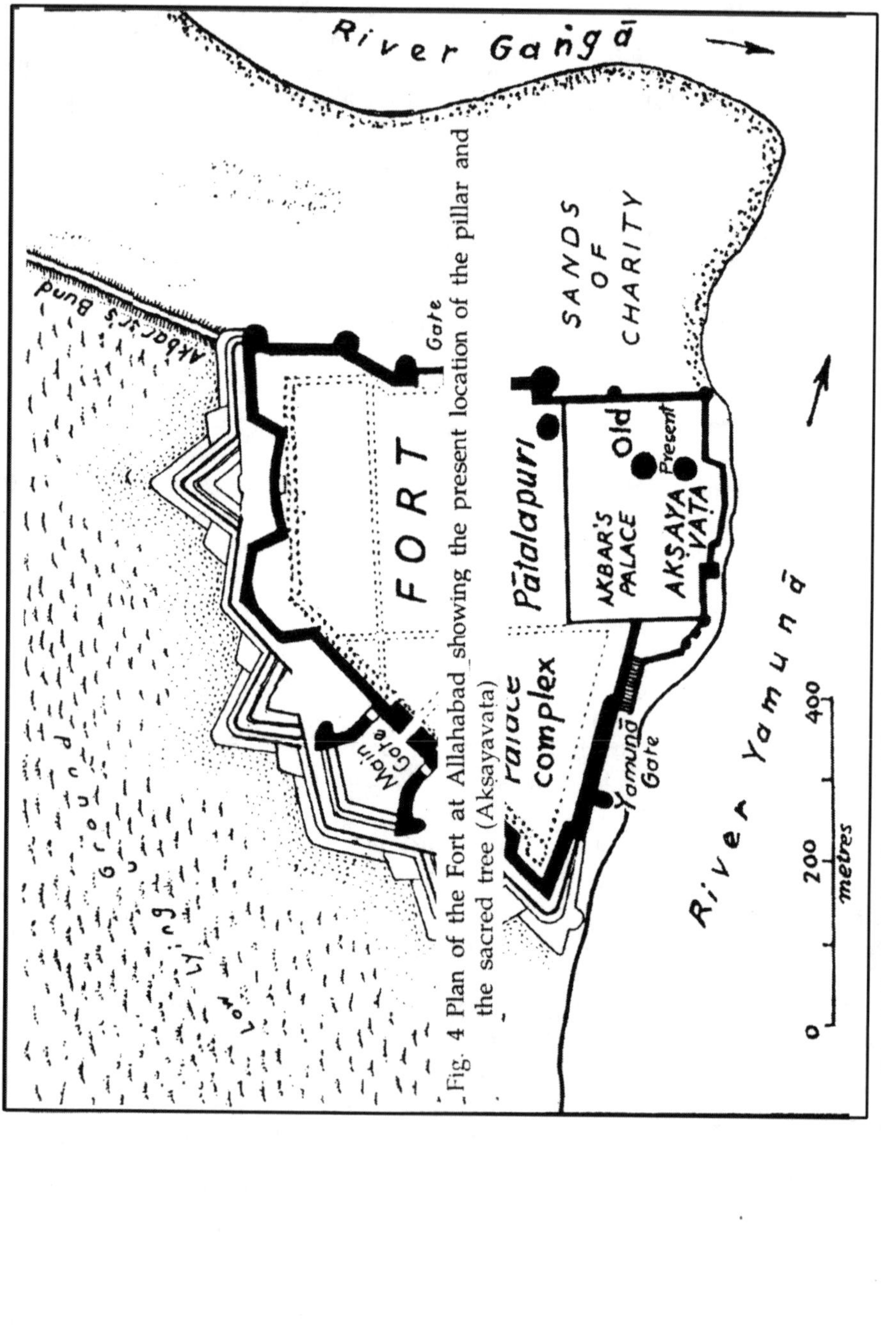

Fig. 4 Plan of the Fort at Allahabad showing the present location of the pillar and the sacred tree (Akṣayavata)

Fig. 4 Plan of the Fort at Allahabad showing the present location of the pillar and the sacred tree (Akṣayavata)

the Hindus reminds of a similar event which occurred in the reign of Akbar. According to Haṁsasoma's *Tīrthamālā*, composed in V.S. 1565 (C.E. 1508), there was the footprint (*caraṇa-cihna*) of Ṛṣabhadeva under the Akhayavaḍa.[89] But the *Tīrthamālā* of Vijayasāgara (C.E. 1607),[90] Jayavijaya (C.E. 1607)[91] and Saubhāgyavijaya (C.E. 1693)[92] record that Rāi Kalyāṇa removed the footprint of Jinendra and established a Śivaliṅga there in V.S. 1648 (C.E. 1591) in the time of Akbar. Fanny Parks does not tell us when the Akṣayavaṭa chamber was built. Her account shows that during the early years of British rule, access to the tree site was allowed possibly on wide demand made by the pilgrims and priests. But on account of the religious rivalry, the commandant of the fort not only closed the way to it for the general public but also bricked up the door of the chamber thereby making the worship-view (*darśana*) of the tree site almost impossible. The fort authorities later on may have decided to shelve the matter on security grounds also.

Thus, the bifurcated log with a green branch, which is found today in the Pātālapurī temple, is merely the trunk of some other Banyan tree, installed by the attendant priests. That the stump being worshipped is spurious is also confirmed by a report published in the daily newspaper named 'Bhārata', dated October 30, 1950, in which the then fort commander Major Kundan Singh admitted having allowed the traditional changeover of the green banyan stump in the Pātālapurī temple by the priests who produced the customary document to this effect. The priests of the Pātālapurī temple also admit the changeover ceremony of the stump every third year.

It is, however, interesting to note that a Banyan tree (Pl. 9) is still standing in the fort. It was discovered by Śivanātha Kāṭjū, a former judge of the Allahabad High Court, in C.E. 1950, in the south-eastern corner of the fort. He claimed that Śrī Ranjan, Professor of Botany in the University of Allahabad, examined it on the request of the defence personnel and suggested that its stump was about 250 years old. This is the tree which was seen by Fanny Parks in C.E. 1831 who says that, 'There is a very fine young ber tree at the gate of the magazine'.[93] It seem that despite the destruction and disappearance of the age-old Banyan tree in the palace complex during the seventeenth century, a small root of it managed to bloom into another tree subsequently at another site in the same area. Thus, the confluence at Prayāga has never been without a Banyan tree in its vicinity.

The antiquity of banyan worship in Prayāga is thus undoubted. It can be traced back at least to the times of the *Rāmāyaṇa*. The banyan worship at the confluence became wide prevalent when a Vaṭa-tree sprouted forth there after the Śyāmavaṭa on the southern bank of Yamunā had become extinct. The Vaṭa-tree at the junction of the holy rivers was of great sanctity for the devotees all over India. The custom of religious suicide not associated with the Śyāmavaṭa, came to be associated with it. The Purāṇas played a leading role in giving it wide popularity. It is not known whether the tree was planted by ordinary devotees in a fit of religious fervour or by representatives of a particular religious sect to commemorate any important event in their history. Possibly it had sprung up at the confluence itself; its situation enhanced its sacredness. The available evidence discussed above reveals its history for about 1,500 years.

The Purāṇas refer to its close association with the prominent gods. Lord Śiva is said to protect it constantly;[94] He has transformed himself into this Vaṭa.[95] Viṣṇu in the form of Mādhava is always present there.[96] Hiraṇyagarbha has the shape of Vaṭa in Prayāga.[97] According to the *Skanda Purāṇa* he, who by resorting to the tree, worships Viṣṇu there gets the merit of residing in the Viṣṇuloka.[98] The *Padma Purāṇa* advises devotees to propitiate Viṣṇu there by tying threads around the tree.[99] The Banyan tree at Prayāga is thus sacred to Śiva and Viṣṇu alike who are supposed to dwell in it. Curiously enough, the *Matsya Purāṇa* says that Śiva was located as Vaṭeśvara at Prayāga by Viṣṇu and the latter in the form of Keśava is always lost under tree in his reveries of yoga.[100] This shows the growth of the Vaiṣṇavite association with the tree. Mārkaṇḍeya is said to have practised penance under it.[101] According to the *Sarvatīrthavandanā* of Nayanasāgara (c. 16th-17th century C.E.), Ṛṣabhadeva, the first Tīrthaṅkara, attained *kevala-jñāna* under the Vaṭa-tree at Prayāga and delivered a sermon there.[102] In the *Prācīna Tīrthamālāsaṅgraha* we find conflicting statements regarding the association of Ṛṣabhadeva with the tree. Haṁsasoma says that Ṛṣabha's initiation took place there,[103] while Jayavijaya maintains that he delivered his first sermon there.[104] Saubhāgyavijaya says that he broke his fast there,[105] but Śīlavijaya is of the opinion that he practised penances for one year under this tree.[106] These statements of Jaina saints of the sixteenth-seventeenth centuries are unacceptable due to their controversial nature. The evidence of the association of Ṛṣabhadeva with the tree at Prayāga found in these late Jaina sources, shows that in the medieval times the Jainas made attempts to associate their religion with this Brāhmaṇical *tīrtha*. We know that Ṛṣabhadeva renounced the world under an aśoka tree in a garden named Siddhārthavana at Ayodhyā,[107] broke his fast at Hastināpur,[108] attained omniscience under a great nyagrodha tree in a grove called Śakaṭamukha at Purimatāla, the chief suburb of Ayodhyā,[109] and delivered his first sermon in the *samavasaraṇa* assembly held there.[110]

The Vaṭa-tree at the confluence is described as the royal umbrella over Prayāga's head.[111] This tree with its dark shade was believed to remove all the three kinds of fatigue (i.e. *daihika*, *daivika*, and *bhautika*) of pilgrims.[112] Its mere sight destroys the sin of Brahmanicide.[113] Everlasting merit accrues from the feeding of brāhmaṇas with devotion under it.[114] It is said that this tree is not burnt in spite of the combined fury of all the twelve suns (*dvādaśa-Ādityas*) that reduces the whole universe to ashes.[115] Lord Viṣṇu in the form of an infant child sucking his toe is said to lie down on its leaf when the whole world is one mass of water.[116] It is the very tree where Mārkaṇḍeya found shelter inside the stomach of the Divine Child at the time of the Great Deluge.[117] The roots of this tree are declared to have spread up to the infernal regions.[118] This tree is indeed known as Akṣayavaṭa, for it does not perish even at the time of the dissolution of the universe.[119]

The reference to the Divine Child resting on the branch of a Banyan tree in the midst of the Great Deluge is found in the *Mahābhārata* and the Purāṇas in the context of the description of creation. But the location of the great nyagrodha with which the child is shown associated is not specified. It is the Vaṭa-tree at Gayā which in the literary and epigraphical records[120] is mentioned first as Akṣayavaṭa/Akṣayakaraṇavaṭa. According to the *Mahābhārata* and the Purāṇas, it was so called because it immortalized the offerings given there to the manes.[121] In the texts, the expression Akṣayavaṭa does not signify an undying Banyan tree. However, one verse in the *Gayāmāhātmya* section of the *Vāyu Purāṇa* says that Viṣṇu in the form of a child lies on its end at the time of the Deluge.[122] It seems that after the legend about Deluge had acquired a respectability people belonging to Prayāga and Gayā tried to acquire for their respective *tīrtha* the prestigious association with the Deluge-story on the ground of the presence of a sacred Vaṭa-tree there. We cannot be sure as to which of the two *tīrthas* was first in establishing a tradition of imperishability for its Banyan tree. That the one at Prayāga was regarded as an eternal tree, the only witness of the creation and destruction of the whole universe, by the tenth century C.E. is proved by the reference in the Maināmāṭī copperplate of Laḍahacandradeva.[123] The tree is called Akṣayavaṭa not because it really was everlasting. There is no reason for literal interpretation; the tree of Prayāga was mythically everlasting, as the archetypal tree of the cosmogony.

The Vaṭa-tree at Prayāga was originally without any specific name. The *Kūrma*, *Agni*, *Narasiṁha* and *Vāmana Purāṇas* neither speak about its imperishability nor give it the name of Akṣayavaṭa; it is mentioned simply as Prayāga-vaṭa.[124] The *Matsya* and *Nāradīya Purāṇas*, which contain verses eulogizing its eternity, also mention it merely as Prayāga-vaṭa.[125] It is in the *Skanda* and *Padma Purāṇas* which refer to its invincibility that the name Akṣayavaṭa occurs for this tree.[126] The name Prayāga-vaṭa is corroborated by foreign travellers to India[127] and some inscriptions.[128] In the Nagardhana copperplate of Svāmirāja it is mentioned as Caṭukavaṭa[129] but we have not come across this designation elsewhere. This tree is also called Śyāmavaṭa in the *Padma Purāṇa*, the lexicon of Hemacandra (c. C.E. 1088-1172) and the Medinīkośa (c. C.E. 1300) in the sense of Prayāga-vaṭa.[130] This name was evidently adopted after the name of Śyāmavaṭa in the *Rāmāyaṇa*.

REFERENCES

1. Cunningham, A., *The Ancient Geography of India*, Vol. I, p.328; Irwin, John C., *JRAS*, 1983, p.265.
2. Katju, S.N., 'Story of the Eternal Tree of Creation', *Leader*, Kumbha Supplement, Feb., 1954; Roy, U.N., *Studies in Ancient Indian History and Culture*, Vol. 1, pp.200-201.
3. Crooke, William, *Religion and Folklore of Northern India*, p.400.
4. Karmarkar, A.P., *The Religions of India*, Vol. I, p.194.
5. यत्राश्वत्था न्यग्रोधा महावृक्षाः शिखण्डिनः ।
   तत् परेताप्सरसः प्रतिबुद्धा अभूतन ॥ *Atharvaveda*, IV.37.4.
   भद्रात् प्लक्षन्निस्तिष्ठस्यश्वत्थात् खदिरात् घवात् ।
   भद्रान्न्यग्रोधात् पर्णात् सा न एह्यरुन्धति ॥ *ibid.*, V.5.5.
   Macdonell and Keith, *Vedic Index of Names and Subjects*, Vol. I, p.462.
6. Śat.Br., XIII.2.7.3.
7. *Ibid.*
8. *Ait.Br.*, 7.5.30.
9. *Ibid.*, 7.5.31.
10. *Ch.Up.*, 6.12.1.3.
11. नैयग्रोध औदुम्बर आश्वत्थः प्लाक्ष इतीध्मो भवत्येते वै गन्धर्वाप्सरसां गृहाः । *Tai.Sam.*, III.4.8.4.
12. अश्वत्थः सूर्यदैवत्यः पलाशो यमदैवतः ।
    न्यग्रोधो वारूणो वृक्षः प्राजापत्यः उदुम्बरः ॥ *Gobhila*, 4.7.24.
13. Coomaraswamy, A.K., *History of Indian and Indonesian Art*, p.47.
14. Agrawala, V.S., *Ancient Indian Folk Cults*, p.115.
15. वारिदा पुरिमा साखा अन्नपानञ्च दक्खिणा ।
    नारिदा पच्छिमा साखा सब्बकामे च उत्तरा ॥
    Jataka, Vol. IV, p.352; Agrawala, V.S., *op.cit.*, p.119.
16. Mehta, R.N., *Pre-Buddhist India*, p.326; *Jataka*, Vol. I, pp.259-261.
17. *Mbh*, III.186.114-115; *BhagP*, XI.30.42; *SkP*, IV. 7.52; *MP*, 167.31; *BP*, 53.27-32, 55.2-11.
18. *MP*, 104.10, 111.10; *SkP*, II.iv.3.38.
19. *BhavP*, II.1.10.
20. *KP*, I.48.6.
21. Allen, A.H., 'The Vaṭa-Sāvitrī-Vrata', *JAOS*, XXI-2, p.58f; Dange, S.A.,

'Sāvitrī and the Banyan', *Purāṇa*,Vol. V(2), pp.258-266. It is to be noted that the tale of Sāvitrī as given in the *Mahābhārata* (III.293-297) is silent about the Banyan tree. It is the Purāṇic version of the tale that brings in the tree. The tale and the ritual of the banyan worship were quite different originally. At a later period the tale was used in the ritual and the banyan came to form an integral part of the tale. Dange, S.A., *op.cit.*, p.264.

22. *Mbh*, I. 25 ff; *Rām*, II.35.27-34.
23. Dange, S.A., *op.cit.*, p.265.
24. *Mbh*, III.82-72, 85.8, 93.13, XIII.88.14; *VaP*, II.44.42, 50.93-99; *AgP*, 115.70-74; *GP*, I.83.25, 43, 84.31-32; *BP*, 25.68; *NP*, II.47.1-4; *PdP*, I.11.72.
25. *BP*, 61.66-67.
26. *BrvP*, III.33.30-32.
27. *BP*, 57.12-15, 60.17-18, 68.65, 77.16; *SkP*, II.ii.4.53, II.ii.10.14, 30.24-27.
28. *BP*, 20.87-88; *KP*, I.48.5.
29. *Rām*, II.55.4.
30. *Ibid.*, 55.5.
31. ततो न्यग्रोधमासाद्य महान्तं हरितच्छदम् ।
    परीतं बहुभिर्वृक्षैः श्यामं सिद्धोपसेवितम् ॥ *Rām*, II.55.6.
32. तस्मिन् सीताञ्जलिं कृत्वा प्रयुञ्जीताशिषां क्रियाम् ।
    समासाद्य च तं वृक्षं वसेद्वातिक्रमेत वा ॥ *Rām*, II.55.7.
33. *Rām*, II.55.8-9.
34. तेषु ते प्लवमुत्सृज्य प्रस्थाय यमुनावनात् ।
    श्यामं न्यग्रोधमासेदुः शीतलं हरितच्छदम् ॥ *Rām*, II.55.23.
35. न्यग्रोधं समुपागम्य वैदेही चाभ्यवन्दत ।
    नमस्तेऽस्तु महावृक्ष पारयेन्मे पतिर्व्रतम् ॥
    कौसल्यां चैव पश्येम सुमित्रां च यशस्विनीम् ।
    इति सीताञ्जलिं कृत्वा पर्यगच्छद्वनस्पतिम् ॥ *Rām*, II.55.24-25.
36. *Rām*, II.55.6.
37. This ghāṭa may be identified with the modern Kakarahāghāṭa in Mīrāpura locality where the bank of the Yamunā is fairly firm and solid forming a ghāṭa in ancient times. This ford does not appear to have been a regular ferry in the days of Rāma, and probably lost its importance during the Mughal period.
38. *Mbh*, III.82.72, 85.8, 93.13.
39. *Mbh*, XIII.88.14.
40. ततः कदाचित् पश्यामि तस्मिन् सलिलसंप्लवे ।
    न्यग्रोधं सुमहान्तं वै विशालं पृथिवीपते ।
    शाखायां तस्य वृक्षस्य विस्तीर्णायां नराधिप ।
    पर्यङ्के पृथिवीपाल दिव्यास्तरणसंस्तृते ॥
    उपविष्टं महाराज पूर्णेन्दुसदृशाननम् ।
    फुल्लपद्मविशालाक्षं बालं पश्यामि भारत ॥ *Mbh*, III.186.81-83.

41. *Mbh*, III.186.91.
42. *Mbh*, III.186.110-115.
43. गङ्गां शतद्रुं सीतां च यमुनामथ कौशिकीम् ।
चर्मण्वतीं वेत्रवतीं चन्द्रभागां सरस्वतीम् ।। *Mbh*, III.186.93.
44. Gode, P.K., 'The History of the Akṣayavaṭa', *Studies in Indian Cultural History*, Vol. I, p.378.
45. *MP*, 166.13-66; *BhagP*, 9.19-32; *SkP*, II.ii.3.3-50; *BP*, *adhyāyas* 52-56.
46. The *SkP* (II.ii.3.5) locates the tree at a place which appeared like Puruṣottama kṣetra. The *BhagP* (XII.9.31) says that the Banyan tree stood on an elevation of earth in the sea of deluge.
47. Bhandarkar, R.G., *Vaiṣṇavism, Śaivism and Minor Religious Systems*, p.45.
48. *MP*, 166.5, 36; *SkP*, II.ii.3.45; *BP*, 55.16-17.
49. Lal B.B., 'The Rāmāyaṇa and Archaeology', p.9.
50. Winternitz, M., *A History of Indian Literature*, Vol. I, p.494.
51. *Ibid.*, p.454.
52. S.M. Bharadvaj assigns the *tīrthayātrā* section to *circa* third century B.C. (*Hindu Places of Pilgrimage*, p.15). According to D.C. Sircar, it was composed earlier than the Gupta Age (*Studies in the Geography of Ancient and Medieval India*, p.178). C. Bulcke places the composition of the *Āraṇyakaparvan* in the second century C.E. (*Rāmakathā* p.33). Jacob Ensink assigns the *tīrthayātrā* section to the first centuries of the Christian era (*Ludwik Sternback Felicitation Volume*, Part I, p.114).
53. त्वया पुरस्तादुपयाचितो यः सोऽयं वटः श्याम इति प्रतीतः ।
राशिर्मणीनामिव गारुडानां सपद्मरागः फलितो विभाति ।।
Raghuvaṁśa, XIII.53.
54. अयमसौ भरद्वाजावेदितश्चित्रकूटयायिनि वर्त्मनि वनस्पतिः कालिन्दीतटे वटः श्यामो नाम ।
Uttararāmacarita, Act I, p.16.
55. श्यामो नाम वटः सोऽयम् एतस्याद्भुतकर्मणः ।
छायामप्यधिवास्तव्यैः पदं ज्योतिर्निषेव्यते ।।
Anargharāghava, VII, 129.
56. *Amarakośa* (*kāṇḍa* I, *varga* 5, verse 14; *kāṇḍ* III, *varga* 3, verse 144) lists Śyāma along with other words for different colours.
57. धत्तेऽभितश्चामरचारुकान्तिं सितासिते यत्र सरिद्वरेण्ये ।
आद्यो वटश्छत्रमिवाति भाति स तीर्थराजो जयति प्रयागः ।।
PdP, VI.23.31.
58. आषाढसंवत्सरे चैत्रामावस्यायां जाह्नवीमध्ये चटुकवटसंस्थितेन ग्रहोपरागे...।
Ep. Ind., Vol. XXVIII, p.9, II. 14-15.

V.V. Mirashi translates *'jāhnavīmadhye caṭuka vaṭa-samsthitena'* as 'staying at the Caṭukavaṭa in the midst of the Ganges' (*Ibid.*, p.111). He suggests that Caṭukavaṭa may be Akṣayavaṭa at Prayāga but this name is not found elsewhere. We feel that the word 'Caṭukavaṭa' is a compound in which the first word is an adjective and the second is a noun. 'Caṭuka' does not give any relevant meaning. Possibly the intended reading was 'Caṭula' which means fine, charming, beautiful, lovely, trembling, unstuffy, etc. 'Caṭula' was corrupted into 'Caṭuka'. Further, the term 'Jāhnavīmadhye' is not to be taken literally. It may mean 'on the very bank of Gaṅgā'.

59. Watters, *On Yuan Chwang's Travels in India*, Vol. I, p.362.
60. *Ibid.*
61. *Ibid.*
62. *Ibid.*, p.364; Beal, *The Life of Hiuen Tsiang*, p.90; Beal, *Buddhist Records of the Western World*, Vol. II, p.253.
63. Sachau, *Alberuni's India*, Vol. II, pp.170-171.
64. Gardizi, p.639 (40).
65. *Pakistan Archaeology*, No. 3, p.40; Sircar, D.C., *Epigraphic Discoveries in East Pakistan*, p.73.
66. प्राप्ते प्रयागवटमूलनिवेशबन्धौ सार्द्धं शतेन गृहिणीभिरमुत्र मुक्तिम् ।
    The Khairā plate of Yaśaḥkarṇa dated C.E. 1071-72, *Ep. Ind.*, Vol. XII, p.211; The Jabalapur plate of Yaśaḥkarṇa dated C.E. 1122, *Ep. Ind.*, Vol. II, p.4; The Jabalapur plate of Jayasiṁha dated C.E. 1167, *Ep. Ind.*, Vol. XI, p.94; The Kumbhī plate of Vijayasiṁha dated C.E. 1181, *JASB*, Vol. XXXI (1862), p.117.
67. Elliot and Dowson, *History of India*, Vol. I, p.55, fn. 2; Elliot, *Bibliographical Index*, Vol. I, p.35 fn.
68. *Muntakhb-ut-Tawārīkh*, Vol. II, p.179; Elliot and Dowson, *History of India*, Vol. I, pp.328-329.
69. संगमु सिंहासनु सुठि सोहा । छत्रु अखयबटु मुनि मन मोहा ।
    चंवर जमुन अरु गंग तरंगा । देखि होहिं दुख दारिद भंगा ॥
    Rāmacaritamānasa, II.105.7-8.
70. Roy, U.N., *Studies in Ancient Indian History and Culture*, Vol. I, pp.194-195, 200.
71. Cunningham, A., *The Ancient Geography of India*, Vol. I, p.328.
72. Elliot and Dowson, *History of India*, Vol. I, p.55, fn. 2; Elliot, *Bibliographical Index*, Vol. I, p.35 fn.
73. वटश्च तत्र गणशस्तुरुष्कैश्छिन्नोऽपि मुहुर्मुहुः प्ररोहति ।
    Vividhatīrthakalpa, p.68.
74. Foster, William (ed.), *Early Travels in India*, p.178.
75. *Khulāṣat-ut-Tawārīkh*, folio 37a; Sarkar, J.N., *India of Aurangzeb*, p.27.
76. *Prācīna Tīrthamālāsaṅgraha*, p.77.
77. *De Imperio Magni Mogolis*, tr. by J.S. Hoyland under the title 'The Empire of Great Mogol', pp.63-64.
78. Sen, S.N. (ed.), *Indian Travels of Thevenot and Careri*, pp.92-94.
79. Bonazzoli, G., 'Prayāga and Its Kumbhamelā', *Purāṇa*, Vol. XIX(1), pp.86-88.
80. *Prayāga Māhātmya Śatādhyāyī*, 32.6-10.
81. Bonazzoli, *op.cit.*, p.145.
82. Sinha, S.N., *The Mid-Gangetic Region in the Eighteenth Century* (Some

Observations of Joseph Tieffenthaler), pp.34-35. *Description Historique et Geographique de Inde* was published from Berlin in 1786-89. Tieffenthaler had extensively toured the mid-Gangetic region for about ten years (C.E. 1760-1770).

83. Thornton, who wrote his Gazetteer in the middle of the nineteenth century, has referred to Tieffenthaler for recording that there was a dead forked tree in the temple. See *Statistical, Descriptive and Historical Account of the North-western Provinces of India*, Vol. VIII, part II, p.62. See also Ojha, K.C., *Journal of Allahabad Historical Society*, 1962, pp.1-5.
84. I have received an abstract translation of the *sanad* from Mr. Nagendra Nath Yogeshvara, one of the priests of Pātālapurī Akṣayavaṭa.
85. Cunningham, A., *The Ancient Geography of India*, Vol. I, p.328; Irwin, John C., 'The Ancient Pillar-cult at Prayāga (Allahabad): Its pre-Aśokan origins', *JRAS*, 1983, p.265.
86. Foster, William (ed.), *Early Travels in India*, pp.177-178. The famous pool called Kāmyakūpa was filled in and obliterated when the East India Company made attempts to convert the fort into a modern stronghold in 1798. The tower-like building forming part of the Palace Complex was known to have incorporated at ground level the sacred reservoir. Irwin, John C., *JRAS*, 1983, p.269.
87. Parks, Fanny, *Wanderings of a Pilgrim in Search of the Picturesque*, Vol. I, pp.213-214.
88. *Ibid.*, p.215.
89. *Prācīna Tīrthamālāsaṅgraha*, Vol. I, p.14, *śloka* 4.
90. *Ibid.*, p.3, *ḍhāla* 2, *śloka* 2.
91. *Ibid.*, p.24, *ḍhāla* 1, *śloka* 11.
92. *Ibid.*, p.77, *ḍhāla* 3, *śloka* 11.

    Rāi Kalyāṇa is mentioned as an important dignitary of the time of Akbar in the *Akbarnāmā*, Vol. III, p.683 and *Muntakhab-ut-Tawārīkh*, Vol. II, p.49. According to Saubhāgyavijaya, the Śivaliṅga was destroyed during the reign of Aurangzeb. *Prācīna Tīrthamālāsaṅgraha*, Vol. I, p.77, *ḍhāla* 3, *śloka* 12.
93. Parks, Fanny, *op.cit.*, Vol. I, p.214. The magazine was built after destroying the Mughal battlements and royal apartments during the first decade of the nineteenth century. It stands almost on the top of the underground temple.
94. तं वटं रक्षति सदा शूलपाणिर्महेश्वरः । *MP*, 103.9a =*TvK*, 137 =*TS*, 5 =*TP*, 323; *KP*, I.34.25a=*TS*, 9=*Śabdakalpadruma*, p.288; *PdP*, III.41.10a.
95. महेश्वरो वटो भूत्वा तिष्ठते परमेश्वरः ।
    PdP, III.48.6a; *MP*, 110.10a=*Tvk*, 151=*TS*, 7.
    यत्र देवो महादेवो देव्या सह महेश्वरः ।
    आस्ते वटेश्वरो नित्यं तत् तीर्थं तत् तपोवनम् ॥ *KP*, I.37.9.
    दृष्ट्वा वटेश्वरं रूद्रं...। *VamP*, 57.28b.

96. माधवाख्यस्तत्र देवः सुखं तिष्ठति नित्यशः ।
तस्य वै दर्शनं कार्यं महापापैः प्रमुच्यते ॥ *PdP*, VI.14.10.
यत्र लक्ष्मीपतिः साक्षाद्वैकुण्ठादेत्य मानवान् ।
श्रीमाधवस्वरूपेण नयेद्विष्णोः परं पदम् ॥ *SkP*, IV.7.53=*TS*, 11.
97. हिरण्यगर्भो विज्ञेयः स साक्षाद्वटरूपधृक् ।
SkP, IV. 7.52a=*TS*, 11 =*TP*, 326.
98. *SkP*, IV. 7.53b=*TS*, 11.
99. *PdP*, VI. i.24.9.
100. *MP*, 21.9.
101. प्रयागमासाद्य पुनः स्नात्वा तीर्थे गरीयसि ।
मार्कण्डेयो महातेजास्तेपे वटतले तपः ॥ *NarP*, 12.4.
102. Joharapurakara, Vidyadhara, *Tīrthavandanasaṅgraha*, p.160; Jain, Balabhadra, *Bhārata ke Digambara Jaina Tīrtha*, Vol. I, pp.135, 136.
103. *Prācīna Tīrthamālāsa=mgraha*, p.14.
104. *Ibid.*, p.24.
105. *Ibid.*, p.77.
106. *Ibid.*, p.108.
107. *Kalpasūtra*, 7.211; *Padmapurāṇa* of Raviṣeṇācārya, 3.280-282, *Tṛṣaṣṭiśalākāpuruṣacarita*, I.3.61-74; *Ādipurāṇa* of Jinasenācārya 17.181, 201.203; *Prakrita Proper Names*, Vol. II, p.787.
108. *Harivaṁśapurāṇa* of Jinsenācārya, 9.157-189; *Tṛṣaṣṭiśalākāpuruṣacarita*, I.3.249-295.
109. *Kalpasūtra*, 7.212; *Harivaṁśapurāṇa* of Jinasenācārya, 9.205-210; *Tṛṣaṣṭi*, I.3.389-398, 512; *Ādipurāṇa* of Jinasenācārya, 20.218-220, 268.
110. *Tṛṣaṣṭi*, I.3.422ff.
111. *PdP*, Vi.i.23.31.
112. *Ibid.*, Vi.i.23.27.
113. *Ibid.*, Vi.i.2.7.
114. तत् समीपे द्विजान् भक्त्या सम्भोज्याक्षयपुण्यभाक् ।
SkP, IV.7.52b.
115. तत्र ते द्वादशादित्यास्तपन्ति रुद्रसंश्रिताः ।
निर्दहन्ति जगत्सर्वं वटमूलं न दह्यते ॥
MP, 105.12=*Tvk*, 142=*TS*, 5=*TP*, 344; NP, II.63.140b-141a; *PdP*, III.43.12b-13a=*TC*, 48.
116. नष्टचन्द्रार्कपवनं यदा चैकार्णवं जगत् ।
स्वपित्येव वै विष्णुर्जायमानः पुनः पुनः ॥
PdP, III.43.13b-14a; *MP*, 105,13=*TvK*, 142=*TS*, 5=*TP*, 344.
हरिश्च भगवांस्तत्र प्रजापति-पुरस्कृतः ।
आस्ते तत्र पुटे देवि पादांगुष्ठं धयञ्छिशुः ॥
NP, II.63.141-142a.
स चाक्षयवटः ख्यातः कल्पान्तेऽपि च दृश्यते ।
शेते विष्णुर्यस्य पत्रे अतोऽव्ययः स्मृतः ॥ *PdP*, VI.i.24.8.

117. प्रलयेऽपि यमारुह्य मृकण्डुतनयोऽवसत् ।
SkP, IV.7.51b=*TS*, 11 =*TP*, 326.
मृकण्डुसूनुना यत्र प्रविश्य मन्मुखे स्थितम् ।
PdP q. in *TS*, 60.
118. तत्राक्षयवटोऽप्यस्ति सप्तपातालमूलवान् ।
SkP, IV.7.51a=*TS*, 11 =*TP*, 325.
अक्षयोऽयं सुरैः सेव्य आपातालजटो वटः ।
PdP q. in *TS*, 60.
119. *PdP*, VI.i.24.8; *SKP*, IV.7.51=*TS*, 11=*TP*, 325-26.
120. *Mbh*, III.82.72=*TvK*, 169; *PdP*, III.38.3; *Mbh*, III.85.8, 13-14, XII.88.14-15; *AgP*, 115.70; *NP*, II.47.1-4; *VaP*, II.44.42, 50.93-100; *Viṣṇusmṛti*, 88.5, 66; *Bṛhaspatismṛti*, III, 67; GP, 83.22, 38, 84.30; *Bhāratamañjarī* (*Āraṇyakaparva*, 654-655), p.57. The Gayā Ins. of Yakṣapāla of the middle of the 11th cent. C.E. mentions the Akṣayavaṭa at Gayā (*vaṭech=ākṣye*), *Ep. Ind.*, XXXVI, p.94.
121. तत्राक्षयवटो नाम त्रिषु लोकेषु विश्रुतः ।
पितृणां तत्र वै दत्तमक्षयं भवति प्रभो ॥
Mbh, III.82.72=*TvK*, 169.
यत्रासौ कीर्त्यते विप्रैरक्षय्यकरणो वटः ।
यत्र दत्तं पितृभ्योऽन्नमक्षय्यं भवति प्रभो ॥
Mbh, III.85.8.
गयायां धर्मपृष्ठे च सदसि ब्रह्मणस्तथा ।
गयाशीर्षेऽक्षयवटे पितृणां दत्तमक्षयम् ॥
Bṛhaspati, III.67=*TvK*, 167; *PdP*, III.38.3, I.11.72; *NP*, II.47.1-4; *VaP*, II.50.93.
122. एकार्णवे वटस्याग्रे यः शेते योगनिद्रया ।
बालरूपधरस्तस्मै नमस्ते योगशायिने ॥
VaP, II.50.98b-99a.
123. सोप्यत्रैव युग-क्षयाखिल-जगद्ध्वंसैक-साक्षी वटः ।
Pakistan Archaeology, No. 3, p.40; Sircar, D.C., *Epigraphic Discoveries in East Pakistan*, p.73.
124. *KP*, I.34.25a, 35.18a; *AgP*, 111.13a; *NarP*, 10.4; *VamP*, 57.28b.
125. *MP*, 103.9a, 105.11a, 110.10a; *NP*, II.63.139a-140b.
126. *SkP*, IV.7.51; *PdP*, VI.i.24.7.9.
127. Watters, *On Yuan Chwang*, Vol. I, p.362; Gardizi, p.639 (40); Sachau, *Alberuni's India*, Vol. I, p.200, Vol. II. p.170; Elliot, *Bibliographical Index*, Vol. I, p.35.
128. प्राप्ते प्रयागवटमूलनिवेशबन्धौ सार्द्धं शतेन गृहिणीभिरमुटत्र मुक्तिम् ।
JASB, Vol. XXXI, p.117; *Ep.Ind.*, Vol. XI, p.94; *Ep.Ind.*, Vol. XII. p.211; *Ep.Ind.*, Vol. II, p.4. The *Vividhatīrthakalpa* (p.68) also refers to it as Prayāga-vaṭa.
129. *Ep.Ind.*, Vol. XXVIII, p.9.

130. श्यामो वटोऽश्यामगुणो वृणोति स्वच्छायया श्यामलया जनानाम् ।
श्यामः श्रमं कृन्तति यत्र दृष्टः स तीर्थराजो जयति प्रयागः ।।
PdP, VI.i.23.27.
श्यामोऽम्बुदे शितौ।हरिते प्रयागवटे कोकिले वृद्धदारके । इति हैमः ।
Anekārthasaṅgraha, 346b-347a.
श्यामो वटे प्रयागस्य वारिदे वृद्धदारके। इति मेदिनी । *Medinījkośa*, 25.31b.
Śabdaratnasamanvayakośa of Shahaji (p. 226) reads as श्यामः प्रयागस्थवटे
Gode, P.K., *Studies in Indian Cultural History*, Vol. I, p. 380.

Chapter V

SACRED RITUALS

Pilgrimage is considered as an alternative to religious practice by means of Vedic sacrifices. It is held even more excellent than sacrifice because it may be performed by anyone, be he rich or poor, brāhmaṇa or śūdra.[1] An inseparable relation binds *tīrtha* to *tīrthayātrā*, because to go on pilgrimage means to enjoy the sacredness of the *tīrtha*. Therefore, the Purāṇic *māhātmyas* not only describe religious observances that are to be fulfilled at the beginning and durng the *tīrthayātrā*,[2] but also that which are to be fulfilled in the sacred place. A *tīrtha* is considered especially appropriate for the performance of such religious rites as *homa* (fire oblation), *pūjā* (worship of deities), *vrata* (vows), *upavāsa* (fast), *dāna* (charity), *snāna* (bath), *tarpaṇa* (satiation of gods, sages and ancestors), *piṇḍadāna* (offering funeral cakes), *śrāddha* (ancestral rite), *tapas* (austerities), chanting of hymns, listening to religious discourses, study of scriptures, etc. The performance of rituals are commended at *tīrthas* as infinitely more effective than when done in one's own home. On the rationale of the commendation of such holy performances Aiyangar comments, "None of these rites will ordinarily be approached in one's own home with that feeling of ecstasy and devotion with which the pilgrim, who has made the long tour, after undergoing the rigour of the *yātrā*, will bring it with at a *tīrtha*. The magic which multiplies the efficacy of the rites lies less in the waters of the *tīrtha* than upon the moral discipline which the pilgrim has undergone before reaching it and his mental state after he does so".[3] It may be noted that pilgrimage affords an opportunity for an ascent to spiritual perfection; and the efficacy of a religious observance at the *tīrtha* depends on the mental and physical purity with which it is done.

Tīrthas vary widely not only in degree of spiritual efficacy, but also in the rites considered especially appropriate to them. Thus, for instance, Gayā is considered an especially auspicious place for the performance of *śrāddha*, but the tonsure ritual is prohibited there. Tonsure is believed to be more meritorious at Prayāga than done at any other *tīrtha*. The spiritual and religious practices at *tīrthas* are one of the most important factors that have substantially contributed to the strengthening of cultural unity in the country. The solemnity of pilgrimage and the sanctity of the *tīrtha* are enforced by these rites and rituals which are considered as especially auspicious there. However, the real point is not forgotten; namely that, just as a *tīrtha* is ultimately an internal quality rather than a physical place so too the pilgrimage symbolised by the essential rituals is ultimately an internal spiritual experience.

Among the sacred places suggested to the pilgrims, Prayāga is one of the most important. The pilgrim, who full of devotion undertakes the pilgrimage to Prayāga, once arrived has to follow certain rituals and observances which range from simple salutation to offering of flowers and from devoted meditation to elaborate observances. He has not gone to Prayāga as a tourist but as a hankerer after purification and salvation. The Dharmaśāstric texts give the details of what rituals a devotee should perform in the sacred space. This may be a sacrifice, but often it is tonsure and fast, bath, worship of the deities, charity, ancestral rites (*tarpaṇa* and *śrāddha*), and sometimes religious suicide. Immediately upon arrival, the pilgrim is advised to prostrate completely, then he is required to take a preliminary bath in the Saṅgama and has to undergo tonsure in his wet clothing. After shaving he should bathe according to the rule prescribed in the *śāstras*.[4] Then other observances follow. At present three rituals are mainly kept: shaving, bathing and giving gifts. Even these practices are more honoured in the breach than in the observance. The inhabitants of Prayāga need not have their heads shaved and Sikhs have only a symbolical little piece of hair cut off as do married women; widows and south Indian women, however, are as a rule shaved entirely. The vast majority of pilgrims simply bathe, giving a fee to their paṇḍās. *Godāna* (gift of cow) is simply reduced to a nominal ceremony. But the ardent pilgrims and kalpavāsīs generally perform the prescribed rituals properly. Such are the prominent features of religious life in Prayāga. No *tīrtha* presents a more interesting field of observation or more startling diversities of beliefs as Prayāga does. In this chapter an attempt has been made to give a typological description of the various important sacred performances that are usually observed in a place of pilgrimage which is famous as the king of *tīrthas*.

MUṆḌANA

Muṇḍana is a specific ceremony related to the act of purification. It means the tonsure of head, moustaches and beard, and is different from *kṣaura* which means only shaving of the head.[5] It is an indispensable element of the *tīrthasnāna* because of its adoption by the learned and self-abnegating men who have given up all desires. The reason behind this is that when one reaches the sacred centre the multitude of sins committed become centered in the hair and they stay there even after the holy dip at the *tīrtha*,[6] therefore, one should have the hair cut off there, because its removal removes the accumulated sins of the period of a *kalpa* (aeon).[7] The tonsure is generally recommended for performance at all *tīrthas* except at Kurukṣetra, Viśālā (Ujjayinī), Virajā (Jājpur on the Vaitaraṇī river in Orissa) and Gayā.[8]

The ceremony of *muṇḍana* is, however, considered as very auspicious at Prayāga (Pl. 10). It is prescribed to be performed on the Gaṅgā only at Prayāga.[9] It must be preceded by an immersion in the holy confluence of the rivers there.[10] It is prescribed even on the *upavāsa* (fast) day of the arrival at this holy place, though it is contrary to the general rule.[11] It is made compulsory there, and even generally prohibited days for shaving are also overruled and allowed for it.[12] It should be noted that the ceremonial tonsure takes place only once during the pilgrimage at Prayāga,[13] even if a pilgrim stays there for some days.

The authors of the Purāṇas and the writers of the *tīrtha*-treatises insist on pilgrim's obligation to undergo tonsure at Prayāga, though Bhaṭṭa Lakṣmīdhara in his *Krityakalpataru* (*Tīrthavivecanakāṇḍa*) has surprisingly committed the mention of this practice. According to him, one whose parents are dead, must cut one's hair at Prayāga when on pilgrimage.[14]

Despite this general recommendation of the necessity of *muṇḍana* at Prayāga, exceptions have been provided in different cases. As for example, a person, whose parents are alive, should undergo *kṣaura* rite and should not have tonsure at Prayāga.[15] The boy, who is *anupanīta*, should have tonsure provided the *cūḍā* rite has already been performed.[16] In the case of an initiated one (*upanīta*), all the hair except the top-knot (*cūḍā*) is to be cut off.[17] As regards ascetics and śūdras, even the top-knot is to be shaved.[18] In the case of a king or a prince or a learned brāhmaṇa shaving of the head should not be insisted upon, but they should have to undergo double the usual penance and the *dakṣiṇā* (a present to brāhmaṇas at the completion of a religious rite) would have to be double.[19] The tonsure is, however, desired in the case of those kings and learned brāhmaṇas who are guilty of *mahāpātakas* (great sins), of cow-killing or of having violated the vows of chastity.[20]

These prescriptions regarding the ceremony of *muṇḍana* at Prayāga are generally related to the male pilgrims. There are, however, certain authorities who have laid down rules specifically for women pilgrims. Thus, some Śāstrakāras[21] hold that the ladies, whose husbands are alive, must shave themselves at Prayāga. They say that such women with their husband's permission should have the head tonsured, and then they should place the cut hair in their joined palms, place thereon a golden or silver *veṇī* (braided hair) and pearls and corals, and should cast all these into the confluence (Veṇī) of the Gaṅgā and the Yamunā after repeating the *mantra*.[22] But others[23] lay down that in the case of maidens and married women whose husbands are living ones, tonsure of the head should not be carried out at Prayāga, but that only two or three finger-breadth of their tresses at the tip should be cut off and thrown into the Saṅgama with an appropriate invocation. *Muṇḍana* is, however, said to be essential ceremony in the case of widows.[24] This appears to be an enjoiner to keep them devoid of attraction and allurement, so that they may not be led to astray. Thus, there is no unanimity among the writers of scriptures regarding the tonsure of women in general at Prayāga, but they unanimously make it compulsory in the case of widows. It should, however, be noted that women do not shave their heads at *tīrthas* except Prayāga and the only reason for this is that it is the practice of the *śiṣṭas*[25] (*śiṣṭah akāmātmā*—pious and self-abnegating men).

The rite of tonsure at Prayāga is said to yield immense fruits.[26] It is believed that *muṇḍana* at this sacred place absolves one immediately from the effect of all past sins.[27] The devotee enjoys the bliss in heaven for as many thousands of years as the number of hair and nails sacrificed in the waters of Gaṅgā.[28] It is said that one should tonsure at Prayāga, offer *piṇḍas* (ceremonial cake of cooked food) to ancestors at Gayā, make gifts at Kurukṣetra and eschew the body at Vārāṇasī. It is added that if one has tonsured at Prayāga, what is the necessity for the other three at Gayā, Kurukṣetra or Kāśī?[29] The latter statement generally implies that *muṇḍana* at Prayāga secures all the fruits of Gayā-*piṇḍadāna*, Kurukṣetra-*snāna* and *Kāśī-tanutyāga*. But this is only a glorification of the rite of tonsure at Prayāga and the fruit thereof is simply the removal of sins.[30] The pilgrim, who fails to sacrifice his hair at Trīveṇī is, however, condemned to hell with equal emphasis. It is stated that he, who has not had tonsure at Bhāskarakṣetra[31] (i.e. Prayāga) on the Gaṅgā, becomes a traitor unto the *tīrtha*[32] and goes to the hell called Raurava along with the members of his family for the duration of a *kalpa*.[33]

SNĀNA

Purification by bathing is one of the most universal religious practices in Hinduism. The question whether a bath, considered as a rite that absolves sins, was already known to the authors of the Vedic literature is discussed by Ensink.[34] The merit of religious bath continued in later periods also. The

Mahābhārata and the Purāṇic tradition are well acquainted with the ritual ablutions at different sacred places. Most of the *tīrthas* in India lie on the banks of a river and a bath is at least recommended to the pilgrim. It appears that bathing has been the central rite in pilgrimage from the very beginning. In a general way the use of the word *tīrtha* pleads for this hypothesis. Its current acceptance of 'place of pilgrimage in general' has developed from the meaning 'a way down to the level of the water'.[35] Moreover, most of the oldest places of pilgrimage are either rivers or places on the banks of rivers or tanks. The procedure of bathing at the *tīrtha* is laid down in the Purāṇas,[36] which has been taken over by several digests. The procedure of a ritual bath is described and illustrated by Kane[37] and Amado;[38] the latter also tries to explain the implicit symbolism. Bath is, in fact, a symbol of the entering into the Reality in order to get rid of whatever is attached to one's skin, the veil of one's ignorance, laziness, passions, temporality and life itself. When a pilgrim comes out of the waters he is a 'reborn' man, if he is full of faith and understanding; he is really a man who has entered the Reality (*jīvanamukta*), even if still walking in the Unreal to complete his *karman*. Bath is therefore particularly meaningful. It is one of the means of earning merits, easy for everybody and fitting the little time one has for religious purpose in this modern age.

Sojourns to holy waters are fraught with merit; ablutions in such waters are meritorious. The bathing at sacred places is an act of physical purification. It is an act of symbolic purification of soul. More than the impurities of the outer body it is the impurities of the mind that are thus washed away. Cleanliness of the body and pure thoughts do not exist without a bath; therefore, bathing is first prescribed for keeping the mind refreshed.[39] Bath is taken at the *tīrtha* for the purpose of observing holy and religious rites and not merely for the sake of purity and cleanliness of the limbs.[40] Without a change of heart, a mere physical act of bath in holy waters would not be enough. It is the pure mind that makes a bath success. It has been aptly stated in the *Mahābhārata* that bathing does not refer to a body immersed in water; he is bathed, who bathes in self-control and washes away with faith the impurities of his mind.[41] The *Skanda Purāṇa* has almost the same words.[42] This Purāṇa further says that removal of mere physical dirt does not make a person pure. It is only on washing away one's mental impurity that one becomes immaculate.[43] The *Skanda Purāṇa* adds that the watery creatures like fish, etc. are born and die in the waters of *tīrthas*; but they do not go to heaven because the impurities of their minds are not removed.[44] The *Brahma Purāṇa* states that a wicked heart is not purified by bathing at sacred places; though washed with water a hundred times he remains, like a wine vessel, impure.[45] Thus, external cleanliness alone is ineffective without internal purity.

Persons of all the four *āśramas* and *varṇas* are entitled to bathe in the *tīrtha*.[46] There is no question of untouchability when bathing in holy waters.[47] But it is said in the *Mahābhārata* that the dishonest man, the man of uncontrolled spirit, the ignorant, the impure man, the evil-doer, and the false-minded man are unworthy of bathing in *tīrthas*.[48] According to the *Skanda Purāṇa*, a man who is avaricious, slanderous, cruel, hypocritical and immersed in pleasures of senses, though bathed in all the *tīrthas* remains sinful and impure.[49] The *Matsya, Padma*, and *Nāradīya Purāṇas* state that he who speaks the truth, has subdued his anger and the vice of causing pain to living beings, follows *dharma*, knows the *tattva*, and is devoted to the welfare of cows and brāhmaṇas, is freed from his sins and attains the desired fruits by bathing at the confluence of the Gaṅgā and the Yamunā.[50] The custom is also discussed critically in the Pāli texts: whoever is inwardly pure does not need the bath in a *tīrtha*, and who is not so will not be cleansed by all rivers together. In this connection several rivers and sacred places like Gayā, Gaṅgā, Sarasvatī and Prayāga are mentioned.[51]

Special sanctity is attached to bathing at Prayāga. It earns various rewards. It should be noted that except where special reference is made to the sub-*tīrthas*, the reference to a bath at Prayāga in general means bathing in the confluence of the rivers Gaṅgā and Yamunā (Pl. 11). Bathing in the waters of the Saṅgama brings purification from sins and many temporal blessings. In the paralipomena of the *Ṛgveda* there occurs one verse which is generally thought to refer to the junction of the Gaṅgā and the Yamunā and the practice of bathing there. It says that those who plunge into the water where the white and the black rivers meet together ascend to heaven.[52] The *Mahābhārata* and the Purāṇas state that a man of laudable vows, who takes ablutions in the confluence of the Gaṅgā and the Yamunā, acquires the merits equal to that obtainable from the performance of *aśvamedha* and *rājasūya* sacrifices together.[53] The sanctity of a man schooled in the four Vedas and of the true spoken person one obtains by merely bathing in the confluence of the Gaṅgā and the Yamunā.[54] The Purāṇas promise the attainment of heaven to those who bathe at Prajāptikṣetra.[55] According to the *Skanda Purāṇa*, one who bathes at the confluence of the two great rivers is freed from all sins and attains the region of the Supreme Being.[56] By bathing in the Saṅgama one certainly becomes immortal.[57] A bath at Prayāga is said to be the destroyer of all sins.[58] The *Padma Purāṇa* says that one who goes to Prayāga and bathes there undoubtedly becomes rich and enjoys long life.[59] Kālidāsa has noted that the souls of those persons who bathe in the confluence of the two consorts of ocean, i.e. Gaṅgā and Yamunā, are purified.[60] According to the *Matsya Purāṇa*, the regular bathing throughout a month, following the path of restraint of the sense-organs, washes away all sins.[61] The same Purāṇa promises immunity from sin to a murderer who lives on alms and bathes three times a day at Prayāga for a period of three months.[62] A betrayer is also purified of sins in three months by fasting and bathing thrice daily there.[63] The Māyā of Viṣṇu is invincible. But it is burned in the month of Māgha at Prayāga.[64] Even a butcher is assured of the highest goal by an ablution there in the month of Māgha.[65] In fact, ritual ablutions at Prayāga bestow much merits. Here one should bathe facing the current[66] and preferably in the morning.[67]

Holy ablutions in the waters of the confluence of the Gaṅgā and the Yamunā in the month of Māgha have been looked upon with great favour in the Dharmaśāstric texts. Here water is very particularly sacred during the month of Māgha. It is considered a rare occurrence and a thing to be coveted even by the deities who flock to Prayāga in their invisible forms for ablutions in the month of Māgha.[68] Therefore, bathing at Prayāga during the month of Māgha is of special significance. Various rewards are obtained by means of a ritual bath at Prayāga throughout the month of Māgha. The devotee can obtain particular fruits by a bath in a pond (*vāpī*), in a pool of water (*taḍāga*), in a river, in a natural basin (*devakhāta*), in a great river, and, lastly, in the confluence of the two great rivers; the fruits are then multiplied by a thousand times when the sun is in the capricornus.[69] It is said that the Gaṅgā flowing towards the west and mingling with the Kālindī destroys sins accumulated in a hundred *kalpas*. It becomes very auspicious in the month of Māgha,[70] and a bath therein is thousand times more meritorious.[71] The *Padma Purāṇa* says that those who regularly bathe in the Gaṅgā at Prayāga in the month of Māgha are released from sorrow for three hundred *kalpas*.[72] Viṣṇu offers the devotees who bathe there in that month the *salokatva* (residence in the same celestial region of Viṣṇu), the *samīpatva* (rejoicing in His vicinity) and the *sarūpatva* (having the same shape of the God).[73]

The most important baths are those taken on special *tithis* like *makarasaṅkrānti*, *rathasaptamī*, *śuklā-ekādasī*, *amāvāsyā*, *pūrṇimā*, etc.[74] But particularly meritorious are three days in the month of Māgha at Prayāga.[75] Although disputed, they may be as: the three days are *makarasaṅkrānti* (the day of passing the sun into the sign of capricornus), *rathasaptamī* (the seventh day of the bright half of Māgha), and *māghīpūrṇimā* (the full-moon day of Māgha); the three consecutive days from the tenth of the bright half of Māgha; the three consecutive days from the thirteenth day of the bright half of Māgha; the first three days of Māgha; any three days in Māgha.[76] However, these three days of Māgha, according to the current usage, are *makarasaṅkrānti*, *amāvāsyā*, and *basantapañcamī*. In order to extol the propitious and saving qualities of a three-day bath in the month of Māgha at Prayāga interesting legends of Kāñcanamālinī[77] and that of brāhmaṇa Bhadraka[78] are told in the Purāṇic literature. In these legends, observes Giussepe Spera, "A *bhakta* substratum is clearly recognisable: that is the conception of divinity in the *tīrtha* offering motherly salvation to the wicked persons unworthy of it".[79]

According to the *Bhaviṣya Purāṇa*, men of all castes, women and those born of mixed unions can perform this ritual bath; śūdras, women and men of mixed castes should not repeat any *mantra* but should bathe silently or with the word *'namaḥ'*.[80] At the time of bath in Māgha, when the sun is in the capricornus, the devotee is advised to recite the *mantra*: "Oh Govinda, Acyuta, Mādhava, let me get the fruits as promised in the śāstras by this holy bath in the month of Māgha, when the sun is in the capricornus".[81] Uttering this *mantra*, he should bathe silently, always thinking of Vāsudeva, Hari, Kṛṣṇa, and Mādhava.[82] The Purāṇas advise that ablutions at Prayāga in the month of Māgha should be performed before the sunrise. According to the *Brahma Purāṇa* quoted in the *Tristhalīsetu*, one obtains immeasurable merits by a bath, with his mind fixed on the feet of Hari, at Prayāga at the time of the break of day in Māgha.[83] The *Padma Purāṇa* states that the sins of one, who bathes there early in the morning in the month of Māgha when the sun is in the capricornus, vanish immediately as darkness disappears at the sight of the sun.[84] Deliverance to seven generations (paternal as well as maternal), immunity from sins, and attainment of heaven are promised to one who takes ablution in the river early in the morning in Māgha.[85] The *Nāradīya Purāṇa* warns that one, who fails to bathe before the sunrise when the sun is in the capricornus, is neither liberated from sins nor goes to heaven.[86] Ablutions performed between dawn and morning at Prayāga in Māgha are graded into good (when stars are still visible), middling (when stars are invisible), and bad (when the sun has risen); each preceding one being holier than each subsequent one.[87] One is also advised to pray and request the sun to come out if the sky is overcast with clouds in the morning in the month of Māgha.[88]

TARPAṆA

The word *tarpaṇa* is derived form √*tṛp*, 'to be satisfied'. It is an elaborate form of water-offering to the manes.[89] It consists of offering of three handful of water, or of water mixed with sesamum and *kuśa* grass. It has to be done by pilgrims as soon as they arrive at the *tīrtha* whether at an auspicious or an inauspicious time.[90] The *tarpaṇa*, occasioned by arrival at the *tīrtha*, is prescribed as coming immediately after bathing.[91] In fact, it is a subsidiary act of bathing ritual usually done in the stream at a *tīrtha*.

It is believed that on mountains, at sacred places, and especially in rivers, ancestors always dwell anxiously thirsting for water;[92] an offering of water which satisfies their thirst, refreshes them, and thus leads them to peace. It is said that if one bathes at a *tīrtha*, and does not perform the rite of *tarpaṇa* for his *pitṛs*, thirsting for water, they drink the excretions from his body.[93] One has to perform *tarpaṇa* according to the procedure prescribed in one's own Vedic school.[94] And the benefit of this is told in the *Viṣṇu Purāṇa*[95] that by properly offering ablutions to the manes with devotion a man pleases the entire world and obtains that merit which accrues from nourishing all the creatures of the universe. The order of recipients in *tarpaṇa* is: father, grandfather, and great-grandfather; mother, grandmother, and great-grandmother; mother of one's half-brothers, mother's ancestors and their wives; one's own wife and children; brothers and paternal uncles, maternal uncles and their wives; daughters and sisters with their offspring and husbands; father's sisters and mother's sisters, father-in-law; honoured *guru* and pupil, friend and any giver of inheritance.[96] After offering water mixed with sesamum and *kuśa* grass thrice to each of these deceased relatives with joined hands, one should give a single handful of water mixed with sesamum to all the gods, seers, manes, and other beings.[97] The *mantra* for this is given in the *Viṣṇu Purāṇa*[98] and in the *Vāyu Purāṇa*.[99] If one is unable to perform an elaborate *tarpaṇa*, he may offer three handful of water, saying 'May the universe from Brahma down to a clump of grass be satisfied'.[100] A widow, who has no sons, may also perform *tarpaṇa* for her husband and his relatives at a sacred place.[101] But one who carries birth-impurity and an ascetic should not do it.[102] A person whose father is alive has not to perform *tarpaṇa*, but he may offer three handful of water to gods, three to the sages, and one to Prajāpati.[103] One is not only required to perform the subsidiary *tarpaṇa* but also separate ablutions at Prayāga. Such persons who maintain celibacy for a month in that sacred place and offer libations of water to the manes and gods are assured to get what they desire, wherever they are born.[104] The *Padma Purāṇa* also recommends the performance of *tarpaṇa* for the ancestors on the riverside known as Urvaśīpulina at Prayāga, and promises enjoyment with *pitṛs* for sixty thousand and sixty hundred years in heaven and the lordship over thousands of cows and hundreds of Urvaśī-like maidens on rebirth in the world to the performer.[105] The *Nāradīya Purāṇa* advises to offer *tarpaṇa* to the ancestors and gods at Samudrakūpa.[106]

UPAVĀSA

Fasting strictly means total rejection of food and drink for the entire day and night, but generally it means light diet restricted in quality and quantity.[107] However, it does not imply merely abstention from food and drink, but a great deal more. *Upavāsa* is living in union with good qualities with aversion from sins and abandonment of all enjoyments.[108] Fasting (*anāśaka*) is regarded as a kind of penance (*tapas*).[109] Rules regarding *upavāsa* have been framed in the Vedic Saṁhitās[110] and other ancient texts.[111] In the enjoined fasting there is to be starvation from morning to evening, and from evening to dawn.[112] A fast is not broken if one partakes of water, milk, roots, fruits, and medicines.[113] Although generally practised for religious merit, the rules and regulations about fasting ware based on a system of hygiene and ware possibly meant to preserve the purity, physical as well as intellectual and cultural. The *Anuśāsanaparva* of the *Mahābhārata*[114] contains an exaggerated eulogy of fasting and remarks that men of all *varṇas* and even *mlecchas* thought highly of fasts.[115]

Fasting is enjoined during a visit to a *tīrtha*.[116] The fast is done in order to purify the body by means of eliminating sins. The general rule is that fasting and tonsure should be observed at all *tīrthas*, except Gayā, Kurukṣetra, Viśālā, and Virajā.[117] There is nothing greater in merit than fasting at a *tīrtha*. Fasting is proclaimed to be atonement for the sins of sinners and the realization of the desires of the virtuous men. Therefore, one should keep a fast at the *tīrtha*.[118] A fast at a *tīrtha* is declared by Lakṣmīdhara Bhaṭṭa[119] and Vācaspati Miśra[120] to be optional. But Nārāyaṇa Bhaṭṭa[121] and Mitra Miśra[122] dissent from this view and maintain that fasting is obligatory. Nārāyaṇa Bhaṭṭa and Mitra Miśra discuss the proper time for the *tīrtha*-fast. There is an optional choice between the day of arrival and the day before arrival,[123] since both the options are prescribed by authoritative texts.[124] It is enjoined that fasting should be carried on assiduously if one visits the *tīrtha* again after ten months.[125] It is also to be done as a penance before important religious acts like ancestral rites, gift, tonsure, suicide, etc. in absolute or graduated forms at the sacred place.

The observance of fast at Prayāga is regarded a meritorious act. The *Viṣṇu Purāṇa*[126] refers to the fasting there. It is pointed out that if a fast is observed in Prayāga by a person sound in health and with perfect continence, he gets the reward of performing the horse-sacrifice at every step. Such a man gets emancipation from bondage for his manes and posterity for ten generations. He is freed from all sins and attains the much cherished dignity.[127] Fasting at the individual holy spots of Prayāga such as Ṛṇapramocana-tīrtha,[128] Mānasa-tīrtha,[129] and Sandhyāvaṭa[130] is also deemed to be efficacious enabling one to acquire celestial regions or the fulfilment of all desires. *Upavāsa* being a kind of *vrata*, one is also expected to observe the various *vratas* which occur during his visit to the sacred place. The Purāṇas, which extol pilgrimage to the sky, give a systematic exposition of the several *vratas*;[131] a *vrata* usually taken to mean a religious vow observed on some particular day with certain restrictions on food and behaviour.[132] Hence, it was quite logical that the observance of some of these at Prayāga has been recommended to help the pilgrim keeping his fervour and acquire new merits.

ŚRĀDDHA

The rite of *śrāddha* is closely associated with ancestor-worship which forges a permanent bond between the dead and the living. The worship of ancestors by means of *śrāddha* is a very ancient rite and is found even in primitive societies. Kane[133] has observed that it was believed even several centuries before Christ that the institution of *śrāddha* had great antiquity behind it and that it was as old as Manu, the father of mankind, according to the *Ṛgveda*.[134] The word *śrāddha* is derived from *śraddhā*,[135] 'faith' : what is offered with faith and devotion to the manes is *śrāddha*.[136] The *Brahma Purāṇa*[137] defines *śrāddha* as 'whatever is given with faith to deserving brāhmaṇas for the pleasure of *pitṛs* at a proper time, in a proper place, and in accordance with the prescribed procedure is called *śrāddha*. In this definition the connection of *śraddhā* with *śrāddha* is emphasized. The *Skanda Purāṇa*[138] says that *śrāddha* is so called because *śraddhā*, i.e. faith, is the root of this rite. According to the Purāṇas,[139] the performance of *śrāddha* not only pleases gods and *pitṛs*, but also ensures progeny and happiness to the performer.

Śrāddha, though a lengthy and complex ritual, consists of three main elements: the pouring of oblations into the fire (*homa*), the offering of balls of rice or other food (*piṇḍa*) to the ancestors, and the feeding of brāhmaṇas (*brāhmaṇa-bhojana*) who symbolically represent the ancestors.[140] The *piṇḍadāna* and the feeding of the brāhmaṇas are the more important components of the *śrāddha* ritual, *homa* being performed in order to remove the impurities of the performer. Kane is of the opinion that "it need not be necessarily supposed that feeding the brāhmaṇas at *śrāddha* was a later idea and offering food to the dead was the original idea".[141] The credentials of a brāhmaṇa engaged for a *śrāddha* at a *tīrtha* are not to be scrutinised.[142]

Śrāddha is generally classified into regular or mandatory (*nitya*), specially occasioned (*naimittika*), and optional (*kāmya*).[143] *Tīrtha-śrāddha*, with which we are mainly concerned, is generally "specially occasioned", that is, occasioned by the special event of arrival at a *tīrtha*. Although *śrāddha* is performed last among the mandatory *tīrtha* rites, it is clearly the most important of them. According to Richard Salomon, '*tīrtha-śrāddha* does not appear to be very prominent in the Vedic texts, but becomes one of the most important rites in classical and modern Hinduism'.[144]

The predominance of *śrāddha* is especially striking in the *tīrtha* ritual. *Śrāddha* should be performed at all *tīrthas* immediately after the mandatory bathing and *tarpaṇa*, regardless of the time and other circumstances. No delay should be made, nor should one interfere with it.[145] If *śrāddha* can not be done immediately because of some obstacle, it should be done on the following day.[146] Since *pitṛs* are deemed to be always present at *tīrthas*, one should omit the water-offering, the invitation, the placing of the thumb of the invited brāhmaṇa in the food, the question about the satisfaction of brāhmaṇas, and the scattering of the rice.[147] This prohibition, however, applies only to the *śrāddha* occasioned by arrival at the *tīrtha*.[148] There is also no fire-oblation in a *tīrtha*.[149] That *śrāddha* which is not defiled by the sight of dogs, gulls, vultures, or crows is called the *tīrtha-śrāddha*, which brings satisfaction to the ancestors.[150] At a normal *śrāddha*, such unclean animals must be kept out of view, but this rule does not apply to *tīrtha-śrāddha*. The reason for this is that the ancestors come together to a *tīrtha* in the form of these birds.[151] If one is unable to follow the complete procedure of *śrāddha*, one should merely offer *piṇḍas* made of grits, wheat-cake, rice pudding, oil-cake or jaggery.[152] The son, grandson, great-grandson, wife, brother or brother's children, or other descendants who offer the same *piṇḍas* are worthy to perform *śrāddha*.[153] Even a son whose father is alive may perform *tīrtha-śrāddha*, except in certain cases.[154] One who has not been initiated, an inheritor of property, and a śūdra may also perform *śrāddha* at a *tīrtha*.[155] The uninitiated man, women, and śūdras should have *śrāddha* performed with the aid of a brāhmaṇa or perform it themselves without *mantras*, according to local custom.[156] *Śrāddha* for the husband should never be performed by a woman who has a son.[157] Ascetics and outcastes can not perform *tīrtha-śrāddha*.[158] The *śrāddha* performed at a *tīrtha* is said to be eternal and gives immense pleasure to the *pitṛs*.

Amongst the several *śrāddha-deśas* river-sides and *tīrthas* are also included.[159] It is, therefore, but natural that Prayāga, being one of the foremost holy places, has been strongly recommended as one of the right places for the offering of *śrāddha*. The *śrāddha* performed there is said to become inexhaustible in fruits.[160] The *Matsya Purāṇa* calls Prayāga *pitṛ-tīrtha* that fulfils the desires of the worshipper.[161] The *Viṣṇu Dharmasūtra*[162] says that a *śrāddha* offered at Prayāga confers eternal bliss upon the performer. According to the *Garuḍa Purāṇa*,[163] the *piṇḍas* offered at Prayāga for the absolution of the departed souls fully serve their initiating purpose. The *Brahma Purāṇa* says that those, who perform *śrāddha* for their ancestors there, are born in the brilliant *brahma-kula* and attain the Brahmahood. They are transported to the Viṣṇuloka where they thrive under the feet of Viṣṇu. As such they do not have to visit the world again.[164] The *Padma Purāṇa* declares that the *pitṛs* of those who perform *śrāddha* for their pleasures before the image of Viṣṇu at this sacred place attain the region of Viṣṇu.[165] That Prayāga was one of the holy places where it was regarded meritorious to perform *śrāddha* ceremony, is also attested to by the Banaras copperplate inscription of king Karṇadeva of the Kalacuri dynasty. King Karṇadeva issued this land-grant at Prayāga after bathing in the Veṇī and worshipping God Śiva on the occasion of the annual *śrāddha* (*saṁvatsara śrāddha*) of his father, Gāṅgeyadeva, on Saturday, the second lunar day of the dark fortnight of Phālguna in the Kalacuri year 793 corresponding to the 9th of January, C.E. 1042.[166]

DĀNA

Dāna is the generic word for gift with its etymological root in '*dā*'; to give is *dāna*. Therefore, it generally refers to the act of giving, bestowing, granting, yielding and presentation. It consists of the cessation of one's ownership over a thing and creating the ownership of another over that. The latter occurs when the receiver accepts the thing. The acceptance may be mental or vocal or physical.[167] According to Devala, only that is described as *dāna* when wealth is given according to śāstric rites so as to reach a receiver who is a fit recipient as defined in the śāstras.[168] *Dāna* has been eulogised from the *Ṛgveda* onwards. It is said that making gifts is the only piety in the Kali age,[169] and that the creatures have no greater piety on the earth than that of making gifts.[170] The gifts are said to have great purificatory powers. They are said to give pomp and pleasure to donor both in this life and the next. For example, "The man who makes gifts, the man who sees (them), the man who hears (about them), and the *vipra* who accepts them, all become free from sins...the man gets rid of all his sins and attains the abode of Viṣṇu".[171] Miserly habits and deceitful economy in gifts are condemned. For instance, those who are the misers and those who do not give anything to the brāhmaṇas, are condemned to hell and its severe tortures.[172] It is laid down that the offer of a gift should be made only to a brāhmaṇa and never to a kṣatriya, vaiśya or śūdra.[173] *Manusmṛti*[174] and *Viṣṇu Dharmasūtra*,[175] etc. give a list of persons to whom gifts should not be offered. The Purāṇas state that whatever is the most desirable and what one prizes most, be given as gift.[176]

Visits to holy places are to be attended with gifts to the brāhmaṇas, because gifts made there have far more efficacy than made elsewhere. The ancient scriptures specify the names of places like Kurukṣetra, Prayāga, Puruṣottamakṣetra, etc. where gifts given bring good results. Prayāga is, however, generally referred to as a sacred place fit for making charities. In the *Mahābhārata*, it is stated that even a small thing donated there produces enormous proceeds of profit.[177] According to the *Garuḍa Purāṇa*, there is no bigger religious rite for a man to perform in this world than making charities in Prayāga.[178] The *Agni Purāṇa* says that an act of charity done and performed there puts forth immortal fruits.[179] The same Purāṇa again mentions that a man who doles out charities at Prayāga goes to heaven after death and becomes a monarch in his next existence.[180] The *Brahma Purāṇa* says that *dāna* made at this sacred place yields one thousand times more of merit than at any other *tīrtha*.[181] The same Purāṇa declares that gift made there is the very door to heaven and salvation.[182] The Purāṇa assures the pilgrims that whatever gifts are made according to their abilities at Prayāga tend to confer inexhaustible rewards.[183] Therefore, the *Nāradīya Purāṇa* rightly advises that one should give charitable gifts at Prayāga in accordance with the capacity of one's resources.[184]

It is generally mentioned in the Purāṇas that if men make gifts of cows, of gold pieces, of precious stones, of pearls and of their other belongings, their pilgrimage becomes fruitful and they collect religious merits.[185] It is said that when a man makes gifts according to his ability and wealth, the fruit of his pilgrimage increases and he remains in heaven till the dissolution of the world.[186] It is stated that one, who offers a tawny-reddish milch cow with her horns adorned with gold, hoofs with silver and neck covered with silken-cloth, along with a milking pot of bell-metal, cloth and jewels, to a virtuous and dispassionate brāhmaṇa, well-versed in the Vedas, at Prayāga, dwells in heaven or in the region of Rudra for as many thousand years as the cow has hair-pores on her body.[187] At the time of his rebirth, the very same cow saves him from hell. He is born in the Uttara Kuru region and enjoys a long life. The gift of only one milch cow instead of hundred thousands of dry cows alone helps the wife, sons and kinsmen of the donor to cross the sea of troubles with ease. For this reason the gift of a cow is said to be the best of all charities, because a single cow protects the donor from all sins.[188] One who offers his virgin daughter (*kanyā*) in the *ārṣa* form of marriage in the area between the Gaṅgā and the Yamunā at Prayāga, in accordance with the prescribed rites, does not have to visit the frightful hell on account of that deed alone. Rather, he is imported to the Uttara Kuru region and thrives there perpetually.[189] One who offers food (*annadāna*) at this sacred place gets the same as by providing to a crore of brāhmaṇas.[190] The man who makes a gift of garments to yogins for their protection from cold there gets the merit of installing the images of Viṣṇu in all the three worlds.[191] The gifts of edible grains, sesamum (*tila*), blankets, butter, etc. at Prayāga are highly recommended and are considered to be of immense merits.[192] Even a particle of the various kinds of gifts like those of a daughter, a cow, land and gold made there is said to equal the merit of their totality existing in the universe.[193]

The merit of gifts given at Prayāga is, thus, great and endless, and has been sung of from very early times. This is the place which has always attracted religious minded persons and liberal benefactors to make gifts and offerings. The practice of making gifts there was observed not only by the common people but also by the kings. We find frequent references to the fact how princes came to make charities at the site of the holy Saṅgama. Kings from the Deccan often visited Prayāga on pilgrimage and made suitable grants in charity to commemorate the event.[194]

Thus, the Ridhapur copperplate inscription (assigned to 5th-6th cent. C.E.) mentions the grant of a village called Kadambagiri by Mahārāja Bhavattavarman (Bhavadattavarman) of the Nala family to Mātrādhyādattāryya and his eight sons of the Parāśara *gotra*, with libations of water, for blessing the matrimonial relationship of the king and his queen, while he (probably together with his queen) was staying as a pilgrim at Prayāga, "the place blest by the favour of Lord Prajāpati at the confluence of the Gaṅgā and the Yamunā".[195] Similarly, the Nagardhana plate of Svāmirāja (dated C.E. 573) records that while staying at the Caṭukavaṭa (probably Akṣayavaṭa) in the midst of the Gaṅgā, Svāmirāja donated, with a libation of water, the village named Aṅkollikā on the left bank of the river Śūla, (situated) to the west of the *agrahāra* village Acalapur and to the east of Śrīparṇikā, to certain brāhmaṇas of the White and Black *Yajurveda* and of the *Sāmaveda*.[196]

Hsüan Tsang[197] mentions that it was at the confluence of the two rivers that from time immemorial, royal and noble personages, endowed with virtue and love, went and distributed costly presents to the destitute and the infirm, and hence, it came to be known as the 'Arena of Charity'. He refers to how king Harṣavardhana (seventh century C.E.) every fifth year of his regin used to distribute all the surplus of his treasury at Prayāga. He even used to give away his crown and rich clothing and took from his sister Rājyaśrī a common garment which had already been worn.[198] The pilgrim, who attended the sixth quinquennial assembly of the king there, further says that from the three precious objects (Buddha, Dhamma and Saṅgha) down to the poorest orphans, there was no one who had not shared his bounty.[199]

The Maināmāṭī inscription refers to Laḍaḥacandradeva (C.E. 1000-1020) of the royal family of the Candras of south-east Bengal who visited Prayāga and made charitable offerings at this *tīrtha* which is sanctified by the Gaṅgā and the Yamunā.[200] The Jhūsī copperplate of the Pratīhāra king Trilocanapāladeva of Kanauj (C.E. 1027) says that Trilocanapāla, being in residence on the bank of the Gaṅgā near Prayāga, having bathed in the

Gaṅgā and having worshipped Śiva, etc. gave the village Lebhuṇḍaka in the Asurābhaka *viṣaya*, to six thousand brāhmaṇas belonging to Pratiṣṭhāna, who were of various *gotras* and *pravaras* and were followers of various Vedic schools.[201] The Banāras copperplate inscription of the Kalacuri king Karṇadeva (C.E. 1041) informs that king Karṇadeva, having bathed at Veṇī, worshipped the God Trilocana (Śiva), and performed the proper rites at the annual funeral ceremony in honour of his father Gāṅgeyadeva, granted the village Susī to the learned Viśvarūpa, a student of the Vājasaneya *śākhā*, who belonged to the Kauśika *gotra* and whose ancestors had come from the village of Veśala.[202]

A copperplate inscription of the Gāhaḍavāla king Govindacandra of Kanuaj (C.E. 1125) mentions that Govindracandra, having bathed in the Gaṅgā, at Śrīśa-pratiṣṭhāna, having satisfied, in due form, the divinities of the Vedas, the saints, deceased mortals, etc. taking water in his palm purified by bending it into the shape of a cow's ear, and by *kuśa* grass granted the village of Agoḍalī in the *pattalā* (canton) of Haladoya (probably modern Haradoi district of Uttar Pradesh) to the fortunate Chichāśarman and Vāchaṭaśarman of the Gautama *gotra*.[203] The Bhaḍavanā grant (C.E. 1127) of the same king says that the village of Bhaḍavanā (probably the modern village of Budawan in tehsil Karchanā of the Allahabad district) together with the hamlets of Bhaṭavalī and Laghu-Bhaḍavanā in the *pattalā* of Mahāvisa was granted by king Govindracandra to two brāhmaṇas by the name of Kumāraśarman of the Kāśayapa *gotra* and Śīlaśarman of the Bharadvāja *gotra*. The inscription mentions that the grant was made by him after he had bathed at Prayāga according to the sacred rites, holding water in the palm of the hand and having worshipped god Vāsudeva and having made oblations to the fire. The object of the grant is said to be the acquisition of merit and renown for the donor and his parents.[204] The Kamaulī plate of king Jayacandradeva of Kanuaj (C.E. 1171) records that Jayacandradeva, after bathing on the *manvantarādi* at the confluence of the rivers at Prayāga, in the presence of the God Gaṅgāditya, granted the village of Kusuphaṭā (modern Kusūngur near Mānasatīrtha) in the Mahaso *pattalā* (Sahason in the Allahabad district), to the *mahāpurohita* Praharājaśarman, a brāhmaṇa of the Bandhula *gotra*, and a student of the *Yajurveda*.[205]

The *Rājataraṅgiṇī* of Kalhaṇa[206] mentions that king Jayāpīḍa of Kashmir (c. the end of the eighth century C.E.) used to give rich gifts to the brāhamaṇas at this place. Once he came to Prayāga, followed by a large retinue, with great pomp, and made a gift of a lakh less one of horses to the *vipras*, along with rich *dakṣiṇā* (gifts of money). He also engraved a seal with the challenge, "If any one else should grant here (at Prayāga) a complete lakh of horses, my seal may be replaced by his own". The same text informs that this record of king Jayāpīḍa remained unchallenged and the proud princes drank the holy Gaṅgā water from the vessels marked with that king's seal and felt pained in their minds. We should note that the sacred water of the Gaṅgā is still carried in sealed pots and bottles to distant parts of India. It would be interesting to find evidence for Kalhaṇa's (12th century C.E.) statement that a seal with Jayāpīḍa's name was still used in his own time for the sealing of such pots at Prayāga. The *Vikramāṅkadevacarita* informs that its author, Bilhaṇa (11th-12th century), came to Prayāga out of his religious leanings. He spent, in pious gifts, the wealth earned by him, which were the wonder of the universe.[207]

However, there is another side of the picture, where the acceptance of a gift in a *tīrtha* is prohibited. It is generally stated that one should not accept any gift in a holy place or in a sacred shrine. He should, in all needs, remain steady and should not yield to temptations,[208] because greed of money causes degradation. It is said that one who accepts a village, gold, pearl or any other gift within the area between the Gaṅgā and the Yamunā at Prayāga, either for his own purpose or for the purpose of obsequial rites or even in the worship of deities, is to have all his pious deeds in the holy place devoid of benefit as long as he enjoys that treasure.[209] Deceitful economy in making charities at Prayāga is also looked down upon. It is said that he who gives alms to the brāhmaṇas with any feeling of conceit derives no benefits.[210]

Prayāga is, thus, undoubtedly, one of the sacred places where it is as meritorious to give away even a smallest copper coin in gift as it would be to lavish a lakh elsewhere. The gifts of gold, kine, land, and *kanyā*, etc. are highly recommend there. At the same time the acceptance of gifts at Prayāga is reprobated with equal emphasis. This may sound paradoxical, but there are some sound reasons behind this. The prohibitory injunction appears to be a sort of warning to the recipients, so that their chief purpose should not be to collect more and more money in the form of gifts from the pilgrims. The injunction is intended to maintain the sanctity of the institution of *dāna* and not allow it to degenerate into a form of making easy money. Another reason, which is more psychological than religious, is that the institution of *dāna* should not become a tool of extortion on the part of the recipients. Our ancient Śāstrakāras were aware of the working of the human instincts, of which greed for money is one. Thus, while prohibiting brāhmaṇas to accept gifts within the sanctified area of the Tīrtharāja and at the same time eulogising the grant of gifts in Prayāga our law-givers created certain in-built checks in order to keep the institution safe and pure from the unscrupulous and the greedy. While it is difficult to settle the question whether one really obtains the various merits accruing from the performance of charities, as promised by the texts, the conclusion is inescapable that this age-old practice shows the firm faith of the devotees in the sacredness of Prayāga and in the enormous religious significance of the institution of *dāna*.

The beliefs of the people of India visualized the forces of nature, crystallized into the attributes of divinity, operating to promote the production. They also serve a magico-religious function where they are symbolic of communion with the supernatural power. Rituals have their definite and particular forms, and their indigenously, historically and locally defined elements. They are not meaningless symbols. R.S. Sharma rightly puts it, 'Rituals have their origin and growth in reality. Even the wild growth of plants and vegetation is governed by certain laws. Rituals therefore do not grow in a vacuum. They owe their origin to certain material and social environments which they subserve and perpetuate. Even those who suspect their historical value consider many rituals as symbols of fertility. And fertility represents production and reproduction without which human society can not continue'.[211] The tract of land between the Gaṅgā and the Yamunā is personified as the symbol of fertility,[212] the nerve centre of which is Prayāga. The various rituals commended for observance at Prayāga serve as an indispensable guide to both social and economic developments in the region in historical perspectives. The extravagant praises of *tīrtha*-rituals may not be dismissed as mere hyperbole in the light of the fact that pilgrimage is superior to Vedic sacrifices, because of its simplicity and availability to all. However, the details of such rituals are described and analysed by the Dharmaśāstra-writers at great length, often to the point of legalism and pedantry. Though most frequently we meet with the prescription of ablutions, the ancestral rites – *tarpaṇa*, *piṇḍadāna* and *śrāddha* – possibly are the first to become connected with the cult of sacred places. This connection may have lain close at hand because the libations of water are preferably made in a river. Bath, tonsure and fast are acts of self-purification. The rhyme *snāna-dāna* has become current in the *tīrtha-māhātmyas*, as has *bhukti-mukti* (happiness and release from rebirth). When the pilgrim participates in rituals, they reinforce holy beliefs about the sanctity of the *tīrtha*. Prayāga is the king of *tīrthas*. Many rituals and devotional activities carried on there substantially contribute to its glory.

REFERENCES

1. *Mbh*, III.80.34-38; *MP*. 111.12-15=*TSSP*, 38.
2. Kane, *History of Dharmaśāstra*, Vol. IV, pp.572-578, 583-84; Nambiar, K.D., *Nārada Purāṇa — A Critical Study*, pp.352-353.
3. Aiyangar, K.V. Rangaswami, *Tīrthavivecanakāṇḍa* of the *Kṛtyakalpataru*, introduction, p.XXXV.
4. *TSSP*, 204-211.
5. सश्मश्रुकेशवपनं मुण्डनं तद्विदुर्बुधाः ।
   न क्षौरं मुण्डनं सुभ्रु कीर्तितं वेदवेदिभिः ॥
   NP, II.62.55. Vasiṣṭha, Baudhāyana and others provide for the tonsure of hair on the head and lips (except those on the eyebrows, the hair on the trunk, and the top-knot). श्मश्रुकेशान्वापयेद्भ्रुवोक्षिलोमशिखावर्जं० । *Vasiṣṭha Dharmasūtra*, 24.5; केशश्मश्रुलोमनखवापनम् । *Baudhāyana Dharmasūtra*, II.i.98.; Kane, *op.cit*., Vol. IV, 122, 575.
6. मनुष्याणां तु पापानि तीर्थानि प्रतिगच्छताम् ।
   केशमाश्रित्य तिष्ठन्ति तस्मात्तद्वपनं चरेत् ॥
   PdP, V.19.21.
7. गङ्गां प्राप्य सरिच्छ्रेष्ठां कल्पान्तपापसंचयाः ।
   केशानाश्रित्य तिष्ठन्ति तस्मात्तान्परिवर्जयेत् ॥
   NP. II. 62.50.
   केशमूलान्युपाश्रित्य सर्वपापानि देहिनाम् ।
   तिष्ठन्ति तीर्थस्नानेन तस्मात्तांस्तत्र वापयेत् ॥
   NP, II.63.109; *TP*, 51, 57; *TS*, 22.
8. मुण्डनं चोपवासश्च सर्वतीर्थेष्वयं विधिः ।
   वर्जयित्वा कुरुक्षेत्रं विशालां विरजां गयाम् ॥
   NP, II. 62.45; *VaP*, 105.25 q. by *TC*, 14 (ascribes to *SkP*); *TP*, 50 (ascribes to *Devalasmṛti* and *SkP*). The first half is *AgP*, 115.7. *TP* (51) has disapproved it. Only *muṇḍana* is prohibited at these sacred places but *kṣaura* is not forbidden there.
   गयादावपि देवेशि श्मश्रूणां वपनं विना ।
   न क्षौरं मुनिभिः सर्वे निषिद्धं चेति कीर्तितम् ॥
   NP, II.62.54.
9. प्रयागव्यतिरेके तु गङ्गायां मुण्डनं नहि ।
   NP, II.62.52a.
   TP (51) finds fault with Vācaspati Miśra for saying that there is no tonsure on the Gaṅgā. *TS* (22) quotes a passage, ascribed to the *Kāmakalopākhyāna* of the *BrvP*, which refers to this practice at Maṇikarṇikā (in Vārāṇasī) on the Gaṅgā. When there is such a conflict of views, the final decision rests with the usage of each country or the individual's choice.

10. Nārāyaṇa Bhaṭṭa and Mitra Miśra discuss at length the pilgrim's obligation to undergo tonsure before a bath at the confluence. They criticise Vācaspati Miśra for holding that tonsure is unnecessary before a bath on the Gaṅgā, on the ground that the text on which the latter relied is corrupt. *TvK*, intro., iii.
11. *TP*, 27.
12. *TP*, 59.
13. सर्वथा त्वेकस्यां यात्रायामेकमेव मुण्डनमिति सिद्धम् ।
    TS, 21.
14. प्रयागे तीर्थयात्रायां मातृपितृवियोगतः ।
    कचानां वपनं कुर्यात्......... ॥
    NP, II, 62.28; *VisP* q. by *Prāyaścittatattva*, 489; *TC*, 7; *TP*, 28, 50, 53, 54.
15. *NP*, II, 62.53.
16. *TS*, 24; Kane, *op.cit.*, Vol. IV, p.602.
17. *TP*, 50; Kane, *op.cit.*, Vol. IV, p.574.
18. यतिः शूद्रश्च-----सशिखं वपनं चरेत् ।
    TP, 51; Kane, *op.cit.*, Vol. IV, p.575.
19. *NP*, I, 24.52-54; *Parāśarasmṛti*, IX. 52-54; Mitākṣarā on *Yājñavalkyasmṛti*, III. 325; *Prāyaścittaviveka*, 503; *Prāyaścittasāra*, 22; *Prāyaścittatattva*., 519; *Śaṁkhasmṛit* q. by *Prāyaścittamayūkha*, II.1.290-291; Kane, *op.cit.*, Vol. IV, p.123.
20. *Manusmṛti* q. by Mitā. on *Yāj*., III. 325; *Prāyaścittasāra*, 22-23., *Prāyaścittatattva*, 579; Kane, *op.cit.*, Vol. IV, p.123.
21. *Prāyaścittatattva*, 493; *TS*, 22; Kane, *op.cit.*, Vol. IV, p.603.
22. वेण्यां वेणीप्रदानेन सर्वं पापंप्रणश्यतु ।
    जन्मान्तरेष्वपि सदा सौभाग्यं मम वर्धताम् ॥
    TS, 22, 'May all my sins be destroyed by this offering of my braided hair into the confluence. May my auspicious state of wifehood always increase in the lives to come'.
23. *NP*, II.63.108; *Āpastambasmṛti*, I.33-34; *Vṛddhahrītasmṛti*, IX. 386; *Parāśarasmṛti*, IX 54-55; Mit. on *Yāj*., III. 263-264; *TP*, 50-51.
24. *TP*, 51; *TS*, 21.
25. *TS*, 23; Kane, *op.cit.*, Vol. IV, p.603. It is noteworthy that women have to shave their heads at Tirupati Devasthānam. But I have no knowledge of any śāstric injunction about that.
26. *TP*, 337; *YT*, 2.3.6.
27. *TC*, 33; *TP*, 37.
28. *NP*, II.62.51; *TS*, 18; *TP*, 63, 336.
29. *NP*, II.63.105-106; *Gaṅgāvākyāvalī*, 298; *TC*, 32; *TS*, 17; *TP*, 335.
30. *TS*, 17; Kane, *op.cit.*, Vol. IV, p.602 fn.
31. Bhāskarakṣetra is Prayāga according to some and Koṇārka according to others. In this context, Bhāskarakṣetra is really Prayāga and not Koṇārka, because the verse occurs in the *Prayāga-māhātmya* of the *Nāradīya Purāṇa*

(II.62.49). *TP* (57) has the same conclusion (प्रयागस्य भास्करक्षेत्रत्वादिति). So the view of Nārāyaṇabhaṭṭa (प्रजापतिक्षेत्रत्वेन भास्करक्षेत्रत्वाभावात् कोणादित्यादीनामेव भास्करक्षेत्रत्वस्य सामान्यविधावुक्तत्वात् . *TS*, 20) that Bhāskarakṣetra of this verse refers to Koṇārka is not acceptable.

32. गङ्गां सम्प्राप्य यो देवि मुण्डनं नैव कारयेत् ।
क्रिया तस्याक्रिया सर्वा तीर्थद्रोही भवेत्तथा ॥
NP, II.62.48.
33. *NP*, II. 62.49; *PdP*, IV.19.2, 27; *VisP*, III. 12.38; *VaP* q. by *TC*, 14; *TP*, 38; *TS*, 20.
34. Ensink, J., 'Problems of the Study of Pilgrimage in India', *Indologica Taurinensia*, Vol. II, pp.64-71; 'Hindu Pilgrimage and Vedic Sacrifice', in *Ludwik Sternbach Felicitation Volume*, part I, pp.111-113.
35. Ensink, J., 'Problems of the Study of Pilgrimage in India', *Indologica Taurinensia*, Vol. II, p.64.
36. *MP*, 101.2-30; *PdP*, I.20.145-176, V.89.12-42, VI.126.12-24.
37. Kane, *op.cit.*, Vol. IV, pp.591-594.
38. Amado, Pierre, 'Le Bain dans le Gange – sa Signification', *Bull. de l' Ecole Francaise d' Extreme — Orient*, Tome LVIII, pp.197-216.
39. *MP*, 101.1.
40. *NP*, II.31.13.
41. *Mbh*, XIII.111.9.
42. *SkP*, IV.6. 33 = *TSSP*, 69.
43. *SkP*, IV.6. 35 = *TSSP*, 69.
44. *SkP*, IV.6. 36 = *TSSP*, 69; NP, II. 62.19.
45. *BP*, 25.4; *SkP*, IV. 6. 38 = *TSSP*, 69.
46. *Mbh*, III.80.51 = *TP*, 19; *VamP*, 36. 78-79.
47. Kane, *op.cit.*, Vol. IV, p.569.
48. *Mbh*, III. 83.90, 90.11 = *TSSP*, 300-301.
49. *SkP*, IV. 6. 34 = *TSSP*, 69.
50. *MP*, 103.15-16 = *TvK*, 137; *PdP*, III. 41.16-17; *NP*, II.63.71b-73a.
51. *Majjhimanikāya*, I.39; *Jātaka*, VI.198.3ff. (543).
52. *Ṛgveda (khila)*, 22.1a = *TC*, 47 = *TS*, 3.
53. *Mbh*, III. 83.76 = *TvK*, 152; = *KP*, I. 35.12; *NP*, II. 63.43; *MP*, 105.21 = *TvK*, 142-143 = *TS*, 28; *PdP*, III. 39.77, 43.22.
54. *Mbh*, III. 83.78 = *TvK*, 153; *NP*, II. 63.42; *PdP*, III. 39.81, 43.48b-49a; *MP*, 105.48 = *TS*, 30.
55. *KP*, I.34.20 = *TS*, 28; *PdP*, III.41.5, 43.54; *NP*, II.63.130b-131a; *MP*, 103.4b-5a = *TvK*, 136.
56. *SkP*, IV.7.46.
57. *SkP*, IV.7.54; *PdP*, VI. 25.23.
58. *BP*, 59.21; *YT*, II.6.168.
59. *PdP*, VI.24.6.
60. *Raghuvaṁśa*, XIII. 58a.
61. *MP*, 107.14 = *TvK*, 148= *TS*, 29; *PdP*, III. 45.13b-14a; *NP*, II.63.46.

62. *MP*, 107.15 = *TvK*, 148= *TS*, 29; *PdP*, III. 45.15b-16.
63. *NP*, II. 63.102.
64. *NP*, II.63.61b-62a; *PdP*, VI. 126.36.
65. *PdP*, VI. 126.34.
66. *NP*, II. 31.23a; *TSSP*, 322.
67. *PdP*, VI. 24.4.
68. *Mbh*, XIII.26.35 = *TS*, 37; *MP*, 106.7 = *TvK*, 14; *KP*. I. 36.1 = *TS*, 30; *NP*, II. 63.7-12, 37; *SkP*, IV. 7.57; *PdP*, III. 44.7b-8a, VI 126.43, 53-57 = *TC*, 18-19 = *TS*, 31 = *TP*, 330; *PdP*, VI. 127.147 = *TC*, 21 = *TS*, 31 = *TP*, 333.
69. *NP*, II.63.161-*18; PdP*, VI. 126.25-27a= *TS*, 40; *TC*, 19.
70. *NP*, II. 63.5.
71. *NP*, II. 63.20b-21a.
72. *PdP*, VI. 23.11.
73. *PdP*, VI. 91.25.
74. *NP*, II.31.27-28, 63.40, 85; *PdP*, VI. 127.58, 151; *TS*, 31, 37-38, 42; *Cf*. Malaviya, M., 'Māghamāsa ke Vrataparvon kā Māhātmya', in D.P. Dubey (ed.), *Kumbhaparva Prayāga*,pp.98-112.
75. *AgP*, 111.10b-11a; *MP*, 106.8; *PdP*, III.44.8; *KP*, I. 36.2; *NP*, II. 63.74b-75a.
76. *TS*, 33; Kane, *op.cit*., Vol. IV. p.617.
77. *NP*, II. 63.77-79; *PdP*, VI. 126.58-73 = *TC*, 27 = *TS*, 36.
78. *NP*, II. 63.80-89; *PdP*, VI. 127.153-162 = *TC*, 28-29 = *TS*, 34.
79. Spera, G., 'Some Notes on Prayāga Māhātmya', *Indologica Taurinencia*, Vol. V, p.189.
80. *BhavP*, IV. 122.12-14 = *TS*, 39; Kane, *op.cit*., Vol. IV, p.617.
81. मकरस्थे रवौ माघे गोविन्दाच्युत माधव ।
    स्नानेनानेन भो देव यथोक्तफलदो भव ॥
    PdP, VI. 126.20 = *TC*, 19 = *TS*, 43 = *TP*, 331; *NP*, II. 63.13b-14a.
82. *NP*, II. 63.14b-15a; *PdP*, VI. 126.21 = *TC*, 19 = *TS*, 43 = *TP*, 331.
83. अरुणोदये तु सम्प्राप्ते स्नानकाले विचक्षण: ।
    माधवाङ्घ्रियुगं ध्यायन्य: स्नाति सुरपूजिते ।
    प्रयागवारिणि शुभे तस्य पुण्यस्य का मिति: ॥
    TS (*BP*), 41.
84. *PdP*, VI. 91.24.
85. *BhavP*, IV. 122.35 = *TS*, 41.
86. मकरस्थे रवौ माघे न स्नात्यनुदिते रवौ ।
    कथ पापै: प्रमुच्येत कथं वा त्रिदिवं व्रजेत् ॥
    NP, II. 63.104; *TS* (*PdP*), 41.
87. अरुणोदयमारभ्य प्रात: कालावधि प्रभो ।
    माघस्नानवतां पुण्यं क्रमात्तत्र च धारणा ॥
    उत्तमं तु सनक्षत्रं लुप्ततारं तु मध्यमम् ।
    सवितर्युदिते भूप ततो हीनं प्रकीर्तितम् ॥
    TS (*BP*), 41.

88. *NP*, II. 31.14.
89. Kane, *op.cit.*, Vol. II, pp.668-669, 689-695.
90. अकालेऽप्यथवा काले तीर्थे श्राद्धं च तर्पणम् ।
अविलम्बेन कर्तव्यं नैव विघ्नं समाचरेत् ॥
SkP, IV. 6.60 = *TSSP*, 323, 386 = *TP*, 67.
प्राप्तैरेव च कर्तव्यं पितृणां चैव तर्पणम् ।
DvP q. in *TSSP*, 324 = *TP*, 73.
91. तद्युक्तम्, बहुभिर्वाक्यैस्तीर्थस्नानान्तरमेव तद्विधानात् । सुमन्तुवचनं तु येषां शाखिनां श्राद्धाङ्गभूतं तर्पणमस्ति तेषां हिरण्यश्राद्धे तत्पश्चात् विधत्ते । अतएव प्रयोगपारिजाते श्राद्धाङ्गतर्पणमेव प्रकृत्येदमभिहितम् - तस्मात्तीर्थतर्पणं स्नानान्त एव कार्यमिति सिद्धम् ।
TSSP, 330. 2-331; *TP*, 69.
92. गिरिषु ख्याततीर्थेषु नदीषु च विशेषतः ।
साकाङ्क्षाः पितरो नित्यं तिष्ठन्ति सलिलार्थिनः ॥
TSSP, 326; *TP*, 68.
93. यस्तु तीर्थे नरः स्नात्वा न कुर्यात् पितृतर्पणम् ।
पिबन्ति देहनिःस्रावं पितरस्तु जलार्थिनः ॥
TSSP, 325; *TP*, 68.
94. *TSSP*, 322.2.
95. कामोदकप्रदानं ते मयैतत् कथितं नृप ।
यद्दत्वा प्रीणयत्येतन् मनुष्यः सकलं जगत् ॥
जगदाप्यायनोद्भूतं पुण्यमाप्नोति चानघ ।
दत्वा कामोदकं सम्यग् एतेभ्यः श्रद्धयान्वितः ॥
VisP, III. 11.37.38 = *TSSP*, 329.
96. *TSSP*, 332.1 – 334.13; Kane, *op.cit.*, Vol. II(1), p.692.
97. *TSSP*, 326.1.
98. देवासुरास्तथा नागा यक्षा गन्धर्वराक्षसाः ।
पिशाचा गुह्यकाः सिद्धाः कूष्माण्डास्तरवः खगाः ॥
जलेचरा भूमिलया वाय्वाधाराश्च जन्तवः ।
तृप्तिमेतेन यान्त्वाशु मद्दत्तेनाम्बुनाखिलाः ।
नरकेषु समस्तेषु यातनासु च ये स्थिताः ।
तेषामाप्यायनायैतद् दीयते सलिलं मया ।
मेऽबान्धवा बान्धवा वा येऽन्यजन्मनि बान्धवाः ।
ते तृप्तिमखिलां यान्तु ये चास्मत्तोऽभिकांक्षिणः ॥
यत्रक्वचनसंस्थानां क्षुत्तृष्णोपहतात्मनाम् ।
इदमक्षय्यमेवास्तु मया दत्तं तिलोदकम् ॥
VisP, III. 11.32-36 = *TSSP*, 327.
99. आब्रह्मस्तम्बपर्यन्तं देवर्षिपितृमानवाः ।
तृप्यन्तु पितरः सर्वे मातृमातामहादयः ॥

अतीतकुलकोटीनां सप्तद्वीपनिवासिनाम् ।
आब्रह्मभुवनाल्लोकादिदमस्तु तिलोदकम् ॥
VaP, II. 48.21-22 = *TSSP*, 328, 337.

100. आब्रह्मस्तम्बपर्यन्तं जगत् तृप्यत्विति ब्रुवन् ।
जलाञ्जलित्रयं दद्यात् कुर्वन् संक्षेपतर्पणम् ॥
or
आब्रह्मस्तम्बपर्यन्तं जगत् स्थावरजङ्गमम् ।
मया दत्तेन तोयेन तृप्तं यातु परां गतिम् ॥
TSSP, 335, 336; Kane, *op.cit.*, Vol. II, p.668.
101. *TSSP*, 343.2 – 344.4.
102. *TSSP*, 345, 571.
103. Kane, *op.cit.*, Vol. IV, p.592, fn. 1340.
104. *MP*, 103.17 = *TvK*, 138 = *TC*, 25 = *TS*, 17 = *TP*, 324; *PdP*, III. 41.18b-19; *NP*, II.63.59-60a.
105. *PdP*, III. 43.35-39.
106. *NP*, II. 63.93.
107. Kane, *op.cit.*, Vol. IV, p.52.
108. उपावृत्तस्य पापेभ्यो यस्तु वासो गुणैः सह ।
उपवासः स विज्ञेयः सर्वभोगविवर्जितः ॥
BhavP, *Brāhmapava*, 64.4, Vyāsa q. by Aparārka, p.199 = *Smṛticandrikā*, II, p.355.
व्यावृत्तस्यैव दोषेभ्यो यस्तु वासो गुणैः सह ।
उपवासं तमाहुस्तु न शरीरस्य शोषणात् ॥
Haradatta on *Gautama Dharmasūtra*, 19.11.
109. *Bṛhadāraṇayaka Up.*, IV. 4.22; *Gautama Dharmasūtra*, 19.15; *Viṣṇu Dharmasūtra*, 54.29; *Manusmṛti*, XI. 203; *Mbh*, XIII. 109.63; Kane, *op.cit.*, Vol. IV, p.53.
110. *Tait. Sam.*, I. 6.7.3-4.
111. *Gobhila Gṛhyasūtra*, I. 5.26; *Khadira Gṛhyasūtra*, II. 1.4, 6; *Mbh*, XIII. 109; *GP*, I. 128.6-8; *BhavP*, I. 184.27; Devala q. by Aparārka, p.199; *Smṛticandrikā* II, p.355; Kane, *op.cit.*, Vol. IV, p.53; *TvK*, intro., XLVIII-XLIX.
112. *TvK*, intro., XLVIII.
113. अष्टौ तान्यव्रतघ्नानि आपो मूलं घृतं पयः ।
हविब्राह्मणकाम्या च गुरोर्वचनमौषधम् ॥
Baudhāyana Dharmasūtra, 2.10.60. 'हविः' क्षारलवणवर्जम् ।
"ब्राह्मणकाम्या" ब्राह्मणाभ्यर्थना ।
एवम् अहविष्यमपि गुरोर्वचनात् इति गोविन्दस्वामी ।
TvK, intor, XLIX and fn. 2.
114. *Mbh*, XIII. 109. 110.
115. सर्वेषामेव वर्णानां म्लेच्छानां च पितामह ।
उपवासे मतिरियं कारणं च न विद्महे ॥
Mbh, XIII. 109.1.

116. तीर्थोपवासः कर्त्तव्यः शिरसो मुण्डनं तथा ।
SkP, IV. 6.65a = *TSSP*, 229, 249 = *TP*, 47.
तीर्थमासाद्य कुर्वीत नरः शुचिरुपोषणम् ।
उपवासविशुद्धात्मा कर्त्तव्यं कर्त्तुमर्हसि ॥
NP q. in *TSSP*, 214 = *TP*, 48.

117. मुण्डनं चोपवासश्च सर्वतीर्थेष्वयं विधिः ।
वर्जयित्वा कुरुक्षेत्रं विशालां विरजां गयाम् ॥
VaP, II. 43.42; *NP*, II. 62.45; *GP*, I. 84.4; *SkP* and Devala q. in *TP*, 47 and 50; Devala q. in *TSSP*, 226. The first half is *AgP*, 115.7a. *SkP* q. in *TC*, 14, 16, however, mentions Gaṅgā in place of Kurukṣetra: Kane, *op.cit.*,Vol. IV, p.574.

118. तीर्थोपवासाद् देवेशि अधिकं नास्ति किञ्चन ।
पापानां पापशमनं सतामीप्सितकारकम् ॥
उपवासो विनिर्दिष्टो विशेषाद् देवताश्रये ।
तीर्थोपवासं कुर्वीत तस्मात्तत्र वरानने ॥
SkP, VII. i. 28.64 – 65a, 78b. = *TSSP*, 212.

119. तीर्थेपवासश्च फलविशेषार्थः । *Tvk*, 11.

120. तीर्थोपवासो विशेषार्थो न त्वावश्यकः । *TC*, 14.

121. तस्मादावश्यक उपवासः । *TSSP*, 225.6.

122. 'सर्वतीर्थेष्वयं विधिः' इत्यनेन तीर्थप्राप्तिनिमित्तकोपवासस्य नैमित्तिकान्तरवदावश्यकत्वाक्षतेः ।
'उपवास नियमयुक्त' इत्यनेन नैमित्तिक उपवासः कार्य इत्युक्तम् । *TP*, 48.

123. तेन तीर्थोपवासे प्राप्तिदिनं तत्पूर्वदिनं वेति कालविकल्पः सिद्धः ।
TSSP, 224.2. एवं च प्राप्तिदिनतत्पूर्वदिनयोरुपवासे विकल्पः । *TP*, 49

124. इत्युच्चार्य नमस्कृत्वा स्नानं कुर्याद्यथाविधि ।
उपवासं ततः कुर्यात्तस्मिन्नहनि सुव्रते ॥ *SKP*, VII. i. 28.126.
यदह्नि तीर्थप्राप्तिः स्यात् तदह्नः पूर्ववासरे ।
उपवासस्तु कर्तव्यः प्राप्ताह्नि श्राद्धदो भवेत् । *SkP*, IV. 6. 66.

125. संवत्सरं द्विमासोनं पुनस्तीर्थं व्रजेद्यपि ।
मुण्डनं चोपवासञ्च ततो यत्नेन कारयेत् ॥
NP, II. 63.107; *TC*, 35; *TS*, 19; *TSSP*, 278, 551.

126. *ViSP*, VI. 8.29.

127. *MP*, 107.3-5 = *TvK*, 147 = *TS*, 50 = *TP*, 345; *PdP*, III. 45.2-4 = *TC*, 50.

128. *MP*, 106. 20-21 = *TvK*, 147 = *TC*l 30-31 = *TS*, 56 = *TP*, 34l; NP, II. 63.100b-101a; *KP*, I.35.14-15; *PdP*, III. 44.21-22.

129. *MP*, 106.2 = *TvK*, 145 = *TS*, 57 = *TP*, 340; *PdP*, III.44.2.

130. *MP*, 105.43 = *TvK*, 144 = *TS*, 56 = *TP*, 340; *KP*, I. 35.27; *PdP*, III. 43.43b-44a.

131. Kane, *op.cit.*, Vol. V, pp.1-462; Nambiar, K.D., *Nārada Purāṇa – A Critical Study*, pp.232-277; Parui, S.S., *Kurukṣetra in the Vāman Purāṇa*, pp.152-158.

132. *Mbh*, III. 280.3, V. 39.56-57; Kane, *op.cit.*, Vol. V, p.28.

133. Kane, *op.cit.*, Vol. IV, p.349.
134. *Ṛgveda*, VIII. 30.3, 63.1.
135. श्रद्धा प्रयोजनं (कारणं) अस्य इति श्राद्धम् । Pāṇini, V. 1.109.
136. सर्वं श्रद्धया दत्तं श्राद्धम् । *Pratimānāṭaka*, V, p.135.
137. देशे काले च पात्रे च श्रद्धया विधिना च यत् ।
 पितृनुद्दिश्य विप्रेभ्यो दत्तं श्राद्धमुदाहृतम् ॥
 BP q. in *Śrāddha Prakāśa*, pp.3, 6 = *Śrāddhakalpalatā*; p.3 = *Paraśāra Mādhavīya*, I. 2.299; Kane, *op.cit.*, Vol. IV, p.334 with fn.751. Though this verse is ascribed to the *BP*, it is not found in the existing one.
138. *SkP*, VI. 218.3.
139. *BP*, 220.117-118; *NP*, I. 28.82-84; *MarP*, 29.38; *AgP*, 163.41-42; *MP*, 18.11-12; *Yājña.*, I.269.
140. Kane, *op.cit.*, Vol. IV, p.335; Salomon, R., *The Bridge to the Three Holy Cities*, intro., XXX.
141. Kane, *op.cit.*, Vol. IV, p.266.
142. तीर्थेषु ब्राह्मणान्नैव परीक्षेत कदाचन ।
 अन्नार्थिनमनुप्राप्तं भोज्यं तं मनुरब्रवीत् ॥
 DvP q. in *TSSP*, 402 = *TvK*, 10 = *TC*, 10 = *TP*, 73; *NP* II. 62.38.
 न परीक्ष्यो द्विजस्तीर्थेष्वन्नार्थीभोज्य एव च ॥
 SkP, IV. 6. 58a = *TSSP*, 404.
143. Kane, *op.cit.*, Vol. IV, pp.369-370, 380-381.
144. Salomon, R., *The Bridge to the Three Holy Cities*, intro., XXIX.
145. न वारं न च नक्षत्रं न कालस्तत्र कारणम् ।
 यदैव दृश्यते तीर्थं तदा पर्वसहस्रकम् ॥
 Prabhāsakhaṇḍa of the *SkP* q. in *TSSP*, 390 = *Śrāddhakalpalatā*, 108.
 अकालेऽप्यथवा काले तीर्थे श्राद्धं तथा नरैः ।
 प्राप्तैरेव सदा कार्यं कर्तव्यं पितृतर्पणम् ॥
 पिण्डदानं च तच्छस्तं पितृणां चातिवल्लभम् ।
 विलम्बो नैव कर्तव्यो न च विघ्नं समाचरेत् ॥
 PdP, V.29.17-18; NP, II. 62.41-42; *DvP* q. in *TvK*, 10 = *TC*, 11 = *Gaṅgāvākyāvalī*, 129= *TSSP*, 381 = *TP*, 73 = *Śrāddhaviveka*, 15 = *Śrāddhakalpalatā*, 107.
146. *TSSP*, 388.2–389.10.
147. अर्घ्यमावाहनं चैव द्विजाङ्गुष्ठनिवेशनम् ।
 तृप्तिप्रश्नं च विकिरं तीर्थश्राद्धे विवर्जयेत् ॥
 SkP, IV. 28.9; *DvP* q. in *TSSP*, 407 = *TP*, 76; Hemādri q. in *Śrāddhacandrikā*, 141-142; *Śrāddhakalpalatā*, 109.
 आवाहनं न तीर्थे स्यात् नार्घ्यदानं तथा भवेत् ।
 आहूताः पितरस्तीर्थे कृतार्घाः सन्ति वै यतः ॥
 BhavP q. in *TSSP*, 410; *Śrāddhakalpalatā*, 109.
148. *TSSP*, 412.1–463.2.
149. *Smṛti Ratnāvalī* q. in *TSSP*, 411 = *TP*, 76 = *Śrāddhacandrikā*, 142.

150. *PdP*, V. 29.13b-14a; *NP*, II.62.40b-41a; *DvP* q. in *TvK*, 10 = *TC*, 11 = *Gaṅgāvākyāvalī*, 129 = *TSSP*, 381 = *TP*, 73 = *Śrāddhaviveka*, 15 = *Śrāddhakalpalatā*, 107.
151. Devala q. in *TSSP*, 412 = *TP*, 76.
152. सक्तुभिः पिण्डदानं तु संयावैः पायसेन तु ।
कर्तव्यमृषिभिर्दृष्टं पिण्याकेन गुडेन च ॥
PdP, V. 29.12; *SkP*, IV. 6.58b-59a; *NP*, II. 62.39; *DvP* q. in *TvK*, 10 = *TC*, 11 = *Gaṅgāvākyāvalī*, 129 = *TSSP*, 532 = *TP*, 73 = *Śrāddhacandrikā*, 142.
153. *TSSP*, 552-553.2.
154. *TSSP*, 553.3-561.3.
155. *TSSP*, 566.3-568, 570.
156. *TSSP*, 568 = *Smṛtyarthasāra*, 56 = *Śrāddhakalpalatā*, 108.
157. सपुत्रया न कर्तव्यं भर्तुः श्राद्धं कदाचन ।
TSSP, 564; *Śrāddhacandrikā*, 143; *Śrāddhakalpalatā*, 108.
158. न कुर्यात् सूतकं भिक्षुः श्राद्धं पिण्डोदकक्रियाम् ।
त्यक्तं संन्यासयोगेन गृहधर्मादिकं व्रतम् ॥
TSSP, 345, 571; *Śrāddhacandrikā*, 143.
159. Kane, *op.cit.*, Vol. IV, pp.377-378.
160. *AgP*, 111.7b; *KP*, II. 20.29; *VdP*, I. 144.4; *VaP*. II. 15.92b; *BrhP*, II. iii. 13.100a, *Śaṅkhasmṛti*, 14.27.
161. *MP*, 21.8.
162. *Viṣṇu Dharmasūtra*, 85.28.
163. *GP*, I. 81.3a.
164. अस्मत्कुलप्रसूतास्तु समा यास्यन्ति शोभनाः ।
श्राद्धं सपिण्डकं येऽत्र करिष्यन्ति ततो वयम् ॥
विष्णुलोकं गमिष्यामो विष्णुपादैकसंश्रयाः ।
पुनः संसारपदवीं नाऽऽयामः पुण्यभाजनाः ॥
BP q. in *TS*, 26.
165. *PdP*, VI. 91.22 = *TS*, 26.
166. इहैव पितुः श्रीमद्गाङ्गेयदेवस्य संवत्सरे श्राद्धे फाल्गुनबहुलपक्ष-
द्वितीयायां शनैश्चरवासरे वेण्यां स्नात्वा भगवंतं देवदेवं त्रिलोचनम्-------।
Ep. Ind., Vol. II. p.310; *CII*, Vol. IV (i), p.244.
167. Śabara on Jaimini, VII. 1-5, IX. 4.32, IV. 2.2.28; Mitākṣarā on *Yājñavalkayasmriti*, II. 27; Kane, *op.cit.*, Vol. II (2), p.841.
168. Devala q. by Aparārka, 287; *Dānakriyā Kaumudī*, 2; *Dāna Mayūkha*, 3; Kane, *op.cit.*, Vol. II (2), p.842.
169. *Manusmṛti*, I.86; *KP*, 1.28.27.
170. *KP*, II.26.56a.
171. *VP*, 100.12-13.
172. *Ibid.*, 198, 76-78.
173. *NP*, II.2.2-3.
174. *Manusmṛti*, IV. 193-200.

175. *Viṣṇu Dharmasūtra*, 93-7-13.
176. *MarP*, 35.52-52; *MP*, 72.39; Kane, *op.cit.*, Vol. II (2), p.847.
177. *Mbh*, III. 85.82 = *TvK*, 152.
178. *GP*, I. 51-29.
179. *AgP*, 111.78.
180. *Ibid.*, 111.128.
181. *BP*, 59.11b-12a.
182. *BP* q. in *TS*, 27.
183. *Ibid.*, 24; Kane, *op.cit.*, Vol. IV, p.601.
184. *NP*, II.63.113b.
185. *MP*, 105.13-14, 16; *NP*, II, 114-115a; Kane, *op.cit.*, Vol. IV, p.600.
186. *MP*, 106.10.
187. *MP*, 105.16-19; *PdP*, 42.17-21; *KP*, I.34.45-46; *TS*, 25; *TvK*, 140; *NP*, II. 63.115b-119a.

    This Purāṇic statement is referred to in an inscription from Roṇ (Dharwar district Maharashtra) of the reign of Cālukya king Jayasiṁha II, dated C.E. 1022, thus : "To those who maintain this pious endowment will accrue the merit of decorating with gold the horns and hoofs of a thousand kine at Prayāga, ... and giving them, during an eclipse of the sun, to a thousand brāhmaṇas learned in the Vedas..." *Ep. Ind.* Vol. XIX, p.226.
188. *MP*, 105.21-22, *NP*, II.63.119b-122; *PdP*, 42.22-24; *TvK*, 140-141.
189. *MP*, 106.8-9; *PdP*, 43.7-9; *KP*, 1.35.6-7; *NP*, II.63. 125b-126; *TvK*, 141; *TS*, 25.

    Ārṣa is one of the eight forms of marriages generally recognised by the ancient authorities. In it, the father of the bride receives a cow and a bull from the bridegroom. According to some, this form of marriage is nothing but a sale of the girl in a veiled manner. But according to others, *ārṣa* was the marriage of the daughter with a *ṛṣi* (sage). It has been described as lawful for a brāhmaṇa by *Baudhāyana* (I. 11-20, 10.12-13), *Viṣṇu* (XXIV. 27, 28), *Vasiṣṭha* (I. 29, 34) and *Manu* (III.23). Uttara Kuru region has been located in Southern Siberia by S.N. Pandey in his article entitled 'Identification of the Ancient Land of Uttara Kuru' in the *Journal of G.N. Jha Research Institute*, Vol. XXVI, parts 1-3, 1970, p.135. But Zimmer and others place the Uttara Kuru region in Kashmir to the north of Kurukṣetra (Jain, K.C., *Prehistory and Protohistory of India*, p.248). It is called the land of gods in the ancient literature. That is why the attainment of it was coveted by the devotees.
190. *BP* q. in *TS*, 27.
191. *Ibid.*, 27.
192. *Ibid.*, 27-28.
193. *Ibid.*, 27.
194. *Ep.Ind.*, Vol. XIX, p.102; *Vākāṭaka-Gupta Age*, pp.375-376.
195. *Ep.Ind.*, Vol. XIX, p.100ff. The village Kadambagiri has been identified with Kalamba in the Yeotmal taluka of Berar.
196. *Ep.Ind.*, Vol. XXVIII, p.13. Svāmirāja was a certain feudatory of an unknown

paramount sovereign in Vidarbha in the post-Vākāṭaka age. The village of Aṅkollikā is modern Aroli on the right bank of the river Sur (Śūla) about 8 miles south by east of Nagardhana near Rāmaṭeka in the Nagpur district of Maharashtra; but there are no places corresponding to Acalapur and Śrīparṇikā in its vicinity.

197. Watters, *On Yuan Chwang*, Vol. II, p.364.
198. Hui-li, *Life of Yuan Chwang*, Eng. tr. by Beal, pp.183-187; Nehru, J.L., *Discovery of India*, p.127.
199. Watters, *op.cit.*, Vol. II, p.364.
200. 'Maināmāṭī plates', *Pakistan Archaeology*, No.3, pp.22-55; Sarcar, D.C., *Studies in the Religious life of Ancient and Medieval India*, p.255.
201. *Indian Antiquary*, Vol. XVIII, p.33ff.
202. *Ep.Ind.*, Vol. II, p.299ff.
203. *JASB*, Vol. XXVII, p.243-44.
204. *Ep.Ind.*, Vol. XIX, p.291.
205. *Ep.Ind.*, Vol. IV, p.122.
206. *Rājataraṅgiṇī* IV. 414-18; Roy, U.N., *Studies in Ancient Indian History and Culture*, Vol. I, p.227.
207. *Vikramāṅkadevacarita*, 18. 90-91; Roy, *op.cit.*, Vol. I, p.227.
208. *MP*, 105.15; *KP*, I. 34-44; *PdP*, III. 42. 16b-17a; *NP*, II.63. 123a-124a.
209. *KP*, I. 34. 42-43., *PdP*, III. 42. 14b-16a; *NP*, II. 63. 124b-135a. The *TvK* (139) refers only to the gift of a cow.
210. *MP*, 106.7.
211. Sharma, R.S., *Material Culture and Social Formations in Ancient India*, p.8.
212. Upadhyaya, G.P., 'The Origins and Functions of Tīrthas—Some Epic and Purāṇic Testimonies', *Indian History Congress Proceedings*, Calicut: 47th Session, 1976, p.127.

Chapter VI

PRACTICE OF RELIGIOUS SUICIDE

The Hindu scriptures ordain pilgrims to follow some observances and rituals at Prayāga. It is, however, not so well-known that the practice of suicide (*kāyotsarga*) – an important subject of sociological interest in Prayāga—was also believed to yield immense religious merits, and that Prayāga was famous as a sacred place fit for committing suicide in the past. Chattopadhyaya[1] has discussed the popularity of this practice at Prayāga in ancient times. Kane[2] has dealt with this topic briefly in his *History of Dharmaśāstra*. Sircar[3] and Thakur[4] have made sundry references to the practice in their works. Their treatments of this important religious practice in the context of Prayāga are mostly tentative and sketchy. In fact, the rite has not yet been studied critically. The present chapter studies the practice of suicide at Prayāga from various angles drawing upon the vast and varied literary and epigraphic sources with a view to presenting a comprehensive account of the problem in all its ramifications. Hitherto untapped evidences, which have provided valuable information, are collected and examined. An attempt is also made to systematize all available data through critical analysis and proper evaluation. The popularity and gravity of the tradition of suicide at Prayāga from the ancient to the modern times has been rendered in historical perspective and its significance to the religious life of the people of India has been highlighted, and it may be found to be useful in understanding the cultural roles of a place of pilgrimage with reference to the complexities of Indian civilization.

Suicide as a means of escape from the bodily or mental ills or for the acquisition of religious merit in the next world has been a recognized institution in the country from early times. The attitude towards suicide, as revealed in ancient Indian literature, suggests that the Vedic people looked upon it with abhorrence, while certain influential non-Vedic elements in the population approved of it, at least under special circumstances, and that the Vedic approach to the problem was gradually overshadowed by non-Vedic ideas.[5] Therefore, a twofold attitude towards suicide is discernible in the sacred texts.[6] It has been generally deprecated as a great sin by the Dharmaśāstras. But exceptions to the condemnation of suicide are found in the Epics, the Smṛtis, the Purāṇas, and the treatises on *tīrtha* in some cases[7]. Religious suicides are eulogized in them. Persons were allowed to kill themselves, for securing release from this world, at holy places such as Prayāga, Kāśī, Amarakaṇṭaka, Pṛthūdaka, Puruṣottamakṣetra and Śrīśaila.

Among the holy places commended for religious suicide, Prayāga is the place where one is advised to commit suicide. An apocryphal verse from the *Ṛgveda* is cited as sanction for this. It says that those determined men who cast off their body at the confluence of the Gaṅgā and the Yamunā secure immortality.[8] It is paraphrased in the Purāṇas[9] and is quoted by the digest writers.[10] Nīlakaṇṭha, the seventeenth century commentator on the *Mahābhārata*, holds that the *khila* verse does not encourage religious suicide and refers to natural death at Prayāga.[11] But Nārāyaṇa Bhaṭṭa (sixteenth century) is of the opinion that it refers to wilful death at Prayāga.[12] The tradition recorded in the *Mahābhārata*, the Purāṇas, the digests, and foreign accounts shows that the verse is indicative of deliberate separation of the body and the soul at Prayāga.[13] Thus, it is the earliest known reference to the efficacy of religious suicide at Prayāga.

The great popularity enjoyed by the custom of religious suicide at Prayāga can be seen in the Epic-Purāṇic injunction: "You should not pass over your wish about dying at Prayāga on account of the words of the Veda or the words of the people".[14] Here 'the words of the Veda' refer to Vedic passages condemning suicide,[15] and 'the words of the people' to the Smṛti injunctions against suicide.[16] The ancient authorities generally interpreted the passage as laying down an exception to the prohibition of suicide by both the Veda and the people's voice.[17] Thus, in spite of scriptural condemnation the popular practice had accepted the efficacy of suicide at Prayāga.

The Purāṇas furnish detailed references to the practice of suicide at Prayāga and the religious merits accruing from it. The *Matsya Purāṇa* says that one who passes away in the Prayāga-maṇḍala redeems his seven previous and fourteen subsequent generations.[18] It adds that yogic power may or may not be obtained by one who gives all his jewels to the brāhmaṇas, but it surely accrues to one who dies at Prayāga.[19] The *Skanda Purāṇa* asserts that he who abandons his life in this sacred place in any way does not incur the sin of suicide and secures his desired objects.[20] The *Garuḍa Purāṇa* declares that Prayāga is a very holy place conducive to worldly enjoyments and salvation to those who die there.[21] The popular belief fostered by several Purāṇic passages is that *mokṣa* results from dying at Prayāga.[22] Kālidāsa (*circa* fourth – fifth centuries C.E.) also believed that people, killing themselves at the confluence of the Gaṅgā and the Yamunā at Prayāga, became free from the cycle of births and deaths even though they may not have obtained the true knowledge (*tattvāvabodha*).[23]

Five different methods of suicide in Prayāga have been detailed in the Purāṇas: (i) suicide by drowing at the confluence of the Gaṅgā and the Yamunā, (ii) termination of life voluntarily by falling head-long from the Vaṭa-tree, (iii) self-cremation in slowly burning fire, (iv) hanging head-downwards over a blazing fire, and (v) cutting off slices of flesh from the body to feed carnivorous birds and bleeding into death. In the *Kūrma Purāṇa* the merit of suicide at the confluence of the Gaṅgā and the Yamunā is equated with that of a yogī who is devoted to spiritual meditation.[24] A man who commits suicide there is assured a long spell of existence in heaven where he enjoys the sensual pleasures in the company of divine women, till the time of his rebirth in a good family.[25] It is also said that he who drowns himself at the Saṅgama at the time of the lunar eclipse is freed from all his sins as the moon is released from the grasp of Rāhu at the end of the eclipse. He attains the Somaloka where he enjoys pleasures with the Moon-god, and remains in heaven, attended upon by *ṛṣis* and Gandharvas, for sixty thousand and sixty hundred years after which he is reborn in a prosperous family.[26] According to the same Purāṇa, he who breathes his last at the foot of the Banyan tree (*Vaṭa-vṛkṣa*) of Prayāga finds his way to the Rudraloka.[27] The *Brahma Purāṇa* says that a person who jumps from this tree and ends his life attains the highest regions and does not incur the sin of suicide.[28] The *Matsya Purāṇa* states that the man, who without any diseases, with unimpaired limbs and in full possession of his five senses, encompasses death in cowdung-fire at the confluence, is honoured in heaven for as many thousands of years as there are pores on his body. Such a person on rebirth becomes the king of Jambūdvīpa.[29] The same Purāṇa further says that a man who stands upside down with outstretched arms and inhales smoke from below at Prayāga is glorified in heaven for a hundred thousand years after which he is reborn as an *agnihotrin*.[30] It is also mentioned that he who commits suicide by lopping off various limbs of his body and offering them to birds of prey enjoys bliss in the Somaloka for a hundred thousand years. Such a man when reborn becomes a king endowed with good qualities, comely features, learning, and sweetness of speech.[31] Similar post-mortuary advantages are held out for self-destruction on the sands known as Urvaśīpulina[32] and in the contiguous Koṭi-tīrtha.[33] Suicide in the Gaṅgā especially at Prayāga is also commended. The inducements held out are happiness and sensual enjoyment in heaven for many thousands of years and rebirth in a rich family.[34] Emancipation can be obtained by dying in the Yamunā at

Prayāga.[35] Even for such people who remember Prayāga at the moment of death, the Purāṇas paint pictures of heaven as a promised land offering material abundance and sensual pleasure, where every appetite can be freely gratified.[36]

The Purāṇic statements for religious suicide at Prayāga are corroborated by the accounts of foreign travellers and Muslim writers. The seventh century Chinese pilgrim Hsüan Tsang speaks of religious suicide committed by Indians at Prayāga. He describes the confluence of the two rivers as the place where many hundreds of people arrived everyday in the month of Māgha to die by drowning themselves in the waters hoping to be reborn in heaven.[37] He adds that even animals killed themselves at Prayāga.[38] He refers to a 'widespreading umbrageous tree' in front of a celebrated *Deva*-temple in the town itself, and to the presence of numerous bones of people who had sacrificed their lives by jumping from its branches (Pl. 13), a rite which had been practised at that spot from old times.[39] Death by putting oneself to extreme pain and torture is also mentioned by him. He says that some people starved themselves to death on the sands of the river Gaṅgā.[40] He describes in detail an austerity rite performed by the devotees there:

High poles were erected in the Ganges at this place, each with a projecting peg near the top; at sunrise a devotee mounted a pole; holding on to the top with one hand and one foot, and supported by the peg, he stretched out his other arm and leg at full length. In this posture he followed keenly with his eyes the sun's progress to the right, when the sun set the devotee came down from his perch to resume it next morning. This painful austerity was practised with the view of obtaining release from mortal life, and it was carried on for several tens of years without relexation.[41]

The passage has been translated differently by Watters and Beal. The difference is pronounced in respect of the lines concerning the pole or poles. Beal translates the relevant expression referring to 'one high column', whereas Watters mentions many 'high poles'. John Irwin claims to have consulted the original Chinese text *Si-yu-ki* which, according to him, supports Beal's translation.[42] We are not in a position to verify it from the original. However, we wonder if possibly the relevant expressions in the manuscripts consulted by the two English translators caused this difference. But a careful investigation favours Watters' translation of the *She-kia-fang-che* which speaks of many poles. John Irwin identifies the 'high column' with the Aśokan pillar existing in the local fort of Prayāga (he actually takes it to be a pre-Aśokan brāhmaṇical post).[43] This creates difficulty because it would not be possible for devotees to perform the type of rite mentioned by Hsüan Tsang. The Aśokan pillar is a single shaft of polished sandstone thirty-five feet in height, with a lower diameter of two feet eleven inches and an upper diameter of two feet two inches.[44] It is doubtful if several devotees could simultaneously climb it, rest on it, and move with the moving direction of the sun with the help of one hand and one foot only. Thus, possibly the original passage referred to several poles used by devotees for this rite. It may be suggested that these poles were made of wood and were of different dimensions suitable for the religious rite mentioned by the Chinese pilgrim.

Albirūnī in the eleventh century testifies to the continuance of the practice of suicide at Prayāga. He says that the brāhmaṇas and kṣatriyas were in the habit of committing suicide by climbing up the Banyan tree and throwing themselves into the Gaṅgā at Prayāga.[45] He adds that the Hindus tormented themselves with various kinds of tortures, which are described in their religious books, at the confluence of the Gaṅgā and the Yamunā.[46] The custom is recorded also by Mahmūd Gardīzī who composed his famous book *Kitāb Zayn al-Akhbār* in the middle of the eleventh century. He mentions a sect called *'Trisuli'* (holders of trident) which followed the custom of committing suicide at the huge wide-spreading 'batu' (*vaṭa*) tree on the Gaṅgā near the confluence at Prayāga. Under it they had fixed a *triśūla* which was made of iron and rose above the level of the river several tens of cubits. It was fixed in a perpendicular position into the soil. A man desirous of committing suicide climbed on to the tree, flung himself on to the stake, cut himself to pieces on its blades, and fell into the river. And the people who were there prayed for him and said, "He is gone to Paradise".[47] Gardīzī further records that there was a sect of people who assembled daily on the spot where the Gaṅgā unites with the Yamunā. Each brought with him a sharp weapon. One of the devotees who wished to purify himself and sought approach to God, came near them and they threw upon him whatever they had of garments, ornaments, golden necklaces, bracelets and the like, and they slew him with their weapons and cut him into two. They threw one part into the Gaṅgā and the other into the Yamunā. They believed that the two streams would take him to paradise.[48] Jinaprabha Sūri has also recorded that at Prayāga the Hindus (*parasamayinaḥ*) traditionally committed suicide by piercing a sharp weapon (*krakacam*) into their body.[49]

Rashīd-ud-dīn in his *Jāmi-ut-Tawārīkh* (C.E. 1310) mentions that people mounted the Banyan tree to throw themselves into the Gaṅgā to end their lives at Prayāga.[50] According to the *Āin-i-Akbarī* of Abul Fazl (sixteenth century C.E.), the Hindus believed that the desires of a man who dies at Prayāga were gratified in his next birth, and that whoever committed suicide was guilty of a great crime except in this holy place where it met with exceeding reward.[51] Abdul Qādir Badāunī (sixteenth century C.E.) in his *Muntakhab-ut-Tawārīkh* writes that the Hindus considered Prayāga a holy place where they submitted themselves to all kinds of tortures for obtaining religious merits. Some splitted their tongues into two, others placed their heads under saws, and others entered hell by casting themselves down into the deep river from the top of a high tree, i.e., the celebrated Banyan tree of Prayāga.[52] Both the *Khulāṣat-ut-Tawārīkh* of Sujān Khattrī (C.E. 1695) and the *Chahār Gulshan* of Rāi Chatarman (C.E. 1759) mention that in former times there was a saw in the fort, under which devotees used to place their necks and make a sacrificial offering of their heads in the hope of final redemption and obtaining their desires in the next world. This practice was forbidden in the time of emperor Shāhjahān (C.E. 1628-1658).[53] But it appears that later on it was resumed, for Joseph Tieffenthaler has observed in C.E. 1766-67:

> People say that behind this underground Cave (Pātālapurī temple), according to others, behind the thick towers situated to the east, on the way which leads to the Ganges, a long and very sharp axe hung by a cord, serving to cut the heads of those who wished to make a sacrifice to the idols. Others say that those who consecrated themselves sat by the killing axe and cut their throats, or cut their bodies into two. Others assure that it was a long and very sharp saw with which these voluntary victims cut their bodies into two parts.[54]

Walter Hamilton, who visited Prayāga in 1812, says that many persons renounce life there. They go in a boat to the spot where the two sacred streams meet, and, after having concluded certain prescribed ceremonies, and tied three large water-pots round their bodies, they sink into the confluence.[55] To this fact adds Leopold von Orlich in 1843 that many of the fanatics "have thrown themselves with such impetuosity into the sacred depths that they were not seen to rise again".[56]

There are historical instances of religious suicide recorded in literary and epigraphic records. The story of king Pramati attaining emancipation in *samādhi* in the presence of his army at the junction of the Gaṅgā and the Yamunā occurs in the Purāṇas.[57] He was one of the most remarkable rulers of ancient India, who appeared as the saviour of country and culture in the Kali age. It is not exactly known who this king Pramati of the Purāṇic description was. However, V.S. Agrawal and S.N. Roy have identified him with Candragupta II Vikramāditya (C.E. 375-413) of the Gupta dynasty.[58] A.B.L. Awasthi has attempted to associate him with the Candella king Dhaṅgadeva (C.E. 950-1002).[59] No solid arguments have been adduced in support of Pramati's identification either with Candragupta II Vikramāditya or Dhaṅga. S.R. Goyal has suggested his possible equation with the Gupta king Samudragupta (C.E. 350-375).[60] A.M. Shastri, who has recently discussed the problem afresh, holds that "if the authors of the Purāṇic accounts of king Pramati had the career of any historical figure to serve as a model before themselves, it could have been no other than that of Samudragupta. He alone of all the ancient Indian rulers satisfies most of the eulogy of Pramati".[61] The identity of the king Pramati is thus uncertain. But the Purāṇic references alluding his suicide at Prayāga may not be doubted, because the account is not an isolated phenomenon confined to one Purāṇa text, but is deep-rooted in the Purāṇa tradition. The Aphsad stone inscription of Ādityasena mentions that Kumārgupta (*circa* C.E. 354) of the later Gupta dynasty entered a fire of cowdung-cakes at Prayāga.[62] According to Fleet, this necessarily does not imply that Kumāragupta voluntarily embraced death by fire; it indicates that his funeral rites took place at Prayāga.[63] The majority of scholars do not accept his suggestion and hold that Kumāragupta burnt himself alive.[64] There is a view[65] that unable to bear the humiliation of defeat at the hands of his Maukhari adversary Īśānavarman, Kumāragupta took this extreme step. It is, however, more likely that the self-immolation at Prayāga was inspired by the ruler's religious zeal. The Baroda copperplate of the Rāṣṭrakūṭa king Karka Suvarṇavarṣa possibly refers to Dhruva's (*circa* C.E. 794) drowning himself at the junction of the Gaṅgā and the Yamunā.[66]

The *Śaṅkara-digvijaya* of Mādhava Vidyāraṇya (C.E. 1295-1300) records that Kumārilabhaṭṭa (eighth century C.E.), the great authority on Pūrva Mīmāṁsā, burnt himself in the paddy-husk fire at Prayāga to expiate for the sin of betraying his Buddhist teachers.[67] His conduct is described as 'a vow enjoined in the scriptures'.[68] This tradition of violent death by an eminent orthodox Vedist shows that the practice of religious suicide at Prayāga had come in yogue by the eighth century C.E. and that the Vedic attitude towards suicide had been seriously compromised with reference to this holy place.[69] In this syncretism of Vedic and non-Vedic ideas about suicide lay the secret of its wide appeal, and Prayāga's rise to the foremost place as the centre of religious suicides.

The Khajurāho stone inscription refers to the suicide of the Candella king Dhaṅgadeva (C.E. 1001-02) at the age of over a hundred years in the waters of the Gaṅgā-Yamunā-saṅgama.[70] Many Kalacuri inscriptions record that king Gāṅgeyadeva Vikramāditya (*circa* C.E. 1015-41) obtained release together with his one hundred wives at the foot of the Banyan tree of Prayāga.[71] The reference seems to refer to mass suicide but the manner of death is not clear. Fitz-Edward Hall infers that Gāṅgeyadeva committed suicide by jumping from the top of the Banyan tree and his wives, amounting to a hundred, underwent cremation with the mortal remains of their husband.[72] K.C. Chattopadhyaya suggests that they embraced death by falling from the branches of the tree.[72] But the reference to their reaching the foot of the Banyan tree and obtaining salvation there indicates that they died by fasting unto death under the tree. Death by starvation as a means to salvation is mentioned in the Purāṇas as a commendable form of religious suicide. Prayāga was, thus, the *mokṣa-bhūmi* for Gāṅgeyadeva and his queens who died with him.

Somedeva (tenth century C.E.) has cited "the little known story of a brāhmaṇa woman named Brahmabandhū who, although she was fasting unto death at Prayāga, was associated by scandal with a monk named Govinda".[74] The *Karakaṇḍacariu*, a Jaina work of the middle of the eleventh century C.E., says that Mādhava, a brāhmaṇa of Mathurā, went to Prayāga where he wasted his body with abstinence and died.[75] Madhusūdana, another brāhmaṇa of the same place, also went there to terminate his life in sheer disgust.[76] In the *Rājataraṅgiṇī* king Raṇāditya-Tuñjīna III of Kashmir is reported to have renounced his body in his previous birth from the end of a branch of the Banyan tree there (*prayāga-vaṭaśākhāgrāt*).[77] In the *Adbhutasāgara*, the Sena king Vallālasena is said to have committed suicide, together with his queens at the confluence of the Gaṅgā and the Yamunā.[78] According to V.S. Pathak, this tradition is doubtful, as the compilation of the *Dānasāgara* by the royal author in 1091 Śaka (C.E. 1169) militates against the statement that Vallālasena committed suicide in 1089 Śaka (C.E. 1167).[79] But the passage in the *Adbhutasāgara* does by no means indicate that Vallālasena died in 1089 Śaka. According to R.C. Majumdar, 'It simply says that the book was begun in that year but was left incomplete when its author died. It may readily be supposed that the royal author commenced his work in 1089 Śaka and was engaged over it for a few years when he died. In the meantime another work, the *Dānasāgara*, which was probably begun earlier, was brought to completion in the year 1091 Śaka. The statements made in the *Adbhutasāgara* and the *Dānasāgara* are therefore not inconsistent with each other'.[80] The Candella minister Ananta (the middle of the twelfth century C.E.) also drowned himself in the Gaṅgā-Yamunā-saṅgama at Prayāga.[81] The belief in the efficacy of religious suicide at Prayāga was so deep-rooted that it was believed that Akbar (C.E. 1556-1605) committed such a suicide in a past birth and was rewarded by becoming an emperor in the next.[82]

A feeling of revulsion against religious suicide gradually developed in later times. Suicide by falling into fire or from a precipice is regarded by many authorities as forbidden in the Kali age (*kalivarjya*).[83] Some writers denounce it as nonsensical and fanatical. They declare suicide at Prayāga in one of the ways referred to above to be an inferior way of death comparable to the condemned *śyenayāga*, for it is dictated by the desire for a definite gain (*kāmya-phala*) and not by the desire for *mokṣa*.[84] Other oblations of water to the manes and gods, always attain what they desire, wherever they are born". Tradition has so much exalted the necessity of remaining one month at Prayāga that living there for such a period is described as giving the same merits as those acqured by Brahmā in his entire life (= one *kalpa*). It is then natural that Prayāga was chosen as the right place for residing in the month of Māgha, thereby attracting people to gather there, thus giving birth to a fair. Since the fifteenth day of the dark half (*amāvāsyā*) of the month of Māgha is regarded as the mouth of the year,[14] it may be suggested that a popular fair of a catholic character came into existence gradually at the site of the most sacred confluence of rivers in the month of Māgha in ancient times. The view that Kali era started from the full moon day (*purṇimā*) of Māgha[15] also seems to have moved persons to hold a popular fair there.

The antiquity of the Māgha Melā can be traced back to the Gupta period (c. C.E. 300-600), when most of the Purāṇas were composed[16] and the final redaction of the *Anuśāsanaparva* of the *Mahābhārata* was completed.[17] It may even claim a date as early as third century B.C. or the second century C.E. when the principles of zodiacal signs were established in India.[18] An unequivocal reference to the congregation of people in the month of Māgha at Prayāga, however, occurs in the *Narasiṁha Purāṇa,*[19] placed by Hazra[20] between C.E. 400 and 500. This Purāṇa narrates that once, in the month of Māgha, some Veda-knowing sages from different parts of India (viz. Himālaya, Naimiṣāraṇya, Arbudāraṇya, Puṣkarāraṇya, Mahendra mountian, Vindhya mountain, Dharmāraṇya, Daṇḍkāraṇya, Śrīśaila, Kurukṣetra, Kaumāra-parvata, Pampā, etc.), along with their disciples went to Prayāga, took their bath in the holy Saṅgama, offered oblations to the manes, worshipped Lord Mādhava, and saw Bharadvāja in his hermitage. When, after mutual greetings, they were engaged in talks about Kṛṣṇa there arrived a *sūta* named Lomaharṣaṇa who was a disciple of Vyāsa and was well-versed in the Purāṇic lore. After Lomaharṣaṇa had been duly received by the sages, Bharadvāja thanked him for having narrated to them the *saṁhitā* named Varāha (i.e. *Varāha Purāṇa*) during the great sacrifice instituted by Śaunaka and wished to hear from him the Purāṇa-saṁhitā named Narasiṁha. The *sūta* consented and narrated the *Narasiṁha Purāṇa* to the assembled sages.

The first historical reference to the religious festivities at Prayāga is supplied by the Chinese pilgrim-traveller Hsüan Tsang who attended the sixth quinquennial assembly organised by king Harṣavardhana and was an eye-witness to a gathering of half a million pilgrims at Prayāga in the month of Māgha in C.E. 643. He gives a vivid description of the sacred occasion in his travel accounts and says that this was an 'age-long festival' held at the confluence of the rivers to the west of which there was a level plain about 15 li (2^miles) wide covered with white sands. He mentions that king Harṣavardhana with his retinue visited Prayāga every fifth year and bestowed gifts lavishly on people of different religious orders and gave alms to the poor and the infirm; so generous was he that after 75 days he no longer possessed a single personal jewel and returned to his metropolis clad only in a piece of borrowed cloth.[21] Lakṣmīdhara, Vācaspati Miśra, Nārāyaṇa Bhaṭṭa, Mitra Miśra, and other medieval digest writers have referred to the efficacy of *māgha-snāna* at Prayāga. Tulasīdāsa (C.E. 1532-1623) has praised it in eloquent terms. He says that all the sacred places, gods, demons, semi-divinities, and pious men assemble in Prayāga and take bath at Triveṇī when the sun enters the sign of capricornus.[22] They bathe in the waters of the confluence throughout the month of Māgha and return to their respective abodes. There is thus a great rejoicing every year at Prayāga in Māgha.[23] The *Āin-i-Akbarī* has recorded, "Throughout the year it (Prayāga) is considered holy, but especially so during the month of Māgha".[24] Thevenot,[25] a European traveller, observed in C.E. 1666-67 :

> They (faquirs) are many times to be seen in troops at Halabas (Allahabad), where they assemble for celebrating some feasts (for which they are obliged to wash themselves in the Ganges) and to perform certain ceremonies. Such of them as do not hurt, and shew signs of piety are extremely honoured by the Gentiles, and the rich think they draw down blessings upon themselves....Their penance consists in forbearing to eat for many days; to keep constantly standing upon a stone for several weeks or several months; to hold their arms across behind their head, as long as they live; or to bury themselves in pits for a certain space of time. But if some of these faquirs be good men, there are also very rouges amongst them; and the Mughal princes are not troubled when such of them as commit violence are killed.

The reference here is clearly to the Māgha Melā which attracts many ascetics devoted to austere vows. The *Khulāṣat-ut-Tawārīkh*, composed in C.E. 1693-95, says : "In winter, when the sun enters the sign of capricorn, crowds of people assemble together at Prayāga from all sides of the world and staying there for one month, daily engage in ceremonial ablutions, and everyone gives alms to the poor and indigent, as far as he can".[26] There are several accounts of the melā from the pen of the European travellers who visited the place during the eighteenth-nineteenth centuries.[27] Thus, there is a continuous history of the fair from at least the Gupta period to the present day. The traditional scene of the melā has remained almost unchanged; the ascetics' exhibitions of yogic performance, the recitation of religious texts, discourses on socio-religious problems and sectarian propaganda continue to be the main attractions of the fair. With the passage of time the melā seems to be growing in popularity, and the Hindus throughout India observe this occasion with great sanctity.

KUMBHA MELĀ

The Māgha Melā is particularly momentous every twelfth year when it gets the name of the Kumbha Melā. It is considered the greatest religious concourse in the world. On this occasion countless pilgrims from every nook and corner of the land, speaking different languages and dialects, wearing distinct sectarian marks, donning various types of dresses, and observing different manners and customs, meet together for a holy dip in the sacred waters. The Kumbha Melā, which is ritualistically known as the Kumbha Parva, is celebrated in a twelve-year cycle by rotation at four sacred places – Haridvāra on the Gaṅgā, Prayāga on the Gaṅgā-Yamunā-saṅgama, Nāsik on the Godāvarī, and Ujjayinī on the Śiprā (Fig. 5), whenever a particular astronomical conjunction (*yoga*) occurs. One is here confronted with the notion of intersection of the trajectories of cosmic forces, symbolized by the moving planets and constellations, and flowing rivers and human lives. This represents the highest state of water symbolism in Hinduism. The Kumbha Melā, attracting millions of devouts periodically to the above sacred places, has had immeasurable influence in strengthening the religious and cultural foundations of Hinduism. There are rarely a few melās in India as traditionally Hindu and symbolic of the whole Hindu culture as the Kumbha Melā. This denotes the most distinct, elaborate and ancient ritual tradition of pilgrimage reflecting the ultimate sense of sacrality related to a place and time; in fact it shows the sacred emergence and integration of space and time. The untold tremendous faith that attracts people for generations, without any propaganda or publicity, all at one time, to the sacred place is still the vital strength of religious belief and practice. "Only as an immediate witness of some of the melās", says Miloslav Krása.[28] "is it possible to realise the depth and extent of the roots of this faith". The general belief that nectarine waters of the sacred rivers of India mysteriously come together at the sacred place at that time accounts for this faith and desire of cleansing through the ritual bath.

There are few melās in the world as challenging and bewildering to western visitors as the Kumbha Melā. Miloslav Krása[29] found the Kumbha Melā at Prayāga "the greatest fair of all nations and of all times". Sidney Low, who visited one of the melās at Prayāga during the tour of the Prince and Princess of Wales in C.E. 1906, was wonderstruck at its majestic sight; he[30] wrote, "Nothing more impressive, picturesque and pregnant with meaning and significant than the Kumbha Melā can be witnessed in India". He further remarked, "Until you have looked upon one of these tremendous

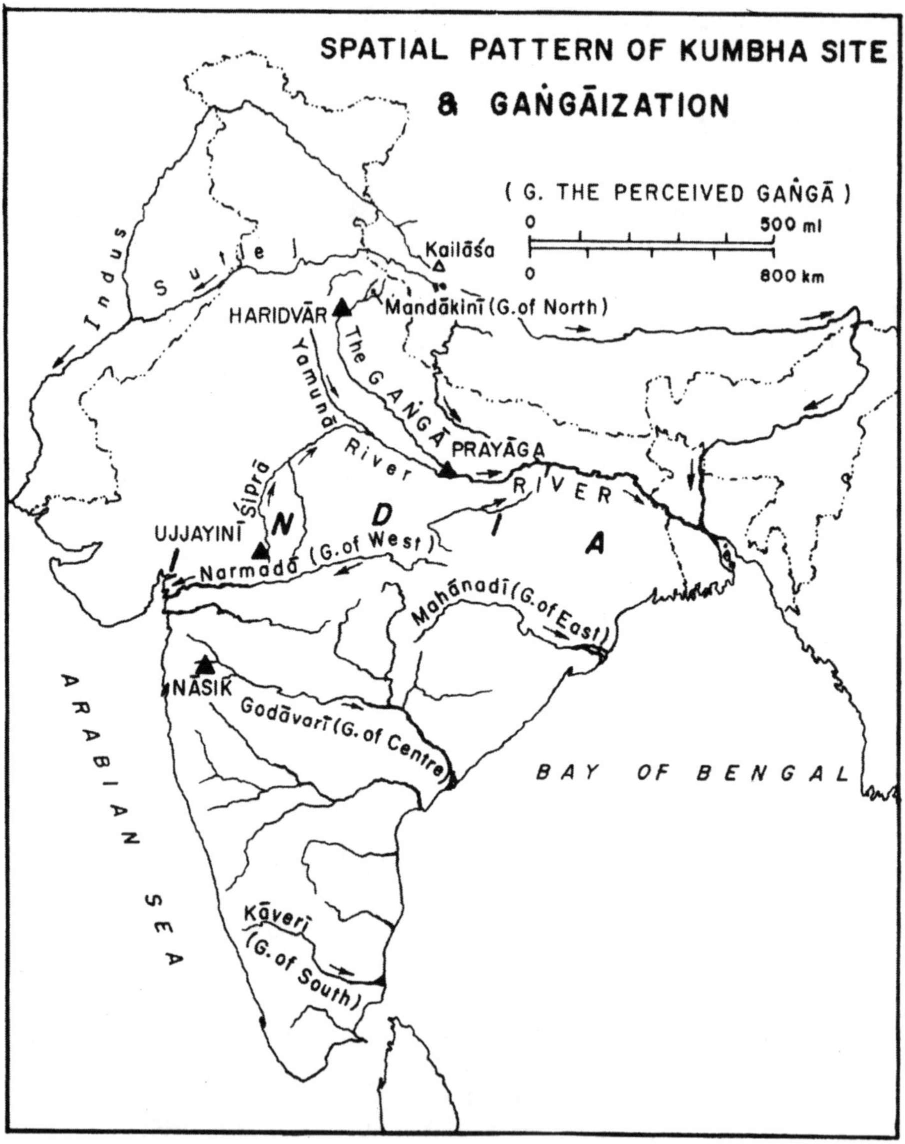

Fig. 5 Spatial pattern of Kumbha Melā sites and Gaṅgāization

gatherings of humanity, many aspects of Indian life and character must be hidden from you.... You see Hinduism at its best and its worst; you begin to realize faintly the hold that this jumble of devotion, metaphysics, and rank idolatry have upon the masses of the people; you observe

26. *KP*, I.36.6-8 = *TS*, 48; *MP*, 106.12-14 = *TvK*, 146 = *TP*, 344-345; *PdP*, III. 44.12b-15a.
27. वटमूलं समाश्रित्य यस्तु प्राणान्परित्यजेत् ।
सर्वलोकानतिक्रम्य रुद्रलोकं स गच्छति ॥
KP, I.35.8 = *TS*, 48; *MP*, 105.11 = *TvK*, 142 = *TP*, 343, *PdP*, III.43.11b - 12a = *TC*, 48; *NP*, II.63.139b-140a; *VsP*, 7.386 (reads चन्द्रलोकम्). The *AgP*, 111.13a (वटमूले सङ्गमादौ मृतो विष्णुपुरीं व्रजेत्) promises the attainment of Viṣṇupurī.
28. प्रयागवटशाखाग्रात् पातनं च करोति यः ।
स्वयं देहविनाशस्य काले प्राप्ते महामतिः ॥
उत्तमान् प्राप्नुयाल्लोकान् नात्मघाती भवेत्क्वचित् ।
महापापक्रियः स्वर्गे दिव्यान् भोगान् समश्नुते ॥
BP q. in *TP*, 248. The *Ādi Purāṇa* q. in Aparārka comm. on *Yājña.*, II.877 and in *TS*, 53 reads प्रयागवटशाखायां देहत्यागं करोति वा।.. महापापक्षयात्स्वर्गे दिव्यान् भोगान् समश्नुते ॥
29. *MP*, 106.9-11 = *TvK*, 146 = *TC*, 50 = *TP*, 344; *KP*, I.36.3-5 = *TS*, 48; *PdP*, III.44.9b-12a; *NP*, II.63.156b-159b.
30. *MP*, 106.15-16 = *TvK*, 146 = *TP*, 345; *KP*, I.36.9-10 = *TS*, 48-49; *PdP*, III.44.15b-17a; *NP*, II.63.127b-129a.
31. *MP*, 106.17-19 = *TvK*, 146-147 = *TC*, 50 = *TP*, 345; *KP*, I.36.11-13 = *TS*, 49; *PdP*, III.44.17b-20a; *NP*, II.63.159b-161.
32. *MP*, 105.34-39 = *TvK*, 144 = *TC*, 48-49 = *TS*, 49-50 = *TP*, 344; *PdP*, III.43.35-39; *NP*, II.63.142b-148a; *KP*, I.35.25-26.
33. *MP*, 105.44-45 = *TvK*, 144-145 = *TC*, 49 = *TS*, 50 = *TP*, 344; *PdP*, III.43.44b-46a; *NP*, II.63.151b-153a; *KP*, I.35.28.
34. *MP*, 106.4-6 = *TvK*, 145 = *TC*, 49-50 = *TP*, 340, 344; *PdP*, III.44.4-7a; *NP*, II.63.153b-156a; *KP*, I.35.38.
35. *MP*, 107.26b = *TS*, 57; *PdP*, III.45.26b = *TC*, 51; *KP*, I.37.3b.
36. *MP*, 104.8-12 = *TvK*, 139 = *TP*, 328; *PdP*, III.42.8b-13 = *TC*, 51-52; *KP*, I.34.36b-41; *NP*, II.63.170-173.
37. Watters, *On Yuan Chwang's Travels in India A.D. 629-645*, Vol. I, p.364; Beal, *Si-yu-ki: Buddhist Records of the Western World*, Vol. II, p.253. Hsüan Tsang visited Prayāga in the month of Māgha in C.E. 643.
38. *Ibid.*
39. Watters, Vol. I, p.362; Beal, Vol. II, p.252.
40. Beal, Vol. II, p.253.
41. Watters, Vol. I, pp.364-365; Beal, Vol. II, pp.253-354.
42. *JRAS*, 1983, p.265.
43. Irwin, John, 'The Prayāga Bull-pillar : Another Pre-Aśokan Monument', *South Asian Archaeology 1979*, pp.313-340.
44. *Corpus Inscriptionum Indicarum*, Vol. I : *Inscriptions of Aśoka*, p.37.
45. Sachau, E.C., *Alberuni's India*, Vol. I, pp.170-171,
46. *Ibid.*, Vol. II, p.200.

47. *Bulletin of the School of Oriental and African Studies*, Vol. XII, p.639 (40).
48. *Ibid.*, pp.639-640 (41).
49. *Vividhatīrthakalpa*, p.68.
50. Elliot, H.M., *Bibliographical Index to the Historians of Muhammedan India*, Vol. I, p.35 fn.; Elliot, H.M. and John Dowson, *The History of India as Told by Its Own Historians*, Vol. I, p.55, fn.2.
51. *Āin-i-Akbarī* of Abul Fazl, Vol. III, p.335.
52. *Muntakhab-ut-Tawārīkh* of Abdul Qādir Badāunī, Vol. II, p.179; *The History of India*, Vol. V, p.512.
53. *Khulāṣat-ut-Tawārīkh* of Sujān, folio no. 37b; *Chahār Gulshan* of Rāi Chatarman, folio no. 67a; Sarkar, Jadunath, *The India of Aurangzeb*, pp.XLVI, 28, 136.
54. Sinha, S.N., *The Mid-Gangetic Region in the Eighteenth Century : Some Observations of Joseph Tieffenthaler*, p.35.
55. Hamilton, Walter, *A Geographical, Statistical and Historical Description of Hindostan and the Adjacent Countries*, Vol. I, p.300.
56. Von Orlich, Leopold, *Travels in India, including Sinde and the Punjab*, Vol. II, pp.117-118.
57. संस्थिता सह सायासे सेना प्रमतिना सह ।

    गङ्गायमुनयोर्मध्ये सिद्धिं प्राप्ताः समाधिना ॥ *MP*, 143.64.

    MP (Bombay : Veṅkṭeshvara Press, 1895), 144.63 reads सहसा या तु for सह सायासे & प्राप्ता for प्राप्ताः, and *MP* (Ānandāshrama Sanskrit Series 54, Poona: Ānandāshrama Press, 1907), 144.63 reads सहसा या तु for सह सायासे, प्राप्ता for प्राप्ताः, and ससाधना for समाधिना.

    स साधयित्वा वृषलान् प्रायशस्तानधार्मिकान् ।

    गङ्गायमुनयोर्मध्ये निष्ठां प्राप्तः सहानुगः ॥

    VaP (Bombay: Veṅkaṭeshvara Press, 1933), I.58.88; *BrhP* (Bombay: Veṅkaṭeshvara Press,1935), II. ii. 31.89.

    In the *Matsya Purāṇa*, the king is specifically called Pramati. The corresponding verses of the *Vāyu Purāṇa* and the *Brahmāṇḍa Purāṇa* do not mention his name. The *Vāyu* (I.58.65) and *Brahmāṇḍa* (II.ii.31.86) Purāṇas like the *MP* (143.61), however, refer to the king as Pramati in the opening verses of the story occurring in their relevant passages.

    Vasudeva S. Agrawala (*Matsya Purāṇa – A Study*, p.230) has interpreted the above passage of the *Matsya Purāṇa* to mean that "His (Pramati's) vast army strong in cavalry (*sasādhanā*) achieved its successful purpose in the country between Gaṅgā and Yamunā". His interpretation is questionable. The verse in the Ānandāshrama edition of the *Matsya Purāṇa*, which Agrawala consulted, reads *sasādhanā* for *samādhinā*. It is surprising how he took the word *sasādhanā* to mean 'cavalry'; the desired expression may be supplanted by the word *sasādhanaḥ* but not by *sasādhanā*. Moreover, the meaning of the words *sasādhanā* and *samādhinā* in the present context is identical and denotes a stage of yoga. This reveals that king Pramati attained final bliss (*siddhim*) by means of *samādhi* or *sādhanā* at the confluence of the Gaṅgā and the Yamunā. The corresponding verses of the *Vāyu Purāṇa* and the *Brahmāṇḍa Purāṇa* also support this interpretation.

58. *Matsya Purāṇa—A Study*, pp.228-231; Roy, S.N., *Historical and Cultural Studies in the Purāṇas*, pp.132-142.
59. Awasthi, A.B.L., *Studies in Skanda Purāṇa*, Part I, pp.182-185; *History from the Purāṇas*, pp.118-133.
60. Goyal, S.R., *Samudragupta Parākramāṅka*, pp.265-267.
61. Shastri, A.M., 'The Purāṇic King Pramati : Some Observations', *Purāṇa*, Vol XXXIII (1), p.59.
62. शौर्य सत्यव्रतधरो यः प्रयागगतो धने ।

    अम्भसीव करीषाग्नौ मग्नः स पुष्पपूजितः ॥

    CII, Vol. III : *Inscriptions of the Early Gupta Kings and Their Successors*, p.203.
63. *Ibid.*, p.206, fn. 3.
64. *JUPHS*, Vol. X, pt. 1, p.74; *History of Dharmaśāstra*, Vol. II, pt. II, p.927, Vol. IV, p.605; *The History of Suicide in India*, p.97; Chattopadhyaya, Sudhakar, *Early History of North India*, p.269.
65. Devahuti, D., *Harṣa—A Political Study*, p.17.
66. यो गङ्गायमुने तरङ्गसुभगे गृह्णन् परेभ्यः समम् ।

    साक्षाच्चिह्ननिभेन चोत्तमपदं तत्प्राप्तवानैश्वरम् ॥

    देहासम्मितवैभवैरिव गुणैर्यस्य भ्रमद्भिर्दशो ।

    व्याप्तास्तस्य बभूव कीर्तिपुरुषो गोविन्दराजः सुतः ॥

    Indian Antiquary, Vol. XII, 1883, p.159.

    James Prinsep (*Journal of the Asiatic Society of Bengal*, Vol. VIII, 1839, p.304ff) and K.C. Chattopadhyaya (*JUPHS*, Vol. X, pt. I, p.76) hold that king Dhruva drowned himself at the confluence of the Gaṅgā and the Yamunā. A.S. Altekar (*Rāṣṭrakūṭas and their Times*, p.58) and V.S. Pathak ('Prayāga in Inscriptions', *JUPHS* (New Series), Vol. VI, pt. II, pp.32-33) controvert this view and suggest that the verse does not refer to the suicide of Dhruva at the confluence.
67. *Śaṅkara-digvijaya* of Mādhava Vidyāraṇya, 7.75; *JUPHS*, Vol. X, pt. 1, p.76; *The History of Suicide in India*, pp.91-92.
68. *Śaṅkara-digvijaya*, 7.110.
69. *JUPHS*, Vol. X, pt. 1, p.76.
70. रक्षित्वा क्षितिमंबुराशिरशनामेतामनन्यायतिम् ।

    जीवित्वा शरदां शतं समधिकं श्रीधङ्गपृथ्वीपतिः ॥

    रुद्रं मुद्रितलोचनः स हृदये ध्यायन्जपन् ।

    जाह्नवी-कालिंद्योः सलिले कलेवरपरित्यागादगान्निर्वृतिम् ॥

    Ep.Ind., Vol. I, p.146.
71. प्राप्ते प्रयागवटमूलनिवेशबन्धौ सार्द्धं शतेन गृहिणीभिरमुत्र मुक्तिम् ।

    Khairā Copperplate of Yaśaḥkarṇadeva dated C.E. 1072, *Ep.Ind.*, Vol. XII, p.211; Jabalapur copperplate of Yaśaḥkarṇadeva dated C.E. 1122, *Ep. Ind.*, Vol. II, p.4; Jabalapur Kotwali Copperplate of Jayasiṁha dated C.E. 1167,

Ep.Ind., Vol. XXI, p.94; Kumbhī Copperplate of Vijayasiṁha dated C.E. 1181, *JASB*, Vol. XXXI, no.2, 1862, p.117; Umariyā Copperplate of Vijayasiṁha dated C.E. 1193, *Ep.Ind.*, Vol. XLI, p.44.

72. *JASB*, Vol. XXXI, no. 2, 1862, p.114.
73. *JUPHS*, Vol. X, pt. 1, p.75.
74. तथा च श्रुतिः-- यथा प्रयागे प्रायोपवेशनस्थितापि
ब्रह्मबन्धूब्राह्मणी गोविन्देन परिव्राजा सह किल
परीवादभागिनी बभूवेति ।
Yaśastilakacampū, p.149.
75. *Karakaṇḍacariu* of Muni Kanakāmara, VI.6.5-10.
76. *Ibid.*, VI.7.7.
77. *Rājataraṅgiṇī*, III.430.
78. शाके नवाष्टखेन्द्वा-1089 ख्य अरिभेऽद्भुतसागरम् ।
गौडेन्द्रकुन्जरालानस्तम्भवाहुर्महीपतिः ॥
ग्रन्थेऽस्मिन्नसमाप्त एव तनये साम्राज्यलक्ष्मीं मुदा ।
दीक्षापर्वणि दक्षिणे निगकृते निष्पत्तिमस्थापयत् ॥
नानादानतिलाम्बुसम्बलनभं सूर्यात्मजासंगमम् ।
गङ्गायां विरचय्य निर्जरपुरं भार्यानुयातो गतः ॥
Adbhutasāgara of Vallālasena, p.4; *Inscriptions of Bengal*, Vol. III, p.174.
Other readings of this couplet give the date as 1090 Śaka. See Banerji, R.D., 'Lakṣmaṇasena', *JASB*, Vol. IV, 1913, p.275; Majumdar, R.C., 'The Chronology of the Sena Kings', *JASB*, Vol. VII, 1921, p.11; Bhattacharya, D.C., 'Date of Lakṣamaṇasena and His Predecessors', *IA*, Vol. LI, 1922, p.146.
79. *JUPHS* (New Series), Vol. VI, pt. II, p.32, fn. 1.
80. *JASB*, Vol. XVII, 1921, p.12, fn. 1.
81. हित्वा देहन्त्रिदश-भानुकन्याजलान्तः श्लाघ्येऽनन्ते--परमं ब्रह्मसायुज्यमाप्ते ।
Mau Stone Inscription of Madanavarman, *Ep.Ind.*, Vol. I, p.201. That Ananta, a minister under the Candella kings Kīrtivarman and Sallakṣaṇavarman, was a brāhmaṇa is mentioned in *Ep.Ind.*, Vol. V, p.29.
82. Anonymous, 'Prayāga or Allahabad', *Modern Review*, December, 1910, p.653; Crook, William, *Religion and Folklore of Northern India*, p.151; Rangaswami Aiyangar, *TvK*, introduction, p.LXXXII; Pandey, B.N., *Allahabad : Retrospect and Prospect*, pp.16-18; *The History of Suicide in India*, p.93.
83. *History of Dharmaśāstra*, Vol. III, pp.939, 948-949.
84. *TS*, 51; *TP*, 346. These works quote this repulsive idea in order to refute it.
85. काम्यमप्यत्र मरणं तत्र च सर्ववर्णानामधिकारः ।
Gaṅgāvākyāvalī, p.305; *TC*, 47; Kane, *op.cit.*, Vol. IV, p.610, fn. 1387.
86. मोक्षार्थं प्रयागमरणे तु सर्वपापक्षये नास्ति विवादः । *TS*, 51.
--- फलान्तरार्थं मोक्षार्थं वा प्रयागमरणे न कश्चिद्दोष इति । *Ibid.*, **52.**
87. तत्सिद्धं ब्राह्मणस्यापि प्रयागे शरीरोत्सर्गेऽधिकार इति । *Ibid.*, 54.

88. तस्मादातुरादेरनातुरादेश्च सर्वस्याधिकारः । *Ibid.*, 55.
89. किंतु वृद्धौ पितरौ तरुणीं भार्यां पोष्यमपत्यं च विहाय नाधिकारः । एवं स्त्रिया अपि गर्भिण्या बालापत्याया भर्त्राननुज्ञाताया वा नाधिकार इत्यादि ज्ञेयम् । *Ibid.*, 55; *History of Dharmaśāstra*, Vol. IV, p.609, fn. 1385.
90. इत्यादि वाक्यात् प्रयागमरणे नाधर्मासम्भवाच्च । *TP*, 346.
91. ब्राह्मणेन कलौ जलादिप्रवेशो न कार्यः । *Ibid.*, 354.
92. न वेदवचनादिति ।--वस्तुतस्तु वाराणसीमरणवद्यादृच्छिकमरणविषय एवायं ग्रन्थो न हठमरणप्रतिपादकः । 'सितासिते सरिते---अमृतत्वं भजन्ते । ब्रह्मज्ञानेन मुच्यन्ते प्रयागमरणेन च' इत्यादि श्रुतयः स्मृतयश्च तादृशा एव ।
Mbh with the comm. of Nīlakaṇṭha, Vol. II, p.146.
93. सिद्धौ वा अचिकित्स्यरोगादिदोषवतां भृगुपतनादि नापिमरणे प्राप्तेऽपि प्रयाग-मरणनियमविधिरियं भविष्यति न च काम्योऽयं मरणविधिर्नित्यस्य मरणनिषेध-विधेर्बाधकः । ---अभ्युपगे वा ब्राह्माव्यतिरिक्तविषय एवायं विधिः । *Ibid.*
94. *Tīrthenduśekhara* of Nāgojī Bhaṭṭa, p.26; *JUPHS*, Vol. X, pt. 1, p.68.
95. Watters, Vol. I, p.362; Beal, Vol. II, pp.252-253.
96. Sachau, Vol. II, p.170.
97. Vaidya, C.V., *History of Medieval Hindu India*, Vol. III, p.399.
98. जइ हिमगिरिहि चडेविणु निवडइ, अह पयायतरुहि विइक्कमणु ।
निक्कइअवें विणु समयाचारेण विणु मण सुद्धिएं लहइन सिव जाणु ॥
Kumārapālacarita, 8.20.
99. *Dohāvalī, dohā* 14.
100. For evidence, see the author's article : 'The Historicity of Akṣayavaṭa at Prayāga', *Purāṇa*, Vol. 28 (1), 1986, pp.45-78.
101. *JRAS*, 1983, p. 271.

Chapter VII

FAIRS AND FESTIVALS

For many centuries Prayāga has been the place of the most amazing meetings of people, of religious fervour, and of sacred rites and rituals. It is one of the most frequented places of pilgrimage, where people come especially during the month of Māgha for bathing in the purifying waves of the holy rivers (*saṅgama*) and every twelfth year they come by hundreds of thousands to India's greatest melā, the Kumbha Melā. A cross-section of the Indian society can be seen here – peasants, merchants, paupers, misers, moneylenders, *paṇḍitas*, illiterates, holy-men, and the sophisticated elite. The focus is on movement, which is what *yātrā* denotes and on 'marching forward' from a less to a more desirable state of being, achieved by a ritual bathing in the holy waters, which is what *tīrtha* signifies. Prayāga becomes the visible manifestation of Indian myths and traditions and the greatest centre for the communication and diffusion of Indian culture on these occasions. Although there are some genuine attempts to understand and appreciate the significance of these two fair-festivals, they have not been studied in a comprehensive manner. They symbolize the best in the socio-religious traditions of the country and bring to the people those noble and enlightening thoughts that foster love and unity. They have helped in stabilizing culture and promoting national integration. In this chapter, these great affairs of national importance have been discussed in historical and cultural perspectives.

MĀGHA MELĀ

The Māgha Melā, held on the vast open sacred sandy site of the rivers, is perhaps the most sanctifying attractive event in the cultural life of the country. It provides a traditional focus for a variety of sects and mendicant orders as well as commonality. It is a colourful, unique aspect, both captivating and crushing. Here mythology is interwoven with history, true religious ignition with simple curiosity.

The Māgha Melā is so-called because the fair is celebrated in the month of Māgha (January-February). What distinguishes this fair from the common run of religious fairs is its long duration, longer than a month, for it covers the month of Māgha both by the lunar and solar calendars. It begins from the *makarasaṅkrānti*, i.e., when the sun enters the sign of capricornus. Thousands of pilgrims, belonging to all strata of society and speaking different languages, and ascetics of various religious orders from all regions of the country flock to Prayāga and dwell in tents and hutments on the sandy tract for *kalpavāsa* within the sacred precincts. It is an annual feature that people perform their purificatory rites in the month of Māgha especially in Prayāga. What attracts them as a magnet, all at one time, to the same place, is the still vital strength of religious tradition. A miniature spiritual India is represented on the dry flood plain between the Gaṅgā and the Yamunā during the shivering cold of Māgha.

The format of the melā is greatly extended, mass-involving ritual. The pilgrims take their baths, make their offerings, observe religious vows, receive religious instructions, and pay visits to holy spots within the framework of scriptural authority. It is a convocation of scholars and saints who sojourn there for the duration to engage in mutual discussions of momentous issues of this world and the next and in preaching to the classes as well as masses. It is perhaps only at the Māgha Melā that saints and laymen feel obliged to talk exclusively about religious subjects; at other places, the monk instructs the laity on all problems, religious and profane. As the melā goes on, monastic and lay religious leaders, including the most famous *paṇḍitas* of the land, address gatherings of many sizes, ranging from 500 to 50,000 persons. Again, doctrinal topics are discussed by the holy ones. It is these meetings alone that coordinate the present state of Hindu theological and exegetical learning in a seemingly informal manner. In previous centuries it was at this melā that Indian learning was solidified and presented to a representative body of Brāhmaṇical, Buddhist, and Jaina religious opinion. The melā may thus be defined as a socio-religious gathering where trade flourished and wealth circulated.

The melā is an old cultural institution. Along with the ritual activities associated with a particular festival come the sensory delights of the fair; and the Māgha Melā is primarily a ritual bathing festival. The wide spreading plain, framed by the branches of the two rivers, is practically deserted most of the year; during the rainy season most of it is covered with mud. And yet when winter comes it becomes one of the beauty spots in the world. The land between the Gaṅgā and the Yamunā was called Madhyadeśa, where the indigenous world attained its final fusion; and the confluence of the rivers at Prayāga was regarded as its visible symbol. The natural importance of the life-giving rivers, the suggestive symbolism of their union, the majestic quiet and beauty of the surrounding nature with its colour play with the river waves, paired with the tradition and fame of the place itself, gave rise to such a festival-fair in ancient times.

Māgha Melā owes its origin to ritual bath at the confluence of the rivers, the supreme bathing site in India since the Vedic age.[1] The *Anuśāsanaparva*[2] of the *Mahābhārata* refers to the living institution of *māgha-snāna* when it says that he who bathes with the restrained mind and observing rigid vows at Prayāga in the month of Māgha is cleansed of all his sins and attains heaven. The Purāṇas[3] also mention it when they wax eloquent over a bath taken thrice a day at Prayāga in the month of Māgha that bears a reward equivalent to a gift of hundred thousand cows. The *Matsya Purāṇa*[4] declares that he who bathes in the waters of the Gaṅgā-Yamunā-saṅgama in the month of Māgha is freed from the cycle of rebirth for hundreds of crores of aeons (*kalpas*). The *Nāradīya Purāṇa*[5] says that even a person enveloped with hundreds of sins becomes liberated from rebirth by bathing at the confluence in the month of Māgha when the sun is in capricornus. The same Purāṇa[6] further states that only the blessed people reach Prayāga in the month of Māgha since the waters of the joint stream lead to non-recurrence of birth. According to the *Padma Purāṇa*,[7] it is the cherished desire of the gods to be present in Prayāga in the month of Māgha. Men who take their holy dip there during those days do not experience the pain of being in a womb. They stay in Viṣṇuloka. It is said that a regular bathing for a period of one month coupled with a continent life at Prayāga washes away all sins.[8] The *Skanda Purāṇa*[9] states that the sins like brahmanicide roar in the body so long as the man does not bathe in the sin-destroying waters at Prayāga in the month of Māgha. By bathing in the Veṇī every day in that month one obtains that benefit which accrues from gifting away a thousand gold pieces at Kurukṣetra at the time of a solar eclipse.[10] Bathing at Prayāga in the month of Māgha is the most efficacious as an incalculable number of holy places, sacred streams, gods, mountains, etc. are believed to assemble on the sands of the Gaṅgā and the Yamunā.[11] Possibly this is one of the factors that makes a bath in the month of Māgha especially purifying and merit-giving at Prayāga. The origin of Māgha Melā seems to lie in the miraculous virtues of bath at Prayāga.

The Purāṇic texts stress the need of undertaking pilgrimage to Prayāga and prescribe the rules about staying there. Going to and remaining in the land of *tapas* and *yajñas* for some days is extremely meritorious. The *Padma Purāṇa*[12] assures immunity from all sins to those who reside with senses restrained for a month in Prayāga and the *Matsya Purāṇa*[13] says, "Those who maintain their sexual purity for a month in that sacred place and offer

Śāstrakāras, however, explain away the time-honoured forms of self-destruction at Prayāga. Viśvāsadevī and Vācaspati Miśra allow religious suicide for people of all communities at Prayāga.[85] Nārāyaṇa Bhaṭṭa in a learned discussion of the ethics of suicide at Prayāga has concluded that there is no sin in suicide at Prayāga for the attainment of salvation and other rewards.[86] that it is not forbidden to brāhmaṇas,[87] and that persons, whether seriously ill or in good health, may resort to suicide at Prayāga.[88] He, however, adds that no one can commit suicide at Prayāga after abandoning one's old parents, young wife and children requiring support, nor can a woman, who is pregnant or who had young children or who has no permission from her husband, commit suicide at Prayāga.[89] Mitra Miśra regards suicide at Prayāga as lawful[90] but restricts it to non-brāhmaṇas, as it is interdicted for the brāhmaṇas in the Kali age.[91] Nīlakaṇṭha explains verses prescribing religious suicide in a different way. He holds that the *Mahābhārata* III.83.78 refers to natural death at Prayāga and the *Ṛgveda khila* verse has the same meaning.[92] But failing to demolish the well established practice of suicide at the place, he suggests that the Epic passage allows persons who are suffering from an incurable disease to commit suicide at Prayāga and that it applies to non-brāhmaṇas only.[93] Nāgojī Bhaṭṭa (first half of the eighteenth century) disapproves of it in the case of the brāhmaṇas. According to him, a brāhmaṇa who kills himself even at Prayāga incurs two sins, one for destroying the soul and another for taking away a brāhmaṇa's life.[94]

The growth of opinion against religious suicide is reflected in the travel accounts of foreigners who visited India. Hsüan Tsang took suicide as a great folly. To substantiate his view, he cites one case. He informs that a wise and learned brāhmaṇa belonging to a good family tried to persuade the people to stop the practice of suicide near the *Deva*-temple. He went to that site and mounted the 'tree' with a view to throwing himself down from it. He declared from its top that formerly he had spoken of the matter as being an illusion but then he had definite proof of it being real because the 'devas' (gods) with their aerial music were coming to meet him and therefore he would cast himself down. His friends tried to dissuade him from resorting to such an act but in vain. Hence, they spread out their garments underneath the place where he was on the tree; so when he jumped down he was unhurt though in a swoon. After recovering, he said to his friends: "What is seen as the 'devas' in the air summoning one is the leading of evil spirits, not the acquisition of heavenly joy".[95]

This account shows that the Chinese pilgrim was opposed to self-destruction at Prayāga. According to him, people wrongly considered suicide at the sacred place to be a means of getting release from transmigration. The observations of Alberūnī on suicide are also significant. He says that it was resorted to by "those who are tired of life, who are distressed over some incurable disease, some irremovable bodily defect, or old age, or infirmity. This, however, no man of distinction does, but only vaiśyas and śūdras.... Burning oneself is forbidden to brāhmaṇas and kṣatriyas by a special law. Therefore, these, if they want to kill themselves, do so at the time of an eclipse in some other manner, or they hire somebody to drown them in the Ganges".[96] The special law mentioned here probably refers to the *kalivarjya* provision on the subject.[97] Hemacandra, a Jaina writer of the twelfth century C.E., has condemned the conventional practice of suicide by jumping down from the tree of Prayāga. According to him, it does not bestow bliss; it only leads to the amputation of limbs.[98] Tulasīdāsa tried to discard the practice by providing an easier substitute for it. He says, "The same merit accrues from one's love to recite the name of Lord Rāma as is produced by the natural death at Kāśī and forced relinquishing the body at Prayāga".[99]

To conclude, Prayāga was the most important centre for suicides and attracted persons inclined to observe this practice from all over the country. It seems that originally religious suicide at the confluence of the Gaṅgā and the Yamunā at Prayāga alone was popular and it was only later that it became associated with other rivers and sacred places. For there is no Vedic authority for this rite in the case of other sacred places and it never became so popular elsewhere as in Prayāga. The practice of suicide at the foot of the Banyan tree and from its top at Prayāga came to an end by the last quarter of the sixteenth century, when Akbar built his fort at the site. However, it continued at the confluence up to the middle of the nineteenth century when it was initially controlled and later on stopped by the British Government on humane considerations in conformity with the thinking of a developing school of Indian reformers. Though there is no evidence of a Jaina monk, or lay believer committing suicide at Prayāga, it is well known that Jaina saints often died by giving up all food and drink and through complete abstinence from all forms of sustenance of life. However, Jaina association with Prayāga is definitely known; references to this have been provided by us elsewhere.[100]

As regards the rationale for this rite, we must remember that religious fanaticism has been one of the most significant causes of suicides in all countries since ancient times. Religious suicide involved no risk of post-mortuary penalties. On the contrary, the person committing suicide thus was believed to have secured a place in the celestial regions with fabulous pleasures, and was expected on the expiry of his religious merit to be reborn as a lord of the Jambūdvīpa. Such attractive temptations must have strengthened the practice. The promised rewards, are, however, not to be taken literally, but to be understood to signify the highest destiny for the devout pilgrim. It is not known for want of relevant evidence whether the growing complexity of socio-economic lift also induced people to take to such extreme steps. 'At the learned level there was a belief that self-inflicted death at the right place and time ensures a future life which is absolute and infinite. Behind this belief is the view that death is simply a rite of passage, a sacral re-entry into a non-physical state of being'.[101] The highest aim of life in Hinduism is to dispense with it once for all. If life is to be laid down, one would like a noble setting for the act of renunciation. Prayāga, saturated with the knowledge of Brahma, where the two holy rivers flowing from the Himālaya mingle their floods, offered the most natural environment to end life under the belief of gratifying religious and material desires in the next birth. Herein lay Prayāga's age-long appeal. Suicide marks the culmination of a scheme of pilgrimage, whose goal lies beyond all physical means of redemption and beyond life itself. The solemnity of the pilgrimage to Prayāga is stressed by this religious practice.

REFERENCES

1. Chattopadhyaya K.C., 'Religious Suicide at Prayāga', *JUPHS*, Vol. X, pt. 1, 1937, pp.65-79.
2. Kane, *History of Dharmaśāstra*, Vol. IV, pp.604-614.
3. Sircar, D.C., 'Religius Suicide', chapter in *Studies in the Religious Life of Ancient and Medieval India*, pp.206-220.
4. Thakur, Upendra, *The History of Suicide in India.*
5. *JUPHS*, Vol. X, pt. 1, p.79; *Studies in the Religious Life of Ancient and Medieval India*, p.206.
6. For details see *History of Dharmaśāstra,* Vol. II, pt. II, pp.924-927, Vol. III, pp.948-949, Vol. IV, pp.604-605; *Studies in the Religious Life of Ancient and Medieval India*, pp.206-211; *The History of Suicide in India*, pp.51-60.
7. Kane, *op.cit.*, Vol. IV, p.604.
8. सितासिते सरिते यत्र संगथे तत्राप्लुतासो दिवमुत्पतन्ति ।
   ये वै तन्वं वि सृजन्ति धीरास्ते जनासो अमृतत्वं भजन्ते ॥
   Ṛgveda, Pariśiṣṭa, 22.1.
9. अत्र स्नात्वा दिवं यान्ति ये मृतास्तेऽपुनर्भवा: ।
   KP, I. 34.20b = *TS*, 28; *MP*, 103.5a = *TvK*, 136 = *TC*, 47 = *TP*, 343; *NP*, II.63.131a; *VsP*, 7.384.
   श्रुतिभि: परिपठ्येते सितासिते सरिद्वरे ।
   तत्राप्लुताङ्गाह्यमृतं भवन्तीति विनिश्चितम् ॥
   SkP, IV. 7.54 = *TS*, 11.

10. *TC*, 47; *TS*, 3; *TP*, 342; it is not quoted by Lakṣamīdhara Bhaṭṭa in his *TvK*.
11. *Mbh* with the comm. of Nīlakaṇṭha, Vol. II, p.146; *History of Dharmaśāstra*, Vol. IV, p.596, fn. 1349.
12. ---बलादपि प्राणत्यागे न दोष इति सूचयति । *TS*, 4.
13. *JUPHS*, Vol. X, pt. 1, pp.73-74.
14. न वेदवचनात्तात न लोकवचनादपि ।
    मतिरुत्क्रमणीया ते प्रयागमरणं प्रति ॥
    Mbh, III.83.78 = *TvK*, 152 (reads वापि for तात); *NP*, II.63. 131b-132a (reads चैव for तात and हि for ते); *PdP*, III.39.79 (reads न देव--) = *TC*, 47 (reads न वेद--); *AgP*, 111.8 (न वेदवचनाद्विप्र--- । मतिरुत्क्रमणीयान्ते प्रयागे मरणं प्रति ॥) = *TS*, 53 and *TP*, 351 (read न लोकवचनाद्विप्र न वेदवचनादपि । मतिरुत्क्रणीयाते प्रयागमरणं प्रति ॥); *MP*, 105.22 (reads न देव--तथा । --प्रयागगमनं प्रति ॥) = *TvK*, 143 (reads न वेद-- प्रयागमरणं प्रति ॥) = *TS*, 49 (reads न लोक वचनात्तात---प्रयागमरणं प्रति ॥) = *PdP*, III.43.23 (reads न देव-- प्रयागगमनं प्रति ॥); *KP*, I. 35.13 is न मातृवचनात्तात--दपि । मति--प्रयागगमनं प्रति ॥

    Some readings entirely change the meaning and assert that one, who has a desire to go to Prayāga, should not heed the words of one's mother or elders or of the people dissuading him from going there.
15. *Śatapatha Brāhmaṇa*, X.2.6.7, 40.3; *Bṛhadāraṇyakoupaniṣad*, IV.4.11; *Īśāvāsvopaniṣad*, verse 3; Medhātithi on *Manu*, V.88, VI. 32; *Uttararāmacarita*, Act IV, after verse 3, p.88; *History of Dharmaśāstra*, Vol. IV, p.606; *Vājasaneyī Saṁhitā*, 40.3.
16. *Āpastamba Dharmasūtra*, I.10.16-17; *Gautama Dharmasūtra*, II.5.11; *Vasiṣṭha Dharmasūtra*, 23.14-15; *Viṣṇusmṛti*, 22.56; *Manusmṛti*, V.89-90; *Yājñavalkya-smṛti*, III.i.6; *Parāśarasmṛti*, IV.1-2; *History of Dharmaśāstra*, Vol. II, pt. II, pp.924-25, Vol. IV, p.606; *Studies in the Religious Life of Ancient and Medieval India*, p.207.
17. लोकवेदविरुद्धस्य हठमरणस्यापवादोऽयम् अहिंसाविधेरिव पश्वालम्भविधिरिति प्राञ्चः ।
    Mbh with comm. of Nīlakaṇṭha, Vol. II, p.146; *JUPHS*, Vol. X. pt. 1, p.68.
18. *MP*, 107.10 = *TS*, 50 = *TP*, 345-346; *PdP*, III.45.9 = *TC*, 51; *NP*, II.63.163.
19. *MP*, 108.11-12 = *TvK*, 150; *PdP*, III.46.11-12 = *TC*, 51; *NP*, II.63.168-169a.
20. *SkP*, IV.22.76 = *TS*, 57 = *TP*, p.352.
21. *GP*, I.81.2b.
22. *History of Dharmaśāstra*, Vol. IV, p.612.
23. समुद्रपत्न्योर्जलसंनिपाते पूतात्मनामत्र किलाभिषेकात् ।
    तत्त्वावबोधेन विनापि भूयस्तनुत्यजां नास्ति शरीरबन्धः ॥
    Raghuvaṁśa, XIII.58.
24. *KP*, I.35.15 = *TS*, 48; MP, 105.24 = *TvK*, 143; *PdP*, III.43.25 = *TC*, 47; *NP*, II.63.133b-134a.
25. *KP*, I.34.31-35 = *TS*, 48; MP, 104.3-7 = *TvK*, 138-139 = *TP*, 343; *PdP*, III.42.3-7 = *TC*, 48; *NP*, II.63.135-139.

Brahmanism working hand in hand with a crude and savage felish worship; you have before you such multitude of men and women as you may not meet twice in a lifetime".[31] The melā brings to life in an organic and cosmic way a personal experience of the Indian folk and Sanskritic traditions on a scale never seen elsewhere.

The origin and historicity of the Kumbha Melā has been a subject of much discussion amongst Indologists. "The Hindus throughout India", regretted Banerjee,[32] "observe this occasion with great sanctity for a very long time and none has given any particular period of its origin". In his *Discovery of India* Nehru[33] observed, "In my old city of Allahabad or in Hardwar I would go to the great bathing festivals, the Kumbha Melā, and see hundred of thousands of people come, as their forebears had come for thousands of years from all over India, to bathe in the Ganges". According to him,[34] "These melās are ancient and lost in an unknown antiquity". Believing participants to this festival hold it as old as the creation itself. Its antiquity has caught the imagination of many, such as Sidney Low[35] who quipped in the context of the Kumbha Melā at Prayāga, "The celebration is older than Mohammadanism, older than Christianity, perhaps older than Brahmanism itself". Some scholars,[36] on the basis of preserved and accessible historical evidence, assert that 'the pilgrimages known as Kumbha Melā do not date back the seventeenth-eighteenth century C.E.' Others[37] hold that the date of the origin of the Kumbha Melā is not exactly known. Much of the discussion on this issue is found inadequate and unsatisfactory. This state of affairs is due to the neglect and insufficiency of the analytical study of myths and legends pertaining to the subject. In spite of some attempts made to discover a pattern, the problem could never be put to a systematic analysis. It may, however, be noted that about the Kumbha Melā there is almost nothing written; most of the information is simply a hearsay and based on oral tradition. There are only bits and pieces of knowledge out of which a coherent account of it remains to be framed.

According to the orthodox view, the antiquity of the Kumbha Melā goes back to the Vedic times. To substantiate this assertion, the following two passages from the *Atharvaveda* are often quoted; other quoted passages are the *Ṛgveda* I.116.7, X.89.7, the *Yajurveda* (*Mādhyandina*) 19.87, and the *Atharvaveda* XVI.6.8.[38]

(i) *caturaḥ kumbhānścaturdhā dadāmi.*

AV, IV.34.7.

(ii) *pūrṇaḥ kumbho=adhi kāla āhitastam.*

AV, XIX.53.3.

The four '*kumbha-s*' in four places mentioned in the first sentence are interpreted by the traditional scholars as the four localities where the Kumbha Melās take place. The expression '*pūrṇaḥ kumbhaḥ*' in the second sentence is understood as signifying the Pūrṇa Kumbha Melā which occurs every twelfth year as distinct from the Ardha Kumbha Melā which takes place every sixth year. Bonazzoli[39] has critically examined the purport of these two sentences and has shown that they have been wrongly adapted to signify the Kumbha Melā by separating them from their original contexts. The first sentence, which belongs to a hymn in glorification of a certain sacrifice called *Viṣṭārī*, indeed, runs like:

I give four pitchers, in four several places, filled to the brim with milk, curds, (*soma*), and water. Abundant with their overflow of sweetness, these streams shall reach thee in the world of *svarga*, whole lakes with lotus-blossom shall approach thee.[40]

The verse is commented upon by Sāyaṇa in the following way:

I put four pitchers full of ingredients like milk, etc. in four ways according to the division of the directions—east, west, etc.[41]

The second sentence is a part of the verse which runs as:

On time is laid an overflowring beaker : this we behold in many a place appearing. He carries from us all these worlds of creatures. They call him Kāla in the loftiest heaven.[42]

Here '*pūrṇaḥ kumbhaḥ*' according to the commentary of Sāyaṇa,[43] refers to the god 'Time', because the hymn is dedicated to him.

It is notable that none of the Vedic verses refers, even in the slightest way, to the Kumbha Melā. The Vedic passages quoted above speak of '*kumbha*' which means a 'pitcher' but there is no symbolic representation of a pitcher in the Melā. Vedic commentators also do not explain these *mantras* to refer to any fair. Even Sāyaṇa, who often superimposes on the Vedic passages the interpretations of his own times (the 14th-15th centuries C.E.) does not connect these *mantras* with the Kumbha Melā, although in his age *tīrthayātrās* were very common. Therefore, possibly one is left with no option but to agree with Bonazzoli[44] that 'the above adaptations are quite recent and possibly restricted to small circles of adherents'. Sāyaṇa's silence about the Kumbha Parva does not, however, necessarily disprove its possible existence in his time. It might be of interest to note that the Kumbha Parva does not figure in the Sūtra-works, Smṛtis, Epic-Purāṇic texts, and Dharmaśāstra-digests also. Kumbha, however, is mentioned in the *Vāyu Purāṇa*[45] as a holy place fit for the performance of the *śrāddha* rite. It is doubtful if it refers to a place where the Kumbha Parva is observed. This

'Kumbha' of the *Vāyu Purāṇa* may be identified with a *tīrtha* named Śrīkumbha on the Sarasvatī river referred to in the *Nāradīya Purāṇa*[46] where a holy bath is believed to bestow the benefit of *yajña* performance upon the devotee. In a brochure the verse—*"aśvamedha-sahasrāṇi vājapeyaśatāni ca/lakṣam pradakṣiṇāḥ pṛthivyāḥ kumbhasnānena tatphalam"*—is found quoted from the *Viṣṇu Purāṇa* to prove the Purāṇic authority for this Melā.[47] The verse is, however, not found in the printed editions of this Purāṇa. The foregoing discussion thus demonstrates that the tradition of Kumbha Parva possibly does not enjoy a respectable antiquity.

The origin of Kumbha Parva is lost in mythical legends. Myths are created as solutions to mysteries, and legends are formed to perpetuate such solutions. Furthermore, legends may become traditions after passage of time. Two traditions are in circulation about the origin of this festival: one that ties its origin with the pre-existing Epic-Purāṇic myth of the churning of the ocean, and the other that connects it with astrological considerations. Bonazzoli[48] has discussed these two traditions and rightly concludes that "the distinction between the two is not sharp and they could have been one in the beginning".

The so-called Epic-Purāṇic tradition is in relation to the widely circulated legend of the churning of the Ocean of Milk. According to it,[49] the gods and demons churned the milky ocean at the beginning of time to wrench from it its divine treasures. Following all the treasures, the pitcher filled with the nectar (*amṛta-kumbha*), the potion of immortality, emerged finally from the Milky Ocean. Immediately a fight for its acquisition began between the gods and the demons. In the scramble, the gods were baffled and the demons succeeded in getting hold of the nectarine pitcher. When the cause of the gods was thus lost, Jayanta, the alert heir-apparent of the paradise, at their incitement, changed himself into a rook and escaped with it into the heights of heaven. The fraud was brought to the notice of the demons by their preceptor Śukrācārya, consequently they chased Jayanta but in vain. By way of precaution the gods sent four planets to accompany Jayanta: the moon to protect the pot from flowing forth, the sun to protect it from bursting, jupiter to protect it from the attack of the demons, and saturn to protect it from the fear of Jayanta lest he should devour its contents. The nectar is said to have splashed the earth in four places as it was whisked away to heaven by Jayanta: Haridvāra, Prayāga, Nāsik and Ujjayinī, the sites becoming especially sanctified by its very touch for all the times to come (cf. Fig. 5). As Jayanta took twelve days to complete his flight and a divine day is equal to one human year, the Kumbha Parva recurs at these four places every twelfth year in a cyclic order. The sun (along with his son saturn), moon, and jupiter were on the vanguard and had protected the jar, therefor the festival is celebrated only on the conjunction of these planets in the specific zodiacal sign, aquarius.

No text supports the above account. Though the story of the churning of the ocean is found in the Epic-Purāṇic texts,[50] the splashing of the nectar at the four places is nowhere mentioned. The relation between the pitcher containing divine liquid and the Kumbha Parva is, therefore, highly fanciful and imaginary. It appears that this Epic-Purāṇic legend has been verbally grafted on the Kumbha Melā to provide it with an antiquity and hoary past.

A somewhat different Epic-Purāṇic story[51] is also in vogue. It is said that Garuḍa brought nectar from heaven to release his mother Vinatā from the bondage of the mother of serpents, Kadrū. He placed the pot of nectar before the sons of Kadrū and Vinatā was freed. But Indra (or his son Jayanta) stole away the pitcher and fled towards heaven being pursued by the serpents. Four drops of nectar fell down from the jar on the aforenamed four places, and therefore these places became fit for celebrating the Kumbha Parva. "The second part of the story, i.e. the falling of the nectar at the four places", opines Bhattacharya,[52] "is not found in any of the known Epic-Purāṇic texts, though Garuḍa's bringing of nectar for his mother is narrated in many of them".[53]

There is no ground for the view that the melā was named after the *kumbha* (pitcher) in which immortality bestowing liquid was kept. Though 'in its entirety the Epic-Purāṇic mythical tradition about the origin of the Kumbha Parva contains a hodgepodge of themes which hardly facilitate rigorous interpretation', as Darian[54] leads us to believe, an analysis of the salient features of the melā would reveal that it served to enhance the grandeur and sublimity of the large life-sustaining river Gaṅgā. Of the four places, where according to legends the *amṛta* fell, two are located on the river Gaṅgā itself; one at the base of the Himālaya foothills where the river enters the plains and the other where it joins the river Yamunā and the invisible Sarasvatī. It appears that the worship of rivers concentrates on certain points in their course. In the case of the Gaṅgā the most important contact points are Haridvāra and Prayāga, the third being Gaṅgāsāgara.[55] The river Godāvarī, on the banks of which Nāsik is situated, is so much identified with the Gaṅgā that, as a matter of fact, it is known as Dakṣiṇa Gaṅgā.[56] The sage Gautama is said to have brought the river Gaṅgā in the form of Godāvarī there, hence it is generally referred to as Gautamī.[57] It is stated in the *Brahma Purāṇa*[58] that to the south of the Vindhya mountains the Gaṅgā is called Gautami and that to its north is known by the name of Bhāgīrathī. There is a temple on Rāmaghāṭa at Nāsik on the Godāvarī.

The temple is opened every twelfth year when jupiter is in leo. At that time, it is believed, the water of the original Gaṅgā comes to the temple. It is also interesting that a similar notion is found in connection with Ujjayinī where the river Śiprā gets added sanctity due to its flow in the northernly direction,[59] the position being comparable with the northward flow of the Gaṅgā in Kāśī; the Gaṅgā is specially holy at places where its stream turns northward. According to the *Skanda Purāṇa*,[60] the Śiprā becomes *pūrva-vāhinī* (one flowing towards east) from the point where it was once embraced by the Gaṅgā. A *liṅga* named Gaṅgeśvara, worshipped by the Gaṅgā,[61] is found on southern bank of the Śiprā in Ujjayinī.[62] Thus, the Kumbha Parva seems to be a ritual bathing festival chiefly associated with the river Gaṅgā in its origin and character. The water in different forms is often an object of worship, especially the flowing water. From very early times, divinity and power are associated to all rivers, but some are more holy than others, and the holiest of all is the Gaṅgā due to its many special qualities such as having been created by the three gods of Hindu trinity[63] and made of all *tīrthas*.[64] The Gaṅgā is the archetype of the sacred waters, to which other water bodies are compared in sanctity; this perception and belief led to establish the process of Gaṅgāization of Indian culture. The sanctity of the Gaṅgā is pre-eminently established in India since the time of composition of the *nadīstuti-sūkta* of the *Ṛgveda* (X.75.5). The Gaṅgā is important in both its physical and symbolic existence. It is deemed to confer immortality to its devotees. In Indian religious life, the Gaṅgā water is equated with the deathless liquid in properties. In support of this belief Darian[65] has quoted an Epic passage which exclaims, "as *amṛta* is to the gods, so Gaṅgā water is to human beings".[66] It may be pointed out that in Ujjayinī the water of the Śiprā is also said to be endowed with the properties of ambrosia.[67] If so, Gaṅgā water might have been *amṛta* to the unknown authors of the Kumbha Parva legend. The *kumbha* (full vessel) itself becomes one of the Gaṅgā's most distinguishing sculptural features; it first appears with the river goddess on the Varāha cave frieze at Udaigiri around C.E. 400 and becomes more and more common as the Gaṅgā theme reaches maturity in Indian art during the medieval period. The *kumbha* is a symbol of fertility and expresses several values, mostly related to the generative and purifying power of water. It may also be understood as an expression of the Gaṅgā's birth from Brahmā's water jug. However, 'It seems', writes Darian,[68] 'highly unlikely that pilgrims at the Kumbha Melā draw any such connections'.

The astrological tradition of the Kumbha Parva is far more complex. The melā takes place when the *kumbhayoga* commences. This astronomical conjunction is said to be of four types, each being associated with one of the aforesaid four sacred places.[69] Some verses, claimed to be from the

Purāṇas but without precise references being given, are often quoted to show the validity of the Kumbha Melā at the specified sacred places. Since much confusion prevails about the auspicious time when the *parva* must be held, it is necessary to produce the verses here.

i. When jupiter (*bṛhaspati*) is in the sign of aquarius (*kumbharāśi*) and the sun enters aries (*meṣarāśi*), Kumbha Parva is held at Haridvāra.[70]
ii. The Kumbha Parva occurs at Prayāga when jupiter enters the zodiac aries and the sun and moon are in capricornus (*makararāśi*) on the new moon day of the month of Māgha.[71]
iii. When the sun and jupiter are in leo (*si=mharāśi*), the Kumbha Parva is celebrated on the Godāvarī at Nāsik.[72]
iv. Kumbha Parva takes place at Ujjayinī when jupiter is in leo and the sun enters aries.[73]

Alternative astronomical conjunctions are also provided for the celebration of the festival at the three sacred places: Prayāga, Nāsik and Ujjayinī :

i. When the sun is in capricornus and jupiter moves into taurus (*vṛṣarāśi*) on new moon day of the month of Māgha, the Kumbha Parva takes place at Prayāga.[74]
ii. When jupiter, sun and moon are in cancer (*karkarāśi*) and it is *amāvāsyā* (new moon day), the Kumbha Parva is held on the Godāvarī at Nāsik.[75]
iii. When jupiter is in the zodiac libra (*tulārāśi*) and the sun and moon dwell together on the new moon day of Kārttika, the salvation bestowing Kumbha Parva occurs in Dhārā/Ujjayinī.[76]

These verses are generally ascribed to the *Skanda Purāṇa*. They are, however, not traceable in the extant editions of this Purāṇa; therefore nothing can be said about their authenticity. Though the authorship and chronology of the verses recorded above are unknown, they might have been composed at a time when the tradition of Kumbha Parva had already become quite popular in India. It may be noted that P.V. Kane,[77] while dealing with the Kumbha Parva in the 'list of *vratas*', has not cited the source of his statements. There is no mention of any such astronomical conjunction as the *kumbhayoga* in astronomical/astrological works. Even the *Sanskrit-English Dictionary* of Monier-Williams does not contain the word '*kumbhayoga*', though it mentions the names of several astronomical conjunctions. Therefore, this *kumbhayoga* is apparently a later interpolation.

The verses usually quoted for holding the Kumbha Melā at Prayāga, Nāsik and Ujjayinī do not contain the word 'kumbha'; the name Kumbha fits in only with the melā of Haridvāra. The Epic-Purāṇic version of the story about the origin of the Kumbha Parva shows that it should be celebrated at the specified sacred places in the year in which there is a conjunction of the sun, moon and jupiter in the zodiac aquarius.[78] It appears that the Kumbha Parva derives its name from an auspicious occasion of ritual bathing that used to take place at Haridvāra every twelfth year when jupiter was in aquarius and the sun entered aries. Such an astronomical conjunction is referred to in the *Nāradīya Purāṇa*[79] as a sacred time for bathing in the river Gaṅgā at Haridvāra. This shows that the Kumbha Parva was originally observed at Haridvāra and was named after the *kumbha-rāśi* (aquarius), for the festival occurs mainly at the time of jupiter being in aquarius which is represented in astrology as a water-carrier. At Prayāga, Nāsik and Ujjayinī, the *kumbhayoga* is not connected with any celestial body being in the *kumbharāśi*. Therefore, there is no apparent reason as to why the melās held in these sacred places should be styled Kumbha Melā at all. The Purāṇas praise bathing in the Gaṅgā-Yamunā-saṅgama at Prayāga in the month of Māgha when the sun is in the sign of capricornus (*makara*). Certain days are held in high esteem for the purpose and fifteenth day of the dark-half (*amāvāsyā*) of that month, being regarded as the mouth of the year, is one of them. The idea of holding the Kumbha Parva at Prayāga may be explained in the light of the ritual bath on this day of the month of Māgha. This day of the *makarasaṅkrānti* month becomes doubly auspicious every twelfth year when jupiter happens to be in aries. Moreover, the first year called *prabhava* of the sixty-year Jovian (*bārhaspatya*) Cycle begins on Māgha-*śukla* 1 when the sun and the moon occupy the *nakṣatra* Dhaniṣṭhā and are in conjunction with jupiter.[80] The promulgators of the Kumbha Melā might have utilized this rare occasion to serve their purpose and called it the Makara Kumbha Parva. Similar may have been the notions behind the celebrations of the Kumbha Parva at Ujjayinī and Nāsik. Ablution in the river Śiprā at Ujjayinī in the month of Vaiśākha in general and on the full moon day (*pūrṇimā*) of that month in particular is eulogized in the *Skanda Purāṇa*.[81] According to the *Śiva Purāṇa* and the *Varāha Purāṇa*, bathing in the river Godāvarī at Nāsik is highly meritorious when the sun and jupiter are in leo.[82] The *Brahma Purāṇa*[83] says that three and half crores of *tīrthas* that exist in the three worlds (heaven, earth and the netherworld) come for a bath in the river Godāvarī when jupiter is in leo and that bathing in the Bhāgīrathī (Gaṅgā) every day for sixty thousand years confers the same merit as a single bath in the river Godāvarī at that auspicious time. Similarly in the *Tristhalīsetu*[84] it is said, "Bathing in the Godāvarī when jupiter is in leo is everywhere equal to bathing in the Jāhnavī (Gaṅgā)". Thus, there is no evidence to show that the melās held at these three places were called Kumbha Melā in the beginning; the melā at Nāsik always being known as Siṁhastha.[85] The nomenclature of Kumbha Melā in this regard does not seem to be a right one. Therefore, there is some weight in the suggestion of Bhattacharya[86] that "the term Kumbha was prefixed to the melās held at Prayāga, Nāsik and Ujjayinī later on after the nomenclature of the Kumbha Parva at Haridvāra".

The place, time of occurrence, and the positions of planets and zodiac determining the Kumbha Melās are given in Table 2 which shows that the melā occurs mainly on the conjunction of jupiter with some specific constellations and the factor *saṅkrānti* (the point of time when the sun leaves one zodiacal sign and enters another) is not a desideratum. Midway between the two Kumbha Melās comes the Ardha Kumbha Melā at Haridvāra and Prayāga. Of this division there is no śāstric authority, except the solitary verse[87] of doubtful authorship. It appears that the tradition of Ardha Kumbha Melā is not of much religious significance; two sites Nāsik and Ujjayinī do not deem it fit for celebrations.

Table 2 also shows that the melā is celebrated regularly at an interval of three years, starting from Haridvāra and followed by Prayāga, Nāsik and Ujjayinī, respectively. But this conceptual position does not appear to have been observed in practice. It is true that the Kumbha Melā at Prayāga takes place after three years of that at Haridvāra and the gap between the melās of Prayāga and Nāsik is also of three years. But interval between the Kumbha Melā at Nāsik and that at Ujjayinī is not of three years; they are celebrated the same year. This deviation in practice from theory is intriguing and is not adequately explained by astronomical or any other exercises. When the Kumbha Melā at Ujjayinī falls in the month of Vaiśākha, it takes place at Nāsik in the month of Bhādrapada the same year. Sometimes the melā at Nāsik occurs earlier than that of Ujjayinī. In that case the Kumbha Melā at Ujjayinī follows that of Nāsik the next year. The gap is, however, never of one full year, though the Vikrama Saṁvata may change. Their precession is not fixed. The melā at Nāsik precedes the melā at Ujjayinī for three consecutive terms and the latter comes before the former at five times (see Table 3). This phenomenon is ascribable to the interconnection of jupiter in leo at these two places; jupiter is in leo for one year once in twelve years. This knotty problem may, however, be solved by adhering to the astronomical provision which requires the Kumbha Melā of Ujjayinī to be held in the month of Kārttika when the sun is in libra. This tradition has somehow become obscure and has fallen into disuse for quite a long period. This accounts for the non-existence of the gap for three years between the Kumbha Melā at Ujjayinī and that at Nāsik.

TABLE 2

	Year	Place	Hindu Roman Month	Position of Cosmic forces	Name of the Parva
|	0	Haridvāra	Caitra (March-April)	Jupiter x Aquarius, Sun x Aries	Kumbha
|	3	Prayāga	Māgha (January-February)	Jupiter x Aries or Taurus, Sun & Moon x Capricornus	Kumbha
|					
|	6	Nāsik	Bhādrapada (August-September)	Jupiter x Leo, Sun x Leo or	Kumbha
↓				Sun, Moon & Jupiter x Cancer	Kumbha
	—	Haridvāra	Caitra	Jupiter x Leo, Sun x Aries	Ardha Kumbha
↑	9	Ujjayinī	Vaiśākha (April-May)	Jupiter x Leo, Sun x Aries or	Kumbha
|				Jupiter, Sun & Moon x Libra	
|		Prayāga	Māgha (January-February)	Jupiter x Scorpio, Sun x Capricornus	Ardha Kumbha
|	12	Haridvāra	Caitra (March-April)	Jupiter x Aquarius, Sun x Aries	Kumbha

The pilgrimage to Kumbha Melā lasts for a whole month, but certain days are supposed to be especially favourable for mass-bathing. The day for actual bathing at Hari kī Pauṛī in Haridvāra is the *pūrnimā* (the full moon day) of Caitra. The main bath at Saṅgama in Prayāga and Rāmaghāṭa in Nāsik is taken on the *amāvāsyā* (the new moon day) of Māgha and Bhādrapada, respectively. The *pūrṇimā* of Vaiśākha is the auspicious day of Kumbha bath at Rāmaghāṭa in Ujjayinī. The *tithi* (lunar day), being governed by the lunar system of reckoning, may vary at Haridvāra (see Table 3), but the solar day is always the same; the sun's passing the first point of aries marks the end of Caitra and the beginning of Vaiśākha. Similarly, when the *parva* is observed, according to the alternative astronomical conjunctions at Nāsik and Ujjayinī it is the *pūrṇimā* of Śrāvaṇa month and the *amāvāsyā* of Kārttika respectively. There is no variation in the *tithi* of melā at Prayāga.

Opinions differ regarding the cyclic period of the Kumbha Parva. According to some scholars[88], it occurs regularly every twelfth year at a sacred place. Others[89] are of the view that unless the particular astronomical conjunctions come into existence the *parva* cannot be held. They assert that a Kumbha Parva may be celebrated even in the eleventh or thirteenth year after the holding of the earlier one. It seems that the Kumbha Melā has not always followed the twelve-year cycle, and that it may recur in the eleventh year or even in the thirteenth year. The view is supported by the calculation of years for the celebrated melās at Prayāga; the figures are: Vikrama Saṁvata 1950, 1962, 1974, 1985, 1997 and 2010.[90] This is due to the retrograde movement of the planet jupiter and the period taken by it in revolving round the sun; jupiter takes 11.86 years for its revolution round the sun[91] which is less than 50 days in twelve solar years, i.e. 4,343 days. According to astronomical calculations, jupiter moves one house further after eighty four years. Therefore, out of seven Kumbha Parva six recur every twelfth year and the seventh one comes in the eleventh year. The argument that the Kumbha Parva occurs every twelfth year is maintained in the same way as it is often said that such and such village is a village of wrestlers (*mallānām grāmaḥ*) which, of course, only means that there the wrestlers are in majority in that village. This problem can be understood with the help of Table 3.

The celebrating years of some of the melās had been controversial. The Kumbha Melā at Ujjayainī was announced by the State Government to be held in C.E. 1956. But it came to be postponed for a year because ascetics did not do so in that year.[92] Some astrologers ruled that the Kumbha Melā at Prayāga should come off in C.E. 1965; others advocated its celebration the next year in C.E. 1966. The melās of 1929 and 1941 met

TABLE 3 : KUMBHA MELĀ

1. Haridvāra : Meṣasaṅkrānti*						2. Prayāga : Māgha amāvāsyā					3. Ujjayinī : Vaiśākha pūrṇimā					4. Nāsik : Bhādrapada amāvāsyā				
V.S.	C.E.	Tithi	P_1	P_2	Difference (in years)	V.S.	C.E.	P_1	P_2	Difference (in years)	V.S.	C.E.	P_1	P_2	Difference (in years)	V.S.	C.E.	P_1	P_2	Difference (in years)
1972	1915	Vk30	10/24^0	0/0^0	12	1962	1906	1/6^0	9/23^0	12	2002	1945	4/24^0	0/27^0	12	1989	1932	4/8^0	4/0^0	12
1984	1927	Cs 15	10/28^0	0/0^0	12	1974	1918	1/10^0	9/23^0	12	2014	1957	4/28^0	0/29^0	12	2001	1944	4/11^0	4/1^0	12
1995	1938	Vk 13	10/2^0	0/0^0	11	1985	1929	0/11^0	9/23^0	11	2025	1968	4/2^0	0/27^0	11	2013	1956	4/17^0	4/18^0	11
2007	1950	Vk 11	10/6^0	0/0^0	12	1997	1941	0/15^0	9/23^0	12	2037	1980	4/6^0	0/15^0	12	2025	1968	4/19^0	4/6^0	12
2019	1962	Cs 9-10	10/10^0	0/0^0	12	2010	1954	1/23^0	9/18^0	13	2049	1992	4/10-1^0	0/29^0	12	2037	1980	4/26^0	4/23^0	12
2031	1974	Vk 7	10/14^0	0/0^0	12	2021	1965	0/23^0	9/4^0	11	2061	2004	4/15^0	0/20^0	12	2049	1992	4/24^0	4/0^0	12
2043	1986	Cs 5	10/18^0	0/0^0	12	2033	1977	0/27^0	9/4^0	12	2073	2016	9/19^0	0/27^0	12	2060	2003	4/4^0	4/0^0	11
2055	1998	Vk 2-3	10/22^0	0/0^0	12	2045	1989	1/2^0	9/18^0	12	2085	2028	4/23^0	0/25^0	12	2072	2015	4/8^0	4/1^0	12
2067	2010	Vk 30	10/26^0	0/0^0	12	2057	2001	1/7^0	9/4^0	12	2097	2040	9/27^0	0/27^0	12					
2078	2021	Cs 1	10/0-1^0	0/0^0	11	2068	2012	0/7^0	9/4^0	11	2101	2051	4/0-1^0	0/29^0	11					
2090	2033	Cs 15	10/5^0	0/0^0	12	2080	2024	0/12^0	9/4^0	12										

P1, Position of Jupiter in Zodiac/degree. P2, Position of Sun in Zodiac/degree. Vk, Vaiśvākha Kṛṣṇa. Cs, Caitra śukla.

* The meṣasaṅkarānti, which now-a-days occurs on April 13/14, occurred on April 8 (*AR*, VI.312) in C.E. 1796.

with the similar fate. As a matter of fact, such controversies are a regular feature in determining almost all the Hindu festivals, which arise on account of the difficulties in calculating the astronomical conjunctions.

The number twelve has its own astronomical importance. It has a philosophico-spiritual significance also. As Gupta[93] puts its, "Man has two kinds of organs: *pañca jñānedriyas* (five organs of perception) – the skin, tongue, eyes, ears, and nose; and *pañca karmendriyas* (five organs of action) – the anus, the organ of generation, hands, feet and speech; the eleventh organ is the mind and the twelfth is the intellect. Since attendance at the Kumbha Melā is piously regarded as the stepping stone for *mokṣa*, which is vouchsafed as the ultimate reward, it is expected that the religious minded and virtuous people, who have shunned all carnal passions by mastering these twelve components to become real recipients of salvation, would attend the Kumbha assemblage. Further, it is incumbent on them to demonstrate to others by their own example the efficacy of this practice".

The antiquity of the Kumbha Melā is shrouded in mystery. The Chinese pilgrim Hsüan Tsang, who attended the sixth quinquennial assembly organised by king Harṣavardhana at Prayāga in the month of Māgha in C.E. 643, supplies the first historical reference to religious festivities at Prayāga.[94] Some scholars[95] think that this account of the Chinese pilgrim implies the visit of Harṣavardhana to Prayāga on the occasion of Ardha Kumbha Melā which occurs after five years. But it is wrong to assume that the Kumbha fair was being held in the times of king Harṣavardhana, for in the accounts of Hsüan Tsang there is no mention of a fair called Kumbha. The fair associated with king Harṣavardhan was a religious occasion in the month of Māgha, in which he used to distribute his accumulated wealth of five years. The king cannot be said to be the instigator of this religious congregation.[96] Moreover, the practice of holding quinquennial assemblies and donating everything in them has been a common phenomenon observed by foreign travellers with reference to a number of kings of India and abroad. Fa-hien, for example, noted the particular case of the king of Kashgar, while Hsüan Tsang referred to the examples of the kings of Kapis and Malwa besides Harṣavardhana who resorted to this practice.[97]

Tradition credits Śaṅkarācārya (ninth century C.E.) with the organisation of the Kumbha Melā at Prayāga. He is believed to have transformed it from a gathering of single group and of local significance into a pan-Indian meeting of ascetics and extended it to other three sacred places.[98] But for want of proof it cannot be corroborated. Other stories are also in circulation among the faithful ones. Some say that the interval of twelve years is due to the fact that the congregation of the Maharṣis Sanaka, Sanandana, etc.

used to take place every twelfth year at Haridvāra and Prayāga.[99] Others maintain that as special rites had to be performed by yogīs every twelfth year, they used to gather at Haridvāra, etc. to get facilities in their yogic practices.[100] Some others claim that this festival has to be traced back to Buddhists who convened their *dharmapariṣads* from time to time.[101] None of these traditions are supported by written records.

It has already been pointed out that the Kumbha assemblage at Haridvāra has been there from the very beginning and was later on grafted on the age-old melās at Prayāga, Nāsik, and Ujjayinī. Hazra[102] thinks that the chapter of the *Nāradīya Purāṇa*, which contains the relevant verse referring to the particular conjunction of planets and zodiacal signs at Haridvāra, is a later interpolation. According to him, it may have been compiled in its surviving form as recently as the sixteenth century C.E. The *Pratisargaparva* of the *Bhaviṣya Purāṇa*[103] mentions the celebration of a great festival (*mahotsava*), attended by kings and commoners, men and women, dressed according to their means, from different regions, at Gaṅgādvāra (Haridvāra) when jupiter entered the zodiac sign of aquarius in the month of Caitra. This provided an opportunity to the brāhmaṇa-poet Mitra Śarmā of Māyāvatī (Haridvāra) and princes Citriṇī, the daughter of king Kāmasena of South India, to meet and fall in love with each other. The *Pratisargaparva* is particularly considered to be a late interpolation as is shown by references to medieval emperors Akbar and Nādir Shāh with their descendants and saints like Kabīr, Caitanya, Raidāsa and others; it even knows the British rule in India and narrates Calcutta and the parliament (*aṣṭakauśalya*). The episode of Mitra Śarmā-Citriṇī love affair in this section can not but be fabricated. The chapter in which it occurs is devoted to the account of births and lives of Nimbārka and Rāmānanda. But this tract of fourteen verses[104] within this chapter is not thematically connected with the subject-matter of the chapter and appears to be a totally isolated intervention. Reference to the Kumbha Melā at Haridvāra in this tract lodged in a chapter devoted to Nimbārka and Rāmānanda may be used to assign this intrusion a date reasonably later than the known dates of these two saints, i.e. thirteenth and fourteenth century C.E. respectively. Placing it two centuries still later will not be wide of mark. These Purāṇic chapters, however, incorporate a tradition that is still earlier. Sarkar[105] has noted a very important traditional piece of history which possibly refers to the celebration of the Kumbha Parva at Haridvāra during the thirteenth century C.E. According to it, Nāgā Saṃnyāsīs are reported to have won a decisive victory at Haridvāra over Bairāgīs, the Vaiṣṇava ascetics, in C.E. 1253. Bloody affrays between the Śaivite Nāgās and the Bairāgīs at the time of the Kumbha bath is a well-known fact of Indian religious history.

It is recorded that in C.E. 1398 the Muslim invader Timūr massacred a large number of devotees in Haridvāra.[106] Only on special occasions does Haridvāra attract large number of devotees. It was perhaps an occasion of the Kumbha Melā; for on reckoning the year happens to be a year for that assemblage at Haridvāra.[107]

In the traditional history of Caitanya's life, Caitanya is reported to have been present at the Kumbha Melā at Prayāga in C.E. 1514.[108] A reference to the Kumbha Melā at Haridvāra is found in the *Dabistān-i-Mazāhib*, the Parsee religious text of the seventeenth century C.E. It mentions that a fighting took place between Mundies (Bairāgīs) and Samnyāsīs (Nāgās) at Haridvāra in the year 1050 Hizri/C.E. 1640. The Samnyāsīs became victorious and a number of Mundies were killed.[109] The *Gurucaritra* of Sarasvatī Gaṅgādhara, a book written in Marāṭhī about the end of the fifteenth century, records the celebration of the Siṁhastha Melā at Nāsik.[110] The *Bītaka* of Lāladāsa (composed in Vikrama Saṁvat 1751 = C.E. 1694) says that Prāṇanāth, the founder of the Praṇāmī sect and the preceptor of the Bundela chief Chatrasāl (C.E. 1649-1731), participated in the Kumbha Melā of Haridvāra in Śaka 1600 (C.E. 1678), where he was crowned with the title of 'Vijayābhinanda Niṣkalaṅka Buddha' in *śāstrārtha* (religious debate) after defeating the contestants belonging to Vaiṣṇavism, Daśanāmī Order, and Ṣaḍarśana (six systems of Indian philosophy).[111]

According to a copperplate inscription in possession of Mahanta Rādhāmohanadāsajī of Nāsik, a great massacre of Bairāgīs took place at Nāsik at the time of Siṁhastha Melā in C.E. 1690.[112] The *Khulāṣat-ut-Tawārīkh*, composed in C.E. 1693-1695, informs that every twelfth year when jupiter enters the sign of aquarius and the sun is in aries, large number of people assemble at Haridvāra from remote distance for ritual bathing.[113] The celebration of a festival on the Godāvarī when jupiter moves into leo is also referred to in the same text.[114] Śaiva Samnyāṣīs and Vaiṣṇava Bairāgīs are reported to have fought a pitched battle involving 1800 casualities on the occasion of the Kumbha Parva at Haridvāra in C.E. 1760 to decide the dispute about precedence at that place.[115] Captain Thomas Hardwicke has informed that at the same melā in C.E. 1796 there was a regular fighting between the Śaiva and the Sikh ascetics and that five hundred men of the former were killed while the Sikhs lost only twenty.[116] On the question of precedence a quarrel occurred in C.E. 1906 between the Nirvāṇī Akhāṛā on one side and the Nirmohī and Digambarī Akhāṛās on the other side at Prayāga. It necessitated the intervention of a squadron of cavalry.[117]

On the basis of the evidence culled above, it may be surmised that the Kumbha Melā came to be organised sometime after the twelfth century

C.E., the conclusion also arrived at by Ghurye.[118] The tradition of holding this religious festival possibly crystallized during the heyday of the Bhakti movement, a movement of the socio-religious reforms set on foot by a series of Hindu saints and reformers during the medieval times. That the melā began to be held during the Bhakti movement is supported by the fact that it is the only melā that possesses a strictly catholic character which was the main ideal of the reformers of the Bhakti movement.

It has been suggested that primarily this festival belonged to the Nāgā Samnyāsīs and ascetics of different sects gradually came to be associated with it on account of its highly religious character.[119] All the organisational matters of the Nāgā ascetics, the election of office-bearers, the settlement of disputes in the *akhāṛās*, and the initiation of ascetics into the Nāgā fold are all done in the Kumbha Melā. That the Nāgās are traditionally given priority in the Kumbha bath supports the argument that the organisation of the Nāgā *akhāṛās* is intimately linked with the organisation of the Kumbha Melā. It should be pointed out that all the *akhāṛās* of Nāgā Samnyāsīs claim their origin to be earlier than the establishment of Muslim rule in India. According to Sarkar,[120] no reliable information about the origin and history of the different *akhāṛās* before C.E. 1750 is available. He has, however, tried to reconstruct the chronology of the establishment of different *akhāṛās* on the basis of a manuscript (*pothī*) maintained by the hereditary bards of the Nirvāṇī Akhāṛā.[121] Giri,[122] who wrote a treatise on the history of the Daśanāmī Samnyāsī sect, maintains that "all the *akhāṛās* must have been formed gradually during the period from the reign of Akbar to that of Aurangzeb". He, however, does not preclude the possibility of the existence of the Nāgās in wandering groups under their leaders before the reign of emperor Akbar (C.E. 1556-1605). The term *akhāṛā* means an organisation of militant Nāgās and points to a certain period when Daśanāmī Samnyāsīs took to arms. This might have happened in the period when Hinduism was in peril during the Muslim rule. If the dates worked out by Sarkar for the establishment of the principal *akhāṛās* be accepted, none of the *akhāṛās* appears to be older than the twelfth century C.E. This coincides with the probable period of the organisation of the Kumbha Melā and further supports the view that at first the Nāgā ascetics became interested or involved in this melā and gradually other sects joined it. That is why this melā is regarded as congress of ascetics and monks (Pl. 12).

It is difficult to ascertain the real historical cause for holding the Kumbha Melās at the places of pilgrimage. It seems that a number of monks and reformers introduced this assemblage of saints and householders at precise intervals at sacred places on the banks of the holy rivers to create an environment of mutual understanding amongst different religious sects and also to give an opportunity to householders to derive invaluable benefits from their association with the saintly personalities. Mammoth conferences were evidently being organised under the auspices of prominent religious organisations wherein philosophers, savants, and reformers participated to express their views for augmenting unity and fostering of different faiths. In fact, various orders of different Hindu faiths treat this fair as the occasion for duo-decennial assembly to discuss various spiritual and organisational problems. They congregate there mainly to profit by their contact with other sages and secondarily to take a hand in helping those pilgrims who are ripe for the message of light. In pre-industrial age when there was very poor facility of transport and communication, such periodical congregations at the sacred places were of utmost importance to give wide publicity to new ideas and inventions in short period. The educative aspect of the melā postulates the significance of jupiter in determining the occasion for its celebration; jupiter symbolizes learning and knowledge.

One of the distinctive features of the Kumbha Melā is that corporate bodies of the various sects of ascetics attend it in state and march down the sacred water in grand procession on the important bathing days (Pl. 14a, b). The most practical sect affiliation is seen here; in the procession the ascetics have to move according to their established order. The question of precedence between the Śaiva Nāgās and the Vaiṣṇava Bairāgīs at the time of the Kumbha bath had been in the past an occasion not only for quarrels and strifes but also for regular battles. For, it was a matter of one's dignity, both worldly and spiritual, whether one reached the sacred water just at the appointed time of the sacred bath or whether one reached there some time before or after it. The British Government in 1879, after enquiring into the old time-honoured practice, laid down the following rules which are strictly enforced today. First the Śaiva Nāgā Saṃnyāsīs bathe, then the Vaiṣṇava Bairāgīs, next the Udāsī Nānaka Panthīs, and lastly the Nirmalā Sikh ascetics.[123] Among the *akhāṛās* the following order is generally observed without breach: at Haridvāra, first the Nirañjanī Akhāṛā goes accompanied by the Jūnā, Āvāhana and Ānanda Akhāṛā. At Nāsik, the Jūnā Akhāṛā goes first, and the Nirvāṇī and Nirañjanī Akhāṛās follow it. At Ujjayinī, all the *akhāṛās* go in a line.[124] This arrangement was made to avoid bloody struggles among the *akhāṛās*.

The melā also records a huge mass of visitors from the West. Although they rarely understood what it all meant, they described what they saw with vivid usual detail. Their writings are interesting and important because they provide the only descriptive accounts of the Kumbha Melā in the past centuries. Captain Thomas Hardwicke, who paid a visit to Haridvāra during the melā on April 8 (the day of *meṣasaṅkrānti*), 1796, is the first

English writer to record his impression of the Kumbha Melā. He wrote:

But every twelfth year, when jupiter is in aquarius, at the time of the sun's entering aries, the concourse of people is greatly augmented. The present one is one of those periods, and the multitude collected here, on this occasion may, I think, with moderation, be computed at two and a half millions of souls. Although the performance of a religious duty is their primary object, yet, many avail themselves of the occasion, to transact business, and carry on an extensive commerce. ...

The most troublesome guests were the Goosseyns (Gosāins), who being the first here in point of numbers and power, thought it warrantable to take more freedom than others did.... In the early part of the melā, this sect of fakeers erected the standard of superiority, and proclaimed themselves regulators of the police.... They published an edict, prohibiting all other tribes from entering the place with their swords or arms of any other description.... The Byraagees (Bairāgīs), who were the next powerful sect, gave up the point, and next followed their example. Thus the Goosseyns paraded with their swords and shields, while every other tribe carried only bamboos through the fair. ...

The Goosseyns maintained an uncontested authority till the arrival of about 12 or 14,000 Seek (Sikh) horsemen, with their families, etc. who encamped on the plains about Jualapore (Jwālāpur)....

All was pretty quiet during the few remaining days of bathing; but on the morning of the 10th of April (which day concluded the melā),... about 8 o'clock in the morning the Seeks assembled in force and proceeded to the different watering places, where they attacked with swords, spears and firearms, every tribe of fakeers that came in their way. These people made some resistance, but being on foot, and few, if any, having fire-arms, the contest was unequal and the Seeks who were all mounted, drove the Sannyassees (Saṃnyāsis), Byraagees, Goosseyns, Naagees (Nāgās), etc. before them, with irresistible fury...and having slaughtered a great number, pursued the remainder, until, by flight to the hills, or by swimming the river, they escaped the revenge of their pursuers. ...

Accounts agree that the fakeers lost about five hundred men killed, among whom was one of their mehunts orpriests named Maunpooree (Mānpurī), and they had many wounded: of the Seeks about twenty were killed, but the number of wounded not known.[125]

The Kumbha Melā of 1882 at Prayāga is thus described by T. Benson,[126] I.C.S., in his report:

To each corporation (Akhāṛā) of religious ascetics was assigned a space of ground, within which it erected a temporary village or town for the accommodation of its members, in the centre of which moved the standard of the guild on a lofty flag-staff. These encampments were orderly and well laid out, and of a comfortable description.... The various camps formed were: Nirvāṇī Nāgā Gosāins, Nirañjanī with whom were associated Jūnā, Bairāgīs, Choṭā Akhāṛā Panchāyatī Udāsī Nānaka Panthīs, Baṛā Akhāṛā Panchāyatī with Bandhuā Akhāṛā (Sikhs), and Nirmalā Sikhs with the Brindāvanī.

On the three great days (makarasaṅkrānti), amāvāsyā, and basantapañcamī) each of the six sects went separately down to bathe in formal processon, the most noticeable feature being the body of naked faquirs closing the procession of each of the first two sects (the Nirvāṇī and the Nirañjanī) and the gorgeous silken banners and elephant trappings of the wealthier guilds.

A graphic description of the Kumbha Melā at Prayāga is also given by Sidney Low,[127] which is quoted below:

There were said to be two millions at the (Kumbha) Melā (of 1906) during one of the great processional days on which I visited it; and to the casual spectator, surveying to immense encampment and the morning crowds, the estimate did not seem exaggerated. The camp, indeed, should not be called by that name. It is a town – a temporary town, it is true; but while it lasts one of the great cities of the world, more populous than Peking or Vienna, with as many inhabitants as Liverpool, Manchester and Glasgow rolled into one.

The Kumbha Melā is an affair of the priests and the ascetics. They keep it going mainly for their own benefit and in essentials it probably does not differ greatly from what it was three centuries or ten centuries ago. The Government does not interfere with the religious ceremonies. Hinduism even in its ridiculous and offensive manifestations, is given a free hand.

The various sects and akhāṛās are active rivals, and some care has to be taken that they do not come into collision during the Allahabad Melā. The most turbulent are the Bairāgīs...who are always a source of anxiety to the police officials during the melā; for they are noisy and aggressive, and, unlike the other bodies, they are not under the regular control of their mahants. All the akhāṛās are encamped upon the left bank of the Ganges, with the Bairāgīs separated by a broad road and a fence from the others.

From bank to bank two temporary bridges of boats are laid during the melā. On the Allahabad side is the camp of the pilgrims. It is a town of many streets. The avenues and crossroads are laid out by the Government, which also builds huts of plaited straw, and allow them to be occupied at a very low rent by the visitors. A few hundred thousands are lodged in this way. Others make tiny sheds for themselves of logs and brushwood, or put up little shelters of canvas, or are content with the bare ground, and it may be an umbrella.

To go his rounds at the fair is an interesting experience. Strange scenes and figures are met at every turn. There is a separate enclosure for the barbers, a whole village of them, for no less than 2,800 of these useful persons are needed to perform the offices of the toilet for the pilgrims. The main street of the camp is a seething bazaar, where traders and merchants of all kinds have set up shops. Brass pots and pans, clothing provisions, toys, jewellery, native shoes and Austrian kidboots, books, perfumes, cheap haberdashery, sewing machines, and numberless other things, are on sale.... There are numerous shows and performances.

Religion, trade and amusement go hand in hand everywhere. The ground is dotted with tiny shrines and makeshift temples.... Dust-strewn faquirs sit under big umbrellas, wrapped in meditation, but with an ear for the clinking of coppers in the begging bowl beside them. Some of them rest immovable, hour after hour, on wooden bedsheets, studded with iron nails, the points upwards. Others exhibit hideous deformities.

The Kumbha Melā occurs at Prayāga and Haridvāra in its gorgeous form and in a minor form at other two sites. On certain days of the melā, Prayāga is the scene of what is almost certainly the greatest assemblage of people gathered together in a confined space for a single purpose anywhere on the earth (Pl. 15a, b). It is a sight to see. On 3rd February 1954, during the Kumbha Melā it was estimated that six million people were present[128] on an area of 1,300 acres. The crowd was divided in 1965-66 due to the emergence of a difference among astrologers. In 1965 more than 4 million pilgrims were reported there. The Kumbha Melā of 1977 was advertised as a rare event, participation in which could earn untold religious merits. So it attracted about thirteen million people.[129] More than fifteen million souls are reported to have participated in the Kumbha Melā of 1989. Haridvāra represents the 'supra-regional' level, attracting pilgrims from all over Northern India from Kashmir to Bengal.[130] There were two and a half million people competing for the sacred bath in 1962, it is reported. In 1974 the melā is said to have attracted four million bathers on April 13, the principal bathing day.[131] Elaborate arrangements were made to meet the rush of seven million persons in 1986 and of about nine million devotees in 1998.[132] The Kumbha Melā at Ujjayinī ranks third in importance, attracting pilgrims mostly from Central India. On 13th May, 1957, 25,000 ascetics belonging to various orders took a dip in the holy waters of the Śiprā at the crack of dawn, and about three hundred thousand lay people followed their example.[133] In 1968 about twenty lakh people bathed in the sacred water on the Vaiśākha Pūrṇimā (12th May) and in 1980 three million persons were estimated to be present there on an area of 535 hectares.[134] About 4 million devotees are reported to have participated in the melā of 1992. The event at Nāsik is somewhat localized; only Nāgās, a few saffron-clad sādhus and people from Mahārāṣṭra and Gujarāta attend it.

The Kumbha Melā attracted a record gathering but also had its share of unpleasant incidents. The desire to bathe at the propitious moment and at the sanctified bathing spot has led great loss of life time and again. In 1820 at Haridvāra, in consequence of a desperate rush made by the infatuated crowd, 430 persons were crushed to death, including several sepoys stationed there as guards.[135] In 1950, on the main bathing day elaborate arrangements were made there but 22 persons lost their lives.[136] When panic broke out among the crowds due to the confusion created during the procession of ascetics about three hundred pilgrims were trampled (Pl. 16a, b) into the muddy ground just below the bund at Prayāga in 1954.[137] The 1986 Kumbha Melā, Haridvāra, was also marked with such a sad stampede; 40 persons were killed and more than one hundred were injured.[138] The number of the dead and injured according to popular calculation was, however, above the limit of official figures.

Crowds at the Kumbha Melā nowadays are bigger than in the past; facilities of transport and explosion of population make the participation more numerous. The management of the melā is not an easy task. Past experiences have opened the eyes of the government. Problems of lodging, food, transport, sanitation, etc. are faced by the local administration. Private bodies and voluntary organisations rise to the occasion to render all possible help to the pilgrims. The Kumbha Melā of 1977 at Prayāga was planned on a lavish scale on an area of 2,665 acres of the sandy tract. Elaborate arrangements were made for the regulation of traffic and for bathing at the confluence which was luckily duplicated by the river Gaṅgā flowing into two streams joining the Yamunā some distance apart. The melā ground had the privileges of a modern town. Temporary hospitals, railway booking offices, post and telegraph offices, fire brigade stations, and enquiry offices were set up for the use of the general public. Numerous tents and hutments for providing lodging for pilgrims and ascetics were erected on the grid pattern in the melā area. Eight temporary bridges on the Gaṅgā and one on the Yamunā for easy communication were constructed, loudspeakers were installed at different corners and barricades were erected to facilitate one-way traffic. Special trains were run and roadways buses and private vehicles operated from all directions. Health facilities were appropriate; and cholera inoculation was made compulsory. The layout of 1989 melā (Fig. 6) was based on that of 1977. Two more pantoon bridges on the Gaṅgā were constructed for smooth circulation of pilgrims in the melā area. Due to the expected increase in number of visiting devotees, it was spread over an area of 3,500 acres of land which was divided into nine sectors for administrative purpose. It is likely to grow bigger and therefore more and more space will be required in future.

Similar arrangements were made by the administrative machinery to provide all possible facilities to pilgrims during the Kumbha Melā of 1986 at Haridvāra. The area of Kumbha Melā was spread over 130 square kilometres embracng parts of Sahāranpur, Bijnor, Dehrādūn, Pauṛī Garhwāl and Ṭehrī Garhwāl districts. The melā region was divided into 20 sectors; and a sector Magistrate, a Deputy Superintendent of Police, and a Regional Health Office/Officer-in-charge Medical Services were posted in each sector. Twenty-one police stations and 42 police posts were set up to keep traffic and law and order situation under control. Safety zones were

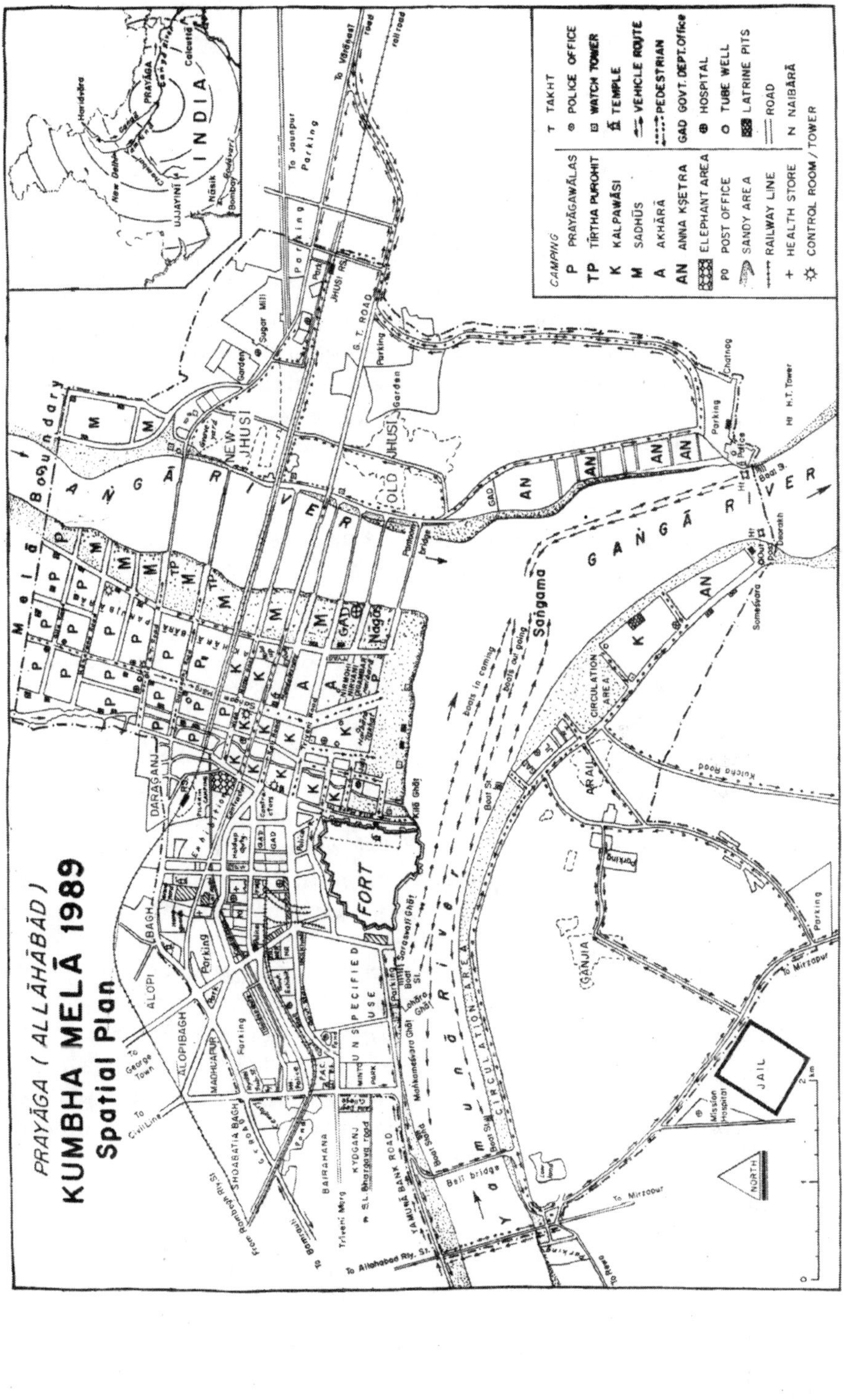

Fig. 6 Kumbha Melā 1989 : Spatial Plan

demarcated by iron chains at the bathing ghātas. Seventeen temporary bridges had been constructed at different points to facilitate the easy movement of traffic. Continuous power and water supply had also been ensured in the region. Hospitals and fair price shops were opened with a view to providing medical facilities and essential commodities to the pilgrims. The melā administration took all measures to provide lodging and transport facilities to pilgrims.[139]

The Kumbha Melā, as the greatest religious fair and the highest state of water symbolism, represents the microcosm of Indian civilization and also the totality of Indian cultural traditions. In fact, it shows how the energy of an entire civilization is converted into culture. Moreover, it serves as a vehicle for learning about the wider world and allows people of different backgrounds to meet each other and join in the common experiences of faith and belief. As an organic emergence of sacred space and sacred time, this melā shows the best in the socio-religious traditions of the country and brings to the people those noble and enlightening thoughts that foster cultural integration through the psycho-historical way of acceptance of a tradition from generation to generation. The melā is based upon the Indian concept of ritual bath, so it remains subjugated to the dominating influence of a ritual pattern, representing life as waterflow in a sense of existence and continuity what is referred as "lifeflow". This idea reveals the quest to understand "human creativity" as water is the basic essential need for life, this quest being symbolically transformed into India's greatest "water ritual" referring to the sensitivity about life as a whole and the motivation to explore its invisibility as it forms the whole of nature, cosmos and humanity—ultimately perceived as holy.[140] According to Bhardwaj,[141] "Purification by bathing, one of the most universal religious practices in Hinduism, finds its full expression at the super climatic times of the Kumbha Melās when the reactualization of a life-giving cosmic event occurs. Pilgrimage is made here to earn merits and experience sanctity rather than to pray for material gains".

Places associated with sacred waters assume high sanctity on the occasion of Kumbha Parva and are mostly 'trans-sectarian'. Just as a pilgrimage to Mecca makes the Muslims of different countries and nationalities feel as one, so does the pilgrimage to the Kumbha Melā by the Hindus make them realize that they are one on the common platform of the virtues of bath with experiences and understanding of the invisible Ultimate Reality of wholeness and oneness.

REFERENCES

1. सितासिते सरिते यत्र संगथे तत्राप्लुतासो दिवमुत्पतन्ति ।
ये वै तन्वं वि सृजन्ति धीरास्ते जनासो अमृतत्वं भजन्ते ॥
Ṛgveda, khila–sūkta, 22.1.
2. माघमासं प्रयागे तु नियतः संशितव्रतः ।
स्नात्वा तु भरतश्रेष्ठ निर्मलः स्वर्गमाप्नुयात् ॥
Mbh, XIII.26.36 = *TS*, 32.
3. गवां कोटिप्रदानाद्यात् त्र्यहं स्नानस्य तत्फलम् ।
प्रयागे माघमासे तु एवमाहुर्मनीषिणः ॥ *AgP*, 111.10b-11a.
गवां शतसहस्रस्य सम्यग्दत्तस्य यत्फलम् ।
प्रयागे माघमासे तु त्र्यहं स्नातस्य तत्फलम् ॥
MP, 106.8; *PdP*, III.44.8; *KP*, I.36.2; *NP*, II.63. 74b-75a.
4. सितासितेषु यत्स्नानं माघमासे युधिष्ठिर ।
न तेषां पुनरावृत्तिः कल्पकोटिशतैरपि ।
MP q. in *TvK*, 152 = *TS*, 30; *TC*, 26 & *TP*, 334 ascribe it to *Mbh*.
5. सितासिते तु यो मज्जेदपि पापशतावृतः ।
मकरस्थे रवौ माघे न स भूयस्तु गर्भगः ॥
NP, II. 63.60b-61a; *PdP*, VI (i). 126.33 = *TS*, 31 = *TP*, 334; *TC*, 25 ascribes it to *MP*.
6. माघस्तु प्राप्यते धन्यैः प्रयागे विधिनन्दिनि ।
अपुनर्भवदं तत्र सितासितजलं यतः ॥
NP, II. 63.36; *PdP*, VI (i). 127.146 = *TC*, 21 = *TS*, 31 = *TP*, 333.
7. गायन्ति देवा सततं दिविष्ठा माघः प्रयागे किल नो भविष्यति ।
स्नानान्नरा यत्र न गर्भवेदनां पश्यन्ति तिष्ठन्ति च विष्णुसन्निधौ ॥
PdP, VI (i), 127.147 = *TC*, 21 = *TS*, 31 = *TP*, 333; *NP*, II, 63.37.
8. *MP*, 107.14.
9. ब्रह्महत्यादिपापानि तावद् गर्जन्ति देहिषु ।
यावन्मज्जन्ति नो माघे प्रयागे पापहारिणि ।'
SkP, IV. 7.62.
10. *NP*, II. 63.73b-74a; *PdP*, VI (i). 126.40.
11. *Mbh* XIII. 26.35 = *TS*, 37; *MP*, 106.7 = *TvK*, 146; *KP*, I. 36. 1 = *TS*, 30; *PdP*, III. 44. 7b-8a, VI (i). 126.43, 53-56 – *TC*, 18-19 = *TS*, 31 = *TP*, 330; *NP*, II.63.7-11; *SkP*, IV. 7.57.
12. *PdP*, III. 45.13b-14a.
13. *MP*, 103.14; *PdP*, III. 41.19.
14. Bhattacharya, R.S., 'The Kumbhaparva', *Hindutva*, Vol. VII (9-10), p.8.
15. माघस्य पौर्णमास्यां च घोरं कलियुगं तथा ।
युगारम्भास्तु तिथयो युगाद्यास्तेन विश्रुताः ॥
BP q. in *Puruṣārthacintāmaṇi*, p.506.

त्रयोदशी नभस्येतु द्वापरेण समागता ।
माघे पञ्चदशी राजन्कलिकालादिरुच्यते ॥
BhavP, IV. 101.6.
भाद्रे त्रयोदशी कृष्णा द्वापरेण समा तु सा ।
माघे पञ्चदशी राजन्कलिकालसमा तु सा ॥
BhavP q. in *Puruṣārthacintāmaṇi*, p.506

16. Jaiswal, S., *The Origin and Development of Vaiṣṇavism*, pp.16-17.
17. *Ibid.*, p.13.
18. Kane, *History of Dharmaśāstra*, Vol. V (i), p.638; Hazra, R.C., *Studies in the Purāṇic Records on Hindu Rites and Customs*, p.23.
19. *NarP*, 1. 1-24.
20. Hazra, R.C., *Studies in the Upapurāṇas*, Vol. I, p.242.
21. Beal, *The Life of Hiuen Tsiang*, pp.90, 184-187; Walters, *On Yuan Chwang's Travels in India*, Vol. I, p.364.
22. माघ मकरगत रबि जब होई । तीरथपतिहिं आव सब कोई ॥
देव दनुज किंनर नर श्रेनीं । सादर मज्जहिं सकल त्रिवेनी ॥
Rāmacaritamānasa, I. 43.3-4.
23. एहिं प्रकार भरि माघ नहाहीं । पुनि सब निज-निज आश्रम जाहिं ।
प्रति संबत अति होइ अनंदा । मकर मज्जि गवनहिं मुनिवृन्दा ॥ *Ibid.*, I. 44. 1-2.
24. *Āin-i-Akbarī*, Vol. III, p.335.
25. Sen, S.N. (ed.), *Indian Travels of Thevenot and Careri*, pp.93-94.
26. *Khulāṣat-ut-Tawārīkh*, folio 37b; Sarkar, Jadunath, *India of Aurangzeb*, p.27.
27. Parks, Fanny, *Wanderings of a Pilgrim in Search of the Picturesque*, Vol. I, pp.227, 253-262; Leopold von Orlich, *Travels in India*, Vol. II, p.118; Caine, W.S., *Picturesque India*, pp.375-377.
28. Krása, M., 'Kumbha Melā : The greatest pilgrimage in the World', *New Orient*, Vol. VI, p.181.
29. *Ibid.*, p.180.
30. Low, Sidney, *A visiion of India as seen during tour of the Prince and Princess of Wales*, p.193.
31. *Ibid.*
32. Banerjee, N.N., 'Pūrṇa Kumbha at Prayāga', *Hinduttva*, Vol. VII (9-10), editorial, p.i.
33. Nehru, J.L., *The Discovery of India*, p.51.
34. *Ibid.*
35. Low, Sidney, *op.cit.*, p.195.
36. Krása, M., *op.cit.*, p.180.
37. Giri, Swami Sadananda, *Society and Sannyāsin : A History of the Daśanāmī Sannyāsins*, p.60.
38. Gauda, Venirama Sharma, *Kumbhaparva Māhātmya*, pp.4-6.
39. Bonazzoli, G., 'Prayāga and its Kumbha Melā', *Purāṇa*, Vol. XIX (1), pp.106-108.

40. चतुरः कुम्भांश्चतुर्धा ददामि क्षीरेण पूर्णाँ उदकेन दध्ना ।
एतास्त्वा धारा उप यन्तु सर्वाः स्वर्गे लोके मधुमत् पिन्वमाना उप त्वा तिष्ठन्तु पुष्करिणीः समन्ताः ॥ *AV*, IV. 34.7.
41. क्षीरादिद्रव्येण पूर्णान् चतुरः कुम्भान् चतुर्धा प्रागादिदिग्भेदेन चतुष्प्रकारं दधामि दिक्षु निदधामि। एताः क्षीरादिधाराः त्वाम् उप यन्तु इत्यादि योज्यम् ॥ Sāyaṇa on *AV*, IV.34.7.
42. पूर्णः कुम्भोऽधि काल आहितस्तं वै पश्यामो बहुधा नु सन्तः ।
स इमा विश्वा भुवनानि पत्यङ् कालं तमाहुः परमे व्योऽमन् ॥ *AV*, XIX.53.3.
43. काले सर्वजगत्कारणभूते नित्ये अनवच्छिन्ने परमात्मनि स्वरूपरूपे ।---पूर्णः सर्वत्र व्याप्तः कुम्भः कुम्भवत् कुम्भः अहोरात्रमासर्तुसंवत्सरादिरूपः अवच्छिन्नो जन्यः कालः आहितः निहितो वर्तते। ---तं जन्यं कालं सन्तः सत्पुरुषा बहुधा नानाप्रकारकम् अहोरात्रादिभेदेन पश्यामो नु अनुभवामः खलु।--- स कालः इमा इमानि परिदृश्यमानानि विश्वा विश्वानि व्याप्तानि भुवनानि भुतजातानि प्रत्यङ् प्रत्यञ्चनः अभिमुखाञ्चनः आव्याप्नुवन् भवति। तं कालं परमे उत्कृष्टे सांसारिकसुखदुःखादिद्वन्द्वदोषरहिते व्योमन् व्योमनि आकाशवन्निर्लेपे सर्वगते विविधं रक्षके परमानन्दप्रदायके स्वस्वरूपे वर्तमानम् आहुः विद्वांसः। Sāyaṇa on *AV*, XIX.53.3.
44. Bonazzoli, G., *op.cit.*, p.107.
45. *VaP*, II.15.47.
46. *NP*, II.65.100.
47. Bhattacharya, R.S., 'The Kumbhaparvan', *Hinduttva*, Vol. VII (9-10), p.2.
48. Bonazzoli, G., *op.cit.*, p. 111.
49. Gauda, Venirama Sharma, *op.cit.*, pp.6-10; Roy, D.K. and Indira Devi, *Kumbha: India's Ageless Festival*, pp.17-19; Dave, J.H., *Immortal India*, Vol. I, p.27; Krása, M., *op.cit.*, p.181; Gupta, S.L., 'The Kumbha Melā: An interpretation', *India Cultures Quarterly*, Vol. 24 (3), pp.44-46; Bonazzoli, G., *op.cit.*, pp.111-115; Saletore, R.N., *Encyclopaedia of Indian Culture*, Vol. 2, p.797.
50. Bedekar, V.M., 'The Legend of the Churning of the Ocean in the Epics and the Purāṇas: A Comparative Study', *Purāṇa*, Vol. IX (1), pp.7-61.
51. Giri, Swami Sadananda, *op.cit.*, p.59.
52. Bhattacharya, R.S., *op.cit.*, p.6.
53. *Mbh*, I. 25ff.; *Rām*, III. 35. 27-34; *GP*, I. 240.26-28; *SkP*, IV. 50.55-125.
54. Darian, S.G., *The Ganges in Myth and History*, p.66.
55. *MP*, 105.54; *PdP*, III.43.54b-55; *BP*, 77.3.
56. *NP*, II.72.5, 25.
57. *BP*, 74-76; *NP*, II.72.11-12; *VP*, I. 71.32-38; Kane, *History of Dharmaśāstra*, Vol. IV, p.708.
58. विन्ध्यस्य दक्षिणे गङ्गा गौतमी सा निगद्यते ।
उत्तरे साऽपि विन्ध्यस्य भागीरथ्यभिधीयते ॥ *BP*, 78.77.
59. शिप्रा च सर्वतः पुण्या पवित्रा पापहारिणी ।
अवन्त्यां च विशेषेण शिप्रा चोत्तरवाहिनी ॥ *SkP*, V (i). 63.7.

60. *SkP*, V (ii). 42.27-29a.
61. त्रिषु लोकेषु विख्यातो देवो गङ्गेश्वरः स्वयम् ।
गङ्गयाऽराधितो यस्मात्समीहित फलप्रदः ॥
एवमुक्त्वा गता गङ्गा कलया तत्र संस्थिता ।
गङ्गेश्वरं तु यः पश्येत् स्नात्वा शिप्राम्भसि प्रिये ॥
SkP, V (i). 42.29bc, 33.
62. *SkP*, V (ii). 42.24.
63. *TSSP*, 58.
64. *TSSP*, 233, 244.
65. Darian, S.G., *op.cit.*, p.67.
66. यथा सुराणाममृतं पितृणां च यथा स्वधा ।
सुधा यथा च नागानां तथा गङ्गाजलं नृणाम् ॥ *Mbh*, XIII.27.48.
देवाः सोमार्कसंस्थानि यथा सत्रादिभिर्मखैः ।
अमृतस्युपजीवन्ति तथा गङ्गाजलं नराः ॥ *Mbh*, XIII.27.52.
67. ततः प्रभृति सा शिप्रा जातानागेऽमृतोद्भवा ।
सर्वलोकेषु विख्याता व्यास शिप्रामृतोद्भवा ॥ *SkP*, V (i). 62.53.
68. Darian, S.G., *op.cit.*, p.67.
69. पृथिव्यां कुम्भयोगस्य चतुर्धा भेद उच्यते ।
विष्णुद्वारे तीर्थराजेऽवन्त्यां गोदावरीतटे ॥ *KM*, 8; KN, 7.
70. कुम्भराशिगते जीवे यद्दिने मेषगे रवौ ।
हरिद्वारे कृतं स्नानं पुनरावृत्तिवर्जनम् ॥ *KM*, 21; KN, 8.
पद्मिनीनायके मेषे कुम्भराशिगते गुरौ ।
गङ्गाद्वारे भवेद्योगः कुम्भनामा तथोत्तमः ॥ *KM*, 16.
वसन्ते विषुवे चैव घटे देवपुरोहिते ।
गङ्गाद्वारे च कुम्भाख्यः सुधामेति नरो यतः ॥ *KM*, 17; *KN*, 8.
71. प्रयागे भास्करक्षेत्रे मकरस्थे रवौ सति ।
मेषे जीवे मृगे चन्द्रे कुम्भाख्यो योग उच्यते ॥ *DTKN*, 10.
मेषराशिगते जीवे मकरे चन्द्रभास्करौ ।
अमावस्या तदा योगः कुम्भाख्यस्तीर्थनायके ॥ *KM*, 17; *KN*, 8.
मकरे च दिवानाथे ह्यजगे च बृहस्पतौ ।
कुम्भयोगो भवेत्तत्र प्रयागे ह्यतिदुर्लभः ॥ *KM*, 17; *KN*, 8; *DTKN*, 22.
72. सिंहराशिगते सूर्ये सिंहराशौ बृहस्पतौ ।
गोदावर्यां भवेत् कुम्भो जायते खलु मुक्तिदः ॥ *KM*, 19.
73. मेषराशिगते सूर्ये सिंहराशौ बृहस्पतौ ।
उज्जयिन्यां भवेत् कुम्भः सदा मुक्तिप्रदायकः ॥ *KM*, 18.
74. मकरे च दिवानाथे वृषराशिगते गुरौ ।
प्रयागे कुम्भयोगो वै माघमासे विधुक्षये ॥ *DTKN*, 10, 22.
75. कर्के गुरुस्तथा भानुश्चन्द्रश्चन्द्रक्षयस्तथा ।
गोदावर्यां तदा कुम्भो जायतेऽवनिमण्डले ॥ *KM*, 19; *KN*, 9.

76. धटे सूरिः शशी सूर्यः कुह्वां दामोदरे यदा ।
धारायां च तदा कुम्भो जायते खलु मुक्तिदः ॥ *KM*, 18; *KN*, 8-9.
77. Kane, *op.cit.*, Vol. V(i), p.287.
78. सूर्येन्दुगुरुसंयोगस्तद्राशौ यत्र वत्सरे ।
सुधाकुम्भप्लवे भूमौ कुम्भो भवति नान्यथा ॥ *KM*, 8; *KN*, 7.
79. अन्यानि वै महाभागे सन्ति तत्र सहस्रशः ।
योऽस्मिन् क्षेत्रे नरः स्नायात् कुम्भगेज्येऽजगे रवौ ॥ *NP*, II.66.44.
80. *VdP*, I., 28.8; *Bṛhat Saṁhitā*, 8.27; Kane, *op.cit.*, Vol. V(i), p.660.
81. प्रतिकल्पामनुप्राप्य दृष्ट्वा देवं महेश्वरम् ।
वैशाखे पौर्णमास्यां वै स्नापयन्त्येकवासरम् ॥ *SkP*, V (i). 48.51.
माधवे मासि सम्प्राप्ते निमज्जन्ति नरोत्तमाः ।
न तेषां निरयनकिच्छिवरूपाश्चरन्ति ते ॥ *SkP*, V (i). 61.39.
अवन्तीयात्रा कर्तव्या प्रयत्नेन मुमुक्षुणा ।
माधवेऽपि विशेषेण ह्यवन्तीस्नानमाचरेत् ॥
यो हि वैशाखमासाद्य अवन्त्यां व्यास मानवः ।
संवत्सरव्रती स्नातस्तीर्थे तीर्थे यथाविधि ।
दत्त्वा दानानि सर्वाणि समूलं फलमश्नुते ॥ *SkP*, V (i). 71.15b-17.
82. गोदावार्यां सिंहमासे स्नायात् सिंहबृहस्पतौ ।
शिवलोकप्रदमिति शिवेनोक्तं तथा पुरा ॥ *ŚP*, I.12.22b-23a.
सिंहस्थे च गुरौ तत्र यो गच्छति समाहितः ।
स्नात्वा च विधिना तत्र पितृंस्तर्पयते तथा ॥
स्वर्गं गच्छन्ति पितरो निरये पतिता अपि ।
स्वर्गस्थाः पितरस्तस्य मुक्तिभाजो न संशयः ॥ *VP*, I.71.47-48.
83. त्वं गौतमि सदा पूज्या सर्वेषामपि मुक्तिदा ।
विशेषस्तु सिंहस्थे मयि त्रैलोक्यपावनी ॥
यानि कानि च तीर्थानि स्वर्गमृत्युरसातले ।
त्वां स्नातुं तानि यास्यन्ति मयि सिंहस्थितेऽम्बिके ॥ *BP*, 152.38-39.
तिस्रः कोट्योऽर्धकोटि च तीर्थानि भुवनत्रये ।
तानि स्नातुं समायान्ति गङ्गायां सिंहगे गुरौ ॥
षष्टिवर्षसहस्राणि भागीरथ्यावगाहनम् ।
सकृद्गोदावरीस्नानं सिंहयुक्ते बृहस्पतौ ॥ *BP*, 175.83-84.
84. *TSSP*, 130.35.
85. *BP*, 152.38.
86. Bhattacharya, R.S., *op.cit.*, p.7.
87. तदर्धे वर्षमाने च कुम्भोर्ध्वं सार्धपञ्चकम् ।
अर्धकुम्भं विजानीयात् फलार्धं मोक्षदायकम् ॥
Pt. Umarao Pandey kindly drew my attention to this *śloka*. His claim that it belongs to the *Saktiyāmala Tantra* could not be verified due to the non-availability of any manuscript of the Tāntric text.

88. देवानां द्वादशाहोभिर्मर्त्यैर्द्वादशवत्सरैः ।
जायन्ते कुम्भपर्वाणि तथा द्वादशसंख्यया ॥ *KM*, 21; *KN*, 6.
89. *DTKN*, 23.
90. *Ibid.*, 25.
91. Kane, *op.cit.*, Vol. V(i), pp.658, 661.
92. Ghurye, G.S., *Indian Sadhus*, p.222.
93. Gupta, S.L., 'The Number Twelve and the Four Kumbha Melā Sites', *India Cultures Quarterly*, Vol. 24 (3), p.51.
94. Beal, *op.cit.*, pp.186-187; Walters, *op.cit.*, Vol. I, p.364.
95. Roy, D.K. and Indira, *op.cit.*, p.xxii; Gupta, S.L., *op.cit.*, Vol. 24 (3), p.47; Roy, U.N., *Studies in Ancient Indian History and Culture*, Vol. I, p.221.
96. Bhattacharya, R.S., *op.cit.*, p.8.
97. Pathak, V., *Pāncavī-sātavi Śatābdiyon kā Bhārata*, p.182.
98. Gauda, Venirama Sharma, *op.cit.*, p.30; Bonazzoli, *op.cit.*, p.110.
99. *Ibid.*
100. *Ibid.*
101. *Ibid.*
102. Hazra, R.C., *Studies in the Purāṇic Records on Hindu Rites and Customs*, p.132.
103. कुम्भराशिं मयि प्राप्ते गंगाद्वारे महोत्सवः ।
बभूव बहुलैर्भूपैः कारितस्तीर्थतत्परैः ॥
तत्रोत्सवे नरा नार्यो बहुभूषणभूषिताः ।
समाययुर्दर्शनार्थे परमानन्दनिर्भराः ॥
BhavP, III (iv).7.37-38.

As the lovers were reportedly devoted to recitation of the *Ādityahṛdayastotra* for securing their romantic objective in the month of Vaiśākha immediately after their departure from the melā, their meeting may be placed in the month of Caitra which should be the month of melā as well. *BhavP*, III (iv).7.43-46.
104. *BhavP*, III (iv).7.36-50.
105. Sarkar, Jadunath, *A History of Dasanāmī Nāgā Sanyāsīs*, p.86.
106. Nevill, H.R., *District Gazetteers of the United Provinces of Agra and Oudh*, Vol. II : *Saharanpur*, p.254.
107. Ghurye, G.S., *op.cit.*, p.160.
108. *Ibid.*
109. *Dabistān-i-Mazāhib*, p.251; Shea and Troyer, Vol. II, pp.196-197.
110. *Gurucaritra*, III. 50.33, 99; Ghurye, G.S., *op.cit.*, p.178 fn.
111. साका सालबाहन का, सोरा सैं पूरंन ।
बैठा साका विजयाभिनन्द का, तब फिराए फिरकें सैयंन ॥
विक्रमाजीत के राज सें, बरस सत्रासै पैंतीस ।
तब जिद हुए फिरकन सों, बुध ईस्वरों के ईस ॥
हरद्वार के मेला में, चार सम्प्रदा ताहिं ।
षटदरसन भी तहाँ मिले, दसनाम सन्यासी जाहिं ॥

जीती फौज सिरें संसार की, कारज कारन विस्तार ।
तहाँ तमासा देख कें, फेर के किया विचार ।।

Bītaka, 32.30-32,87.

112. Ghurye, G.S., *op.cit.*, p.178.
113. *Khulāṣat-ut-Tawārīkh*, folio 34b; Sarkar, Jadunath, *India of Aurangzeb*, p.19.
114. *Khulāṣat-ut-Tawārīkh*, folio 33a; Sarkar, Jadunath, *India of Aurangzeb*, p.51.
115. Nevill, H.R., *op.cit.*, p.255; Ghurye, G.S., *op.cit.*, p.112.
116. *Asiatic Researches*, Vol. VI, p.319; Sarkar, Jadunath, *A History of Dasanāmī Nāgā Sanyāsīs*, p.102.
117. Low, Sidney, *op.cit.*, p.208; Pandey, B.N., *Allahabad: Retrospect and Prospect*, p.222.
118. Ghurye, G.S., *op.cit.*, p.160.
119. Bhattacharya, R.S., *op.cit.*, p.1.
120. Sarkar, Jadunath, *A History of Dasanāmī Nāgā Sanyāsīs*, p.82.
121. *Ibid.*, pp.83-90.
122. Giri, Swami Sadananda, *op.cit.*, p.23.
123. Sarkar, Jadunath, *A History of Dasanāmī Nāgā Sanyāsīs*, p.99.
124. Giri, Swami Sadananda, *op.cit.*, p.61.
125. *Asiatic Researches*, Vol. VI, pp.312-319; Sarkar, Jadunath, *A History of Dasanāmī Nāgā Sanyāsīs*, pp.100-102.
126. Sarkar, Jadunath, *A History of Dasanāmī Nāgā Sanyāsīs*, pp.107-108.
127. Low, Sidney, *op.cit.*, pp.196-199.
128. Krása, M., *op.cit.*, p.181.
129. Gupta, J., 'Kumbha Prayāga Kā', *Dharmayuga*, January 9-15, 1977, p.6.
130. Bhardwaj, S.M., 'Religion and Circulation : Hindu Pilgrimage', in *Circulation in Third World Countries*, p.258.
131. Varun, D.P., *Uttar Pradesh District Gazetteers: Saharanpur*, p.337.
132. *Kumbha Melā Guide*, 1986, p.11.
133. Ghurye, G.S., *op.cit.*, p.222.
134. Sharma, Shiva, 'Ujjain Kā Siṁhastha Parva', *Dharmayuga*, March 30 – April 5, 1980, pp.8, 11.
135. Nevill, H.R., *op.cit.*, p.254.
136. Varun, D.P., *op.cit.*, p.337.
137. Krása, M., *op.cit.*, p.181.
138. Rudra, Shukla, 'Mahākumbha kā Ānkhon Dekhā Hāla : na Gaṅgā milī na gāon', *Dinamāna*, April 20-26, 1986, p.21.
139. *Kumbha Melā Guide*, 1986, pp.11-14.
140. Buttimer, Anne, 'Nature, Water Symbols, and the Human Quest for Wholeness', in *Dwelling, Place and Environment*, pp.262-263.
141. Bhardwaj, S.M., *op.cit.*, pp.258-259.

APPENDIX

PRAYĀGA : LATITUDE AND LONGITUDE OF HOLY SPOTS

Holy Spot	Latitude				Longitude			
	a^0	a'	a"	a^0 dec.	b^0	b'	b"	b^0 dec.
Koṭitīrtha	25	30	12.1241	25.5034	81	52	13.4213	81.8704
Nāgavāsuki	25	27	25.9496	25.4572	81	53	5.0590	81.8847
Veṇīmādhava	25	26	44.4088	25.4457	81	53	0.5163	81.8835
Saṅgama	25	25	44.1450	25.4289	81	52	42,6053	81.8785
Samudrakūpa	25	25	32.8722	25.4258	81	54	0.4494	81.9001
Bharadvāja Āśrama	25	27	26.5059	25.4574	81	51	31.4200	81.8587
Draupadīghāṭa	25	28	42.4402	25.4785	81	49	17.3142	81.8215

Based on two GARMIN GPS 75 receivers' recordings; courtesy: Prof. John McKim Malville, University of Colorado; April 1, 1994.

BIBLIOGRAPHY

Abul Fazl, *Āin-i-Akbarī*, (tr.) H. Blochmann and H.S. Jarrett, Calcutta : Asiatic Society of Bengal, 3 vols., 1873-1894, New Delhi : Oriental Books Reprint Corporation, reprint, 1977-78.

——, *The Akbaranāmā*, (tr.) H. Beveridge, Delhi : Rare Books, second Indian reprint, 3 vols., 1973.

Adbhutasāgara of Vallālasena, (ed.) Muralidhar Jha, Benares: Prabhakari Co., 1905.

Ādi Purāṇa, Bombay : Venkateshwar Steam Press, 1907.

Ādipurāṇa (text and trans. in Hindi) of Jinasenācārya, (ed.) Pannalal Jain, Murtidevi Jain Sanskrit Granthamala No. 9, Kashi: Bharatiya Jnanapitha, second edn., 1965.

Agni Purāṇa, (ed.) Baladeva Upadhyaya, Varanasi : Chowkhamba Sanskrit Series Office, 1966.

Agrawala, V.S., 'The Seven-sea-gift in the Matsya Purāṇa', *Purāṇa*, Vol. I (2), 1960, pp.206-212.

——, *Matsya Purāṇa : A Study*, Varanasi : All India Kashiraj Trust, 1963.

——, *Ancient Indian Folk Cults*, Varanasi : Prithivi Prakashan, 1970.

Ahmad, Nizamuddin, *Tabaqāt-i-Akbarī*, (tr.) B. De, Bibliotheca India Works, Calcutta : The Royal Asiatic Society of Bengal, 3 vols., 1927-39.

Aitareya Brāhmaṇa (with the comm. of Sāyaṇa), (ed.) Kashinath Shastri Agashe, Anandashram Sanskrit Series No. 32, Poona: Anandashrama Press, 1896.

Allen, A.H., 'The Vaṭa-Sāvitrī Vrata According to Hemādri', *Journal of the American Oriental Society*, Vol. XXI (2), 1901, pp.53-66.

Altekar, A.S., *Rāṣṭrakūṭas and Their Times*, Poona Oriental Series No. 36, Poona : Oriental Book Agency, Second revised edn, 1967.

Amado, Pierre, 'Le Bain dans le Gange – sa Signification', in *Bull. de l'Ecole Francaise d' Extreme–Orient*, Tome LVIII, Paris, 1971, pp.197-216.

Amarakośa of Amarasimha (with the comm. of Acharya Krishna Mitra), (ed.) Satyadeva Mishra, Kuala Lumpur: University of Malaya,1972.

Anargharāghava of Murāri Miśra (with the comm. Prakāśa), (ed.) Ramachandra Mishra, Vidyabhavan Sanskrit Granthamala No. 47, Varanasi : Chowkhamba Vidyabhavan, 1960.

Anekārthasaṅgraha of Hemacandra, in *Abhidhānasaṅgraha*, (ed.) V. Upadhyaya, Delhi: S.N. Publications, 1981.

Āpastamba Dharmasūtra (with the Ujjvalā comm. of Haradetta Mishra), (ed.) Umesha Chandra Pandey, The Kashi Sanskrit Series No. 93, Varanasi: Chowkhamba Sanskrit Series Office, Second edn, 1969.

Aṣṭādhyāyī of Pāṇini, (ed.) & (tr.) Srisa Chandra Vasu, Allahabad: Panini Office, 1891-97.

Aṣṭādaśa Smṛtayaḥ, Bombay: Venkateshwar Press, Samvat 1981.

Āśvalāyana Gṛhyasūtra, (ed.) Vinayaka Ganesha Apte, Poona : Anandashrama Press, 1937.

Atharvaveda (with the pada-pāṭha and Sāyaṇa's comm.), (ed.) Vishwa Bandhu, Visheshvarananda Indological Series Nos. 12-17, Hoshiarpur : Vishveshvarananda Vedic Research Institute, 1959-62.

The Hyms of the Atharvaveda, (tr.) with a popular comm. by Ralph T.H. Griffith, Chowkhamba Sanskrit Studies, No. (LXVI), Varanasi : Chowkhamba Sanskrit Series Office, 2 vols., 1968.

Avantisundarīkathā of Daṇḍin, (ed.) K.S. Mahadeva Shastri, University of Travancore, Trivendrum Sanskrit Series No. 172, Trivendrum: City Manuscript Library, 1945.

Āvaśyakacūrṇī, Ratlam : Rishabhadeo Kesarimal Jaina Pedhi, 1928-29.

Āvaśyakaniryukti, Surat : Vijayadanasuri Jain Series, 1939-41.

Āvaśyakavritti of Haribhadra, Bombay: Agamodaya Samiti, 1916-17.

Awasthi, A.B.L., *Studies in the Skanda Purāṇa*, Part I, Lucknow: Kailash Prakashan, 1976.

Badauni, Abdul Qadir, *Muntakhub-ut-Tawārīkh*, (tr.) George S.A., Ranking, W.H., Lowe, Sir Wolseley Haig, 3 vols., Calcutta : The Asiatic Society of Bengal, 1898-1925, Patna : Academica Asiatica, reprint, 1973.

Bahadur, K.P., (tr.) *Selections from Rāmacandrikā*, Delhi: Motilal Banarsidass, 1976.

Bajpai, K.D., (ed.) *The Geographical Encyclopaedia of Ancient and Medieval India*, Part I, Varanasi : Indic Academy, 1967.

Banerjee, N.N., 'Pūrṇa Kumbha at Prayāga', *Hinduttva*, Vol. VII (9-10), 1976-77, pp.i-vi. editorial.

Banerji, R.D., 'Lakṣamaṇasena', *Journal of the Asiatic Society of Bengal*, Vol. IV, 1913, pp.275ff.

Beal, Samuel, *Si-Yu-Ki : Buddhist Records of the Western World, translated from the Chinese of Hiuen Tsiang*, London : Kegan Paul, Trench, Trubner & Co. Ltd., 2 vols.,1906, reprint, Delhi : Bharatiya Publishing House, 4 vols., 1980.

——, *The Life of Hiuen Tsiang by Shaman Huwi-Li*, New Delhi : Munshiram Manoharlal, second edn., 1973. .

Beck, Brenda E.F., 'The symbolic merger of body, space and cosmos', *Contributions to Indian Sociology* (NS), Vol. 10(2), 1976, pp.213-243.

Bedekar, V.M., 'The legend of the Churning of the Ocean in the Epics and Purāṇas : A Comparative Study', *Purāṇa*, Vol. IX (1), 1967, pp.7-61.

Bhāgavantabhāskara of Nīlakaṇṭha Bhaṭṭa, Part IV: *Śrāddhamayūkha*, (eds.) Mahadeva Sharma Bakre and Vyankatesh Shastri Lele; Part VII: *Dānamayūkha*, (ed.) Vyankatesh Shastri Lele; Part X: *Prāyaścittamayūkha*, (ed.) Ananta Yajeshwar Bhatta, Delhi: Chowkhamba Sanskrit Prakashan, 2 vols., reprint, 1985.

Bhāgavata Mahāpurāṇa (with text and English trans.), (tr.) C.L. Goswami, Gorakhpur: Gita Press, 1971.

Bhandarkar, R.G., *Vaiṣṇavism, Śaivism and Minor Religious Systems*, Government Oriental Series, Poona : Bhandarkar Oriental Research Institute, 1929.

Bhāratamañjarī of Kṣemendra, (eds.) Pandit Shivadatta and Kashinath Panduranga Parab, Kavyamala No. 64, Bombay: Nirnayasagar Press, 1898, Delhi: Motilal Banarsidass, reprint, 1984.

Bharati, Aghenanda, 'Pilgrimage sites and Indian Civilization', in *Chapters in Indian Civilization*, (ed.) J.W. Elder, Dubuque : Kendall-Hunt Publ. Co., Vol. I, 1970, pp.85-126.

Bhardwaj, S.M., *Hindu Places of Pilgrimage in India*, Berkeley : University of California Press, 1973.

——, 'Religion and circulation : Hindu pilgrimage', in *Circulation in Third World Countries*, (eds.) R. Manshell Prothero and Murry Chapman, London : Routledge & Kegan Paul, 1985, pp.241-261.

Bhattacharya, Adityaram, 'Prayāga or Allahabad', *The Modern Review*, Vol. VIII (5), 1910, pp.647-670.

Bhattacharya, D.C., 'Date of Lakṣamaṇasena and His Predecessors', *Indian Antiquary*, Vol. LI, 1922, pp.146ff.

Bhattacharya, R.S., 'The Kumbhaparvan', *Hinduttva*, Vol. VII (9-10), 1976-77, p.109.

Bhaviṣya Mahāpurāṇa, Bombay : Venkateshwar Steam Press, 1910.

Bhikhari, Sewanand, 'Rāma's Journey to Chitrakūṭa', *The A.B. Patrika*, September 16, 1945.

Bhūparikramaṇam of Vidyāpati, (ed.) Munishwar Jha, Calcutta : Mithila Sanskritik Parishad, 1976.

Bītaka of Lāladāsa, (eds.) M.B. Jayaswal and D.K. Sharma Shastri, Allahabad: Pranami Sahitya Sansthan, 1966.

Bonazzoli, G., 'Prayāga and its Kumbhamelā', *Purāṇa*, Vol. XIX (1), 1977, pp.81-179.

——, 'Places of Purāṇic Recitation according to the Purāṇas', *Purāṇa*, Vol. XXXIII (1), 1981, pp.48-61.

Bṛhatsaṁhitā of Varāhamihira (with the comm. of Bhaṭṭotpal), (ed.) Sudhakar Dwivedi, Banaras: Chowkhamba Sanskrit Series Office, 2 parts, 1895-97.

Brahma Purāṇa, Gurumandala Granthamala No. XI, Calcutta: Mora Prachya Shodha Sansthan, 1954.

Brahmāṇḍa Purāṇa, Bombay: Venkateshwar Steam Press, 1935.

Brahmavaivarta Purāṇa, Bombay: Venkateshwar Steam Press, 1910; Gurumandala Granthamala No. XIV, Calcutta: Mora Prachya Shodha Sansthana, 2 vols., 1954-55.

Bṛhadāraṇyakopaniṣad, in *Upaniṣatsangrah*, 2 parts, (ed.) J.L. Shastri, Delhi: Motilal Banarsidass, pt. I, 1970, pp.84-134.

Bṛhajjābālopaniṣad, in *Upaniṣatsangrah*, 2 parts, (ed.) J.L. Shastri, Delhi: Motilal Banarsidass, pt. I, 1970, pp.207-217.

Bṛhannārdīya Purāṇa, (ed.) Hrishikesh Shastri, Chowkhamba Amarabharati Granthamala No. 3, Varanasi: Chowkhamba Amarabharati, second edn, 1975.

Bṛhaspatismṛti, (ed.) K.V. Rangaswami Aiyangar, Gaekwad Oriental Series No. 85, Baroda: Oriental Institute, 1941.

Bulcke, Comil S.J., *Rāmakathā: Utpatti aur Vikāsa*, Prayaga: Hindi Parisad Prakashan, Prayaga Vishvavidyalaya, 1962.

Buttimer, Anne, 'Nature, Water Symbols, and the Human Quest for Wholeness', in *Dwelling, Place and Environment*, (eds.) Seaman & R. Mugeraner, Dordrecht: Martinus Nijhaff Publishers, 1985, pp.259-280.

Caine, W.S., *Picturesque India*, London: George Routledge & Sons Ltd., 1898.

Chahār Gulshan of Rai Chatarman, Khuda Baksh O.P. Library, Patna, HL No. 92, Catalogue No. 542.

Chattopadhyaya, K.C., 'Religious Suicide at Prayāga', *Journal of the U.P. Historical Society*, Vol. X(1), 1937, pp.65-79.

Chattopadhyaya, S., *Early History of North India*, Delhi: Motilal Banarsidass, 3rd revised edn., 1976.

Chhāndogyopaniṣad, in *Upaniṣatsangraha*, (ed.) J.L. Shastri, Delhi: Motilal Banarsidass, 2 parts, pt. I, 1970, pp.34-83.

Chhibber, H., *Physical Basis of Geography of India*, Banaras: Nandakishore and Brothers, 1945.

Coomaraswamy, A.K., *History of Indian and Indonesian Art*, New York: Dover Publications, 1965.

Crooke, William, *Religion and Folklore of Northern India*, London: Humphrey Milford, 1896, Oxford University Press, second edn., 1926.

Cunningham, A., *The Ancient Geography of India*, 1871, Vol. I, Varanasi: Indological Book House, reprint, 1963.

——, *Corpus Inscriptionum Indicarum*, Vol. I: *Inscriptions of Aśoka*, Calcutta: Office of the Superintendent of Government Printing, 1877.

Dabistān-i-Mazāhib, (ed.) Moulavi Nazer Ushruf, Calcutta: Oriental Press, 1809; tr. David Shea and Anthony Troyer, Paris: Printed for the Oriental Translation Fund of Great Britain & Ireland, 3 vols., 1843.

Dange, S.A., 'Sāvitrī and the Banyan', *Purāṇa*, Vol. V(2), 1963, pp.258-266.

Dani, A.H., 'Mainamati Plates of the Chandras', *Pakistan Archaeology*, Karachi: Directorate of Archaeology, No. 3, 1966, pp.29-55.

Darian, S.G., *The Ganges in Myth and History*, Honolulu: University Press of Hawaii, 1978.

Dave, J.H., *Immortal India*, Vol. I, 1957, Bombay: Bharatiya Vidya Bhawan, second edn, 1970.

Dānakriyākaumudī of Govindānanda, (ed.) Kamala Krishna Smritibhushana, Bibliotheca Indica Series, Calcutta: The Asiatic Society of Bengal, 1903.

Devabuti, D., *Harṣa—A Political Study*, Oxford: Oxford University Press, 1970.

Dey, N.L., *The Geographical Dictionary of Ancient and Medieval India*, Delhi: Low Price Publications, reprint, 1990.

Devī Bhāgavata Purāṇa, Bombay: Venkateshwar Steam Press,1907.

Devī Purāṇa, (ed.) Panchanana Tarkarata, Calcutta: Vangavasi Press, 1896.

Dīghanikāya, Gen. ed. Bhikkhu J. Kashyap, Nalanda: Pali Publications Board, 2 vols., 1958.

Dohavali of Tulsīdāsa, (ed.) H.P. Poddar, Gorakhpur: Gita Press, 1984.
Dubey, D.P., 'The Sacred Geography of Prayāga: Identification of Holy Spots', *National Geographical Journal of India*, Vol. 31 (4), 1985, pp.319-340.
—— 'The Historicity of Akṣayavaṭa at Prayāga', *Purāṇa*, Vol. 28(1), 1986, pp.45-78.
—— 'The Religious Practice of Suicides at Prayāga', *Archiv Orientalni*, Vol. 55, 1987, pp.355-369.
—— 'Kumbha Melā: Origin and Historicity of India's Greatest Pilgrimage Fair', *National Geographical Journal of India*, Vol. 33(4), 1987, pp.469-492.
—— 'Māghamelā at Prayāga', *Purāṇa*, Vol. 30 (1), 1988, pp.60-68.
—— '*Kumbhaparva Prayāga*, (ed.) Allahabad: Sharada Pustak Bhawan, 1989.
—— 'Sacred Complex of Prayāga: The Myth of Triveṇī', in L. Gopal and D.P. Dubey, (eds.) *Pilgrimage Studies—Text and Context*, Allahabad: Society of Pilgrimage Studies, 1990, p.136-156.
—— 'Significance of Ritual Bath of Prayāga', *Purāṇa*, Vol. 33(1), 1991, pp.72-86.
Eck, Diana L., *Banaras: City of Light*, London: Routledge & Kegan Paul, 1983.
Edward C. Sachu, *Alberuni's India*, London : Kegan Paul, Trench, Trubner & Co., 1910, Delhi: S. Chand & Co., reprint, 1964.
Elliot, Sir H.M., *Bibliographical Index to the Historians of Muhammadan India*, Vol. I, 1850, Delhi: Idarah-i-Adabiyat-i-Delhi, reprint, 1976.
Elliot, Sir H.M. and Dowson, John, *The History of India as Told by its own Historians*, Allahabad: Kitab Mahal, reprint, 8 vols., 1964.
Ensink, J., 'Problems of the Study of Pilgrimage in India', *Indologica Taurinensia*, Vol. II, 1974, pp.57-79.
——, 'Hindu Pilgrimage and Vedic Sacrifice', in *Ludwik Sternbach Felicitation Volume*, (ed.) J.P. Sinha, Lucknow: Akhila Bharatiya Sanskrit Parisad, Part I, 1979, pp.105-118.
Epigraphia Indica, A Collection of Inscriptions, reprint, New Delhi: Archaeological Survey of India, 1979-84.
Fausböll, V., (ed.) *The Jātaka* (together with its comm.), index by Dinesh Andersen, London: Luzac & Co. Ltd., reprint, 1962-64.
Fisher, F.H. and Hewett, J.P., (eds.) *Statistical Descriptive and Historical Account of the North-Western Provinces of India*, Vol. VIII(2), compiled by C.D. Steel, Allahabad: North-Western Provinces and Oudh Govt. Press, 1884.
Fleet, John Faithful, *Corpus Inscriptionum Indicarum*, Vol. III: *Inscriptions of the Early Gupta Kings and their Successors*, Calcutta : Superintendent of Government Printing, 1988.
Foster, William (ed.), *Early Travels in India – 1583-1619*, London: Humphrey Milford, Oxford University Press, 1921, reprint, Delhi: S. Chand & Co., 1968.
Gaṅgāvākyāvalī of Viśvāsadevī, in *The Contribution of Women to Sanskrit Literature*, (ed.) J.B. Chaudhuri, Calcutta : Printed at the Calcutta Oriental Press, Vol. IV, 1940.
Garuḍa Purāṇa, (ed.) Ram Shankar Bhattacharya, *Kashi Sanskrit Series* No. 165, Varanasi: Chowkhamba Sanskrit Series Offices, 1964.

Gauda, Venirama Sharma, *Kumbhaparva Māhātmya*, Kashi: Vyasa Pustakalaya, 2004 Samvat (C.E. 1948).

Gautama Dharmasūtra (with the Mitākṣarā comm. of Haradatta Mishra), (ed.) Umesh Chandra Pandey, Kashi Sanskrit Series No. 172, Varanasi: Chowkhamba Sanskrit Series Office,1966.

Ghosh, N.N., 'Sanctity of Present Bharadwāj Āshram', *The A.B. Patrika*, September 2, 1945.

Ghurye, G.S., *Indian Sadhus*, 1953, Bombay: Popular Prakashan, second edn., 1964.

Giri, Swami Sadananda, *Society and Sanyāsin: A History of the Daśanāmī Sannyāsins*, Rishikesh: Kriyayoga Ashrama, 1976.

Gode, P.K., 'The History of the Akṣayavaṭa at Prayāga and Gayā as revealed by some Sanskrit texts between the first century A.D. and 1900', in *Studies in Indian Cultural History*, Vol. I, Vishweshwarananda Indol. Series No. 9, Hoshiarpur: Vishweshwarananda Vedic Research Institute, 1961, pp.374-383.

Gobhila Gṛhyasūtra (with Bhaṭṭanārāyaṇa's comm.), (ed.) Chintamani Bhattacharya, The Calcutta Sanskrit Series No. XVII, Calcutta: Metropolitan Printing and Publishing House, 1936.

Gupta, A.S., 'Conception of Sarasvatī in the Purāṇas', *Purāṇa*, Vol. IV(1), 1962, pp.55-95.

Gupta, J., 'Kumbha Prayāga Kā', *Dharmayuga*, January 9-15, 1977, pp.6-8.

Gupta, P.L., *The Imperial Guptas*, Vol. I, Varanasi: Vishwavidyalaya Prakashan, 1974.

Gupta, S.L., 'The Kumbha Melā: An Interpretation', *India Cultures Quarterly*, Vol. 24(3), 1967, pp.44-49. 'The Number Twelve and the Four Kumbha Melā sites', *India Cultures Quarterly*, Vol. 24(3), 1967, pp.51-57.

Gurucaritra of Gaṅgādhara Sarasvatī, (ed.) Ramachandra K. Kamata, Bombay: Shri Samartha Sadan, 11th edn., 1983.

Hall, Fitz-Edward, 'An Inscription of Govinda Chandra Gahadvala', *Journal of the Asiatic Society of Bengal*, Vol. XXXI, 1862, pp.123-124.

Hamilton, Walter, *A Geographical, Statistical and Historical Description of Hindostan and the Adjacent Countries*, 2 vols., Delhi: Oriental Publishers, First Indian reprint, 1971.

Hadīqat-ul-Aqālīma of Murtuzā Hussain (Hizari 1142/C.E. 1730), Khuda Baksh O.P. Library, Patna, Catalogue No. 637, HL No. 252; Allahabad Regional Archives Ms. No. 11784.

Hardwicke, Capt. Thomas, 'Narrative of a Journey to Sirinagur', *Asiatic Researches*, Vol. VI, 1809, pp.309-349.

Harivaṁśa Purāṇa, (ed.) Parashuram Lakshaman Vaidya, Poona: Bhandarkar Oriental Research Institute, 2 vols., 1969-71.

Harivaṁśapurāṇa of Jinasenācārya, (ed.) Pannalal Jain, Kashi: Bharatiya Jnanapitha, 1962.

Harṣacarita of Bāṇabhaṭṭa (with the comm. of Śaṅkara), (ed.) Kashinath Panduranga Parab, Bombay : Nirnayasagar Press, 3rd edn., 1912; tr. E.B. Cowell and F.W. Thomas, Delhi : Motilal Banarasidass, reprint, 1961.

Hazra, R.C., *Studies in the Purāṇic Records on Hindu Rites and Customs*, Delhi: Motilal Banarsidass,1940, second edition, 1975.

Indian Antiquary, A Journal of Oriental Research, Bombay: British India Press.

Indian Archaeolgoy — A Review, Publ. of the Archaeological Survey of India, New Delhi.

Irwin, John C., 'The Prayāga Bull-pillar : Another Pre-Aśokan Monument', in *South Asian Archaeology*, 1979, (ed.) Herbert Hartel, Berlin: Dietrich Reimer Verlag, 1981.

—— 'The Ancient Pillar-cult at Prayāga (Allahabad): Its Pre-Aśokan Origins', *Journal of the Royal Asiatic Society*, 1983, pp.253-280.

Īśāvāśyopaniṣad, in *Upaniṣatsaṅgraha*, 2 parts, (ed.) J.L. Shastri, Delhi: Motilal Banarsidass, Pt. I, 1970, pp.1-2.

Jābāladarśanopaniṣad, in *Upaniṣatsaṅgraha*, 2 parts, (ed.) J.L. Shastri, Delhi: Motilal Banarsidass, Pt. I, 1970, pp.572-582.

Jaiminīya Nyāyamālā, (with the author's own comm. by Mādhvācārya), (ed.) Shivadatta Sharma, Anandashrama Sanskrit Series No. 24, Poona: Anandasharma Press, 1892.

Jain, Balabhadra, *Bhārata ke Digambara Jain Tīrtha*, Bombay: Bharatavarsiya Digambara Jain Tirthaksetra Committee, 4 vols., 1974-78.

Jain, J.C., *Life in Ancient India as Described in the Jain Canons*, Bombay: New Book Co., 1947

Jain, K.C., *Prehistory and Protohistory of India*, New Delhi: Agam Kala Prakashan, 1979.

Jain, J.P., *Religion and Culture of the Jains*, New Delhi: Bharatiya Jnanapitha Prakashan, 1975.

Jaiswal, Suvira, *The Origin and Development of Vaiṣṇavism from 200 B.C. to A.D. 500*, New Delhi: Munshiram Manoharlal, 1967, second edn., 1981.

Jayaswal, K.P., *History of India, 150 C.E. to 350 C.E.*, Lahore: Motilal Banarsidass,1933.

Joannes De Laet, *De Imperio Magni Mogolis*, Berlin, 1631, (tr.) J.S. Hoyland, annotator S.N. Banerjee, *The Empire of the Great Mogol*, New Delhi: Oriental Books Reprint Corporation, second edn., 1974.

Joharapurakara, Vidhyadhara, (ed.) *Tīrthavandanasaṅgraha*, Jivaraja Jaina Granthamala No. 17, Sholapur: Jaina Sanskrit Sanrakshaka Sangha, 1965.

Joshi, Esha Basanti, (ed.) *Uttara Pradesh District Gazetteers: Allahabad*, Lucknow: Govt. of U.P., 1968

Kavitāvalī of Tulsīdāsa, (ed.) Pandit Vamadeva Sharma, Allahabad: Ramanarayan Lal Publ. & Book, 1938.

Kalpasūtravṛtti of Śāntisāgara, Ratlam: Rishavhadeo Kesarimal, .

Kalpasūtram of Bhadrabāhuswāmī, Ŕatlam : Rishabhadeva Kesarimal Jaina Pedhi, 1938.

Kane, P.V., *History of Dharmaśāstra*, 1930-62, Poona: Bhandarkar Oriental Research Institute, 5 vols., second edn., 1968-77.

Kantawala, S.G., *Cultural History from the Matsya Purāṇa*, Baroda: M.S. University, 1964.

Karakaṇḍacariu of Muni Kanakamara, (ed.) Hiralal Jain, Murtidevi Jain Granthamala Apavhramsa Series No. 4, Calcutta : Bharatiya Jnanapitha Publication, second edn., 1964.

Karmarkar, A.P., *The Religions of India*, Lonavala: Mira Publishing House, Vol. I, 1950.

Kashinath, 'Serpent worship', *Indian Antiquary*, Vol. 2, 1873, p.124.

Kathāratnakośa of Devabhadrācārya, (tr.) Bejaradas Luvaraj Doshi, Bhavanagar: Shri Jain Atmananda Sabha, 1951-56.

Katju, K.N., 'Where was Bharadwāj Āshram?', *The A.B. Patrika*, August 19, 1945.

——, 'A letter relating to the Akṣayavaṭa controversy', *Leader*, October 18 and 19, 1950.

Katju, S.N., 'Story of the Eternal tree of Creation', *Leader*, Kumbha supplement, Allahabad: The Leader Press, February, 1954.

Keen, H.G., *Handbook for Visitors — Allahabad, Cawnpore, Lucknow and Benares*, second edn., Calcutta., 1896.

Khattrī, Sujān, *Khulāṣat-ut-Tawārīkh*, Khuda Baksh O.P. Library (Patna) Catalogue No. 540, HL No. 94.

Kooij, K.R. Von, *Worship of the Goddess according to the Kālikā-purāṇa*, Leiden: E.J. Brill, 1972.

Krása, M., 'Kumbha Melā: The greatest pilgrimage in the world', *New Orient*, Vol. VI, 1965, pp.180-184.

Kitāb Zain-ul-Akhbār of Abu Said Gardizi, (ed.) M. Nazim, Berlin, 1928, English trans. of some portions by V. Minorsky, 'Gardizi on India', *Bulletin of the School of Oriental and African Studies*, Vol. VII, 1948, pp.625-640.

Krityakalpataru, Vol. VIII : *Tīrthavivecanakāṇḍa* of Lakṣmīdhara Bhaṭṭa, (ed.) K.V. Rangaswami Aiyangar, Gaekwad Oriental Series Vol. XCVIII, Baroda : Oriental Institute, 1942.

Kumārapālacarita of Hemacandra, (with the comm. of Pūrṇakalaśagaṇi), (ed.) Shankar Panduranga, Bombay: Nirnayasagar Press, 1900.

Kumbha Melā Guide, Lucknow: Information and Public Relations Dept. of U.P., 1986.

Kumbhaparvanirṇayaḥ of Swami Shriramakrishnananda Giri, (ed.) Sitaram Sharma, Allahabad: Baghambari Gaddi, Samvat 1965.

Kūrma Purāṇa, (text & trans.), (ed.) A.S. Gupta, Varanasi: All-India Kashiraj Trust, 1972.

Kuṭṭanīmatam of Dāmodaragupta, (ed.) Madhusudan Kaul, Bibliotheca Indica Series, Calcutta: The Asiatic Society of Bengal, 1944.

Lal, B.B. and Dikshit, K.N., 'Śriṅgaverapura: A Key-site for the Proto-history and early history of the Central Gaṅgā Valley', *Purātattva*, Vol. 10, 1978-79, pp.1-7.

——. 'The Rāmāyaṇa and Archaeology', Paper presented at the seminar on *Śrī Rāma in Indian Culture*, Ayodhya, November 12-14, 1983, pp.1-12.

Leopold von Orlich, *Travels in India, including Sindh and the Punjab*, (tr.) from the German, H. Evans Lloyd, London: Longman, Brown, Green and Longmans, 2 vols., 1845.

Liṅga Purāṇa, (ed.) J.L. Shastri, Delhi: Motilal Banarsidas, 1980.

Low, Sidney, *A Vision of India as Seen during Tour of the Prince and Princess of Wales*, London : Smith, Elder & Co., 1906.

Macdonell, A.A. and Keith, A.B., *Vedic Index of Names and Subjects*, London: John Murrary & Co., 1912, Varanasi: Motilal Banarsidass, reprint, 1958.

Mahābhārata, (eds.) V.S. Sukthankar *et al.*, Poona: Bhandarkar Orietnal Research Institute, 19 vols., Critical edn., 1933-1959.

Mahābhārata (with the Bharata Bhavadīpa comm. of Nīlakaṇṭha), (ed.) Pandit Ramchandra Shastri Kunjawadekar, Second edn., New Delhi: Oriental Books Reprint Corporation, 1979.

Mahāvaṁśa, (tr.) Bhadanta Ananda Kaushalya-yana, Prayaga: Hindi Sahitya Sammelana, Samvat 2014.

Mahāvaṁśaṭīkā (*Vamsattha Prakāsinī*), (ed.) Shridhar Vasudev Sohoni, Nalanda: Navanalanda Mahavihar, 1971.

Majumdar, N.N., (ed.) *Inscriptions of Bengal*, Rajashahi: Varendra Research Society, Vol. III, 1929.

Majumdar, R.C., 'The Chronology of the Sena Kings', *Journal of the Asiatic Society of Bengal*, Vol. XVII, 1921, pp. 11ff.

Majumdar, R.C., and Altekar, A.S., (eds.) *A New History of Indian People: The Vākāṭaka Gupta Age*, Lahore: Bharatiya Itihasa Parishad, 1946.

Majjhimanikāya (Gen. ed.), Bhikkhu J. Kashyapa, Nalanda: Pali Publications Board, 3 vols., 1958.

Malalasekhera, G.P., *Dictionary of Pāli Proper Names*, London: Pali Text Society, 1938, reprint, 2 vols., 1974.

Malaviya, M., 'Māgha Māsa ke Vrata-parvon kā Māhātmya', in *Kumbhaparva Prayāga*, (ed.) D.P. Dubey, Allahabad : Sharada Prakashan, 1989, pp.98-112.

Mani, Vettam, *Purāṇic Encyclopaedia: A Comprehensive Dictionary with Special Reference to the Epic and Purāṇic Literature*, reprint, Delhi : Motilal Banarsidass, 1975.

Manusmṛti (with the Manubhāṣya of Medhātithi), (ed.) Ganganath Jha, Bibliotheca Indica Work No. 256, Calcutta: The Asiatic Society of Bengal, 1932.

Mārkaṇḍeya Purāṇa, (ed.) K.M. Banerjea, Bibliotheca Indica Work No.29, Calcutta: The Asiatic Society of Bengal, 1862.

Matsya Purāṇa, Bombay: Venkateshwar Steam Press, 1895; Anandashrama Sanskrit Series No. 54, Poona: Anandashrama Press, 1907; Gurumandala Granthamala No. XIII, Calcutta: Mora Prachya Shodha Sansthan, 1954.

Medinīkośa of Medinī, (ed.) Jagannath Shastri Hoshing, Kashi Sanskrit Series No. 41, Varanasi: Chowkhamba Sanskrit Series Office, 1968.

Mehta, M.L. and Rishabha, C.K. (comb.), *Prākrita Proper Names*, (ed.) Dalsukh Malvania,Lalbhai Dalpatbhai Series No. 28, Ahmedabad: L.D. Institute of Indology, 2 parts, 1970-72.

Mehta, R.N., *Pre-Buddhist India*, Bombay: Examiners Press, 1939.

Mirashi, V.V., *Corpus Inscriptionum Indicarum*, Vol. IV(1): *Inscriptions of the Kalacuri-Cedi Era*, Ootacamund: Govt. Epigraphist for India, 1955.

Mishra, V.N., 'Climate, a Factor in the Rise and Fall of the Indus Civilization — Evidence from Rajashtan and Abroad', in *An Archaeological Tour along the Ghaggar — Hakra River*, (ed.) S.P. Gupta, Meerut: Kasumanjali Prakashan, 1989, pp.125-171.

Mittal, C.P., 'Why Bharadwāj Āshram shifted?', *The A.B. Patrika*, September 2, 1945.

Monier-Williams, M., *A Sanskrit–English Dictionary*, Oxford: Oxford University Press, 1899; Delhi: Motilal Banarsidass, reprint, 1963.

Mukherji, R. and Maity, S.K., *Corpus of Bengal Inscriptions*, Calcutta: Firma K.L. Mukhopadhyaya, 1967.

Mukherji, S.C., 'Allahabad', *The Modern Review*, Vol. VIII (5), 1910, pp.632-640.

Naiṣaddhacarita of Śrīharṣa, (tr.) K.K. Handiqui, Poona: Deccan College Postgraduate and Research Institute, 1965.

Nambiar, K.D., *Nārada Purāṇa : A Critical Study*, Varanasi: All-India Kashiraj Trust, 1979.

Nāradīya Mahāpurāṇa, Bombay: Venkateshwar Steam Press, 1933.

Narasiṁha Purāṇa, (ed.) Udhvacarya, Bombay: Gopal Narayana & Co., 1911.

Nehru, J.L., *The Discovery of India*, New Delhi: Jawaharlal Nehru Memorial Fund, 1961, reprint, 1972.

Nevill, H.R., *District Gazetteers of the United Provinces of Agra and Oudh*, Vol. II : *Saharanpur*, Allahabad: Government Press, 1909.

——, *Allahabad District Gazetteer*, Allahabad: Govt. Press, 1909.

Nirṇayasindhu of Kamalākara Bhaṭṭa, (with the comm. of Krishna Bhaṭṭa), (ed.) Pandit Gopal Shastri Nene, Chowkhamba Sanskrit Series No. 52, Benares : Chowkhamba Sanskrit Series Office, 1930.

Niśīthacūrṇī, Agra: Sanmati Jnanapitha, 1957-60.

Ojha, K.C., 'Ancient Allahabad: A Foreigner's Account', *Journal of the Allahabad Historical Society*, Vols. II & III, 1962, pp.1-5.

Olsson, Gunnar, *Birds in Egg/Eggs in Bird*, London: Pion Ltd., 1980.

Padma Purāṇa, Bombay: Venkateshwar Steam Press, 1927; Gurumandala Granthamala No. XVIII, Calcutta: Mora Prachya Sodha Sansthan, 5 vols., 1957-59.

Pañcavimśa Brāhmaṇa, (ed.) W. Caland, Bibliotheca India work No. 255, Calcutta: The Asiatic Society of Bengal, 1931.

Pande, B.N., *Allahabad : Retrospect and Prospect*, Allahabad : The Municipal Press, 1955.

Pande, S.N., 'Identification of the Ancient Land of Uttara Kuru', *Journal of the G.N. Jha Research Institute*, Vol. XXVI (1-3), 1970, pp.132-140.

Papañcasūdanī (Majjhimanikāyaṭṭhakathā) of Buddhaghoṣācārya, (ed.) I.B. Horner, 5 parts, Pali Text Society, London: Oxford University Press, 1933-38.

Parāśarasmṛti (with the gloss of Mādhvācārya), (ed.) Chandrakanta Tarkalankara, Bibliotheca Indica Works Nos. 303, 298, Calcutta: The Asiatic Society, 3 vols., reprint, 1973-74.

Parui, S.S., *Kurukṣetra in the Vāmana Purāṇa*, Calcutta: Punthi Pustak, 1976.

Pathak, V., *Pācavī-sātavī Śatābdiyon kā Bhārata*, Allahabad: Sahitya Sangam, 1990.

Pathak, V.S., 'Prayāga in Inscriptions', *Journal of the U.P. Historical Society* (New Series), Vol. VI (2), 1958, pp.31-34.

Parāśara Mādhavīya of Mādhavācārya (ed.) Chandrakant, Calcutta: The Asiatic Society of Bengal, 3 vosl., 1973-74.

Parks, Fanny, *Wanderings of a Pilgrim in Search of the Picturesque*, London: Pelhem Richardson, 1850.

Pratimānāṭakam of Bhāsa, (ed.) M.R. Kale, Delhi: Motilal Banarsidass, reprint, 1977.

Prāyaścittatattva in *Smṛtitattva* of Raghunandana Bhattācārya, (ed.) Swami Achintya Bhagawan, 2 vols., Calcutta: Jivananda Vidyasagara, Vol. I, pp.466-558, 1895.

Prāyaścittaviveka (with Govindānanda *tīkā*) of Śūlapāṇi, (ed.) Sadashivacharya Dixit, Varanasi: Prabhakari Medical Hall, Samvat 1959.

Prāyaścittasāra (a part of the *Nṛsiṁha Prasāda*) of Dalapati, (ed.) Nanda Kishore Sharma and Nanda Kumar Sharma, Saraswati Bhawan Text Ni. 54, Banaras: Govt. Sanskrit Libray, 1934.

Prayāga–māhātmya Śatādhyāyī (text with Hindi *ṭīkā*), (tr.) Chandrashekhar Shastri, Prayaga: S.S.S. Sharma Printer, Samvat 1981.

Puruṣārthacintāmaṇi of Viṣṇubhaṭṭa, (ed.) H.N. Apte, Anandashrama Sanskrit Series No. 55, Poona : Anandashrama Press, 1907.

Rāmacandrikā of Keśavadāsa, Allahabad: Ramanarayan Lal Benimadhava, 2 parts, 12th edn, 1972.

Rāmacaritamānasa of Tulsīdāsa, (text in bold letters), Gorakhpur: Gita Press, 9th edn., 1975.

Rājataraṅgiṇī of Kalhaṇa, (tr.) M.A. Stein, Delhi: Motilal Banarsidass, 2 vols., 1961.

Raja Radhakanta Deva (Samvat 2024), *Śabdakalpadruma*, Chowkhamba Sanskrit Series No. 93, Varanasi: Chowkhamba Sanskrit Series Office, 1966.

Raghuvaṁśa of Kālidāsa, in *Kālidāsa Granthāvalī*, (ed.) Reva P. Dvivedi, Varanasi: Banaras Hindu University, 1976.

Rāmāyaṇa of Vālmīki (critical edition), (Gen. eds.); G.H. Bhatt and U.P. Shah, Baroda: Oriental Insitute, 7 vols., 1960-75.

Rāmāyaṇa (with the commentary of Rāma), (ed.) Vasudeva Luxman Shastri Pansikar, Delhi: Indological Book House, 7 vols., 1983.

Ṛgveda Saṁhitā, (ed.) Shripada Damodra Satavalekar, Paradi: Svadhyaya Mandala, 1940; (with the comm. of Sāyaṇa), (ed.) F. Maxmüller, Chowkhamba Sanskrit Series No. 99, Varanasi : Chowkhamba Sanskrit Series Office, First Indian edn., 4 vols., 1966.

Roy, D.K. and Indira Devi, *Kuṃbha: India's Ageless Festival*, Bombay: Bharatiya Vidya Bhavan, 1956.

Roy, S.N., *Historical and Cultural Studies in the Purāṇas*, Allahabad: Pauranic Publications, 1978.

Roy, U.N., 'Prayāga in legend and history', in *Studies in Ancient Indian History and Culture*, Vol. 1, Allahabad: Lokbharti Publications, 1969, pp.172-233.

Śabara-Bhāṣya, (tr.) G.N. Jha, Gaekward Oriental Series Nos. 66, 70, 73, Baroda: Oriental Institute, 3 vols., 1933-36.

Saletore, R.N., *Encyclopeadia of Indian Culture*, New Delhi: Sterling Publishers, 2 vols., 1981-82.

Śaṅkara-digvijaya, of Mādhava Vidyāraṇaya, (tr.) Swami Tapasyananda, Madras: Shri Rama-krishna Matha, n.d.

Saran, B., 'Geomorphology of the Saṅgam Region', *Journal of the U.P. Historical Society* (N.S.), Vol. II, 1954, pp.46-53.

Sarkar, Sir Jadunath, *The India of Aurangzeb* (with extracts from the *Khulāṣat-ut-Tawārīkh* and the *Chahār Gulshan*), Calcutta: Bose Brothers, 1901.

——, *A History of Dasanami Naga Sanyasis*, Allahabad: Shri Panchayati Akhara Mahanirvani, 1958.

Śatapatha Brāhmaṇa, (ed.) A Weber, Chowkhamba Sanskrit Series No. 96, Varanasi: Chowkhamba Sanskrit Series Office, 1964.

Scheftelowitz, J., *Die Apokryphen des Ṛveda*, Breslau: Verlag von M. and H. Marcus, 1906, Otms: Hildesheim, reprint, 1966.

Sen, S.N., (ed.) *Indian Travels of Thevenot and Careri*, New Delhi: National Archives of India, 1949.

Śabdaratnasamanvayakośa of Shahji, (ed.) Vitthalaram Lalluram Shastri, Baroda: Oriental Institute, 1932.

Sharma, R.S., *Material Culture and Social Formations in Ancient India*, Delhi: Macmillan India Ltd., 1983, reprint, 1985.

Sharma, Shiva, 'Ujjain kā Siṁhasthaparva', *Dharmayuga*, March 30-April 5, 1980, pp.8-11.

Sharma, T.R., *Studies in the Sectarian Upaniṣads*, Varanasi: Indological Book House, 1972.

Shastri, K.C., *Jaina Dharma*, Bharatiya Digambara Jainasangha Pustakamala No. 2, Varanasi, 3rd edn., 1955

Shastri, R.M., 'Full Light on the Real Site of the Bharadwāj Āshram', *Journal of the G.N. Jha Research Institute*, Vol. III, 1945, p.159ff.

Shukla Rudra, 'Mahākumbha kā Ānkhon Dekhā Hāla: na Gaṅgā Milī na Gāon', *Dinamāna*, April 20-26, 1986, pp.21-25.

Singh, Ujagir, *Allahabad: A Study in Urban Geography*, Varanasi: Banaras Hindu University, 1961.

Sinha, H.P., *Bhārata ko Prayāga kī Dena*, Allahabad: Ramanarayana Lal & Co., 1953.

Sinha, S.N., *The Mid–Gangetic Region in the Eighteenth Century: Some Observations of Joseph Tieffenthaler*, Allahabad: Shanti Prakashan, 1976.

Sircar, D.C., *Studies in the Geography of Ancient and Medieval India*, Delhi: Motilal Banarsidass, 1960.

——, *Studies in the Religious life of Ancient and Medieval India*, Delhi: Motilal Banarsidass, 1971.

——, *Epigraphic Discoveries in East Pakistan*, Sanskrit College Series No. LXXVII, Calcutta: Sanskrit College, 1973.

Śiva Purāṇa, Bombay: Venkateshwar Steam Press, 1944; Delhi: Nag Publishers, 1981.

Śivopaniṣad, in *Upaniṣatsaṅgraha*, (ed.) J.L. Shastri, Delhi: Motilal Banarsidass, 2 parts, Pt. II, 1970, pp.324-378.

Skanda Purāṇa, Bombay: Venkateshwar Steam Press, 7 vols., 1909; Delhi: Nag Publishers, 1982.

Smṛticandrikā of Devaṇṇabhaṭṭa, (ed.) J.R. Gharpure, Bombay: Nirnayasagar Press, 1954.

Smṛti-Sandarbha, Gurumandala Granthamal No. IX, Calcutta: Mora Prachya Shodha Sansthan, 5 vols., 1952-1955.

Smṛtyarthasāra of Śrīdharācārya, (ed.) H.N. Apte, Anandashrama Sanskrit Series No. 70, Poona: Anandashrama Press, 1912.

Spera, Giuseppe, 'Some Notes on Prayāga – māhātmya', *Indologica Taurinensia*, Vol. V, 1977, pp.179-197.

Śrāddhacandrikā of Divākara Bhaṭṭa, (ed.) Vishnu Prasad Bhandari, Banaras: Chowkhamba Sanskrit Series Office, 1934.

Śrāddhakalpalatā of Nandapaṇḍita, (ed.) Lakshmidhar Pant Dharmadhikari, Banaras: Chowkhamba Sanskrit Series Office, 1935.

Śrāddhaviveka of Rudradhara, (ed.) Anantaram Dogare Shastri, Kashi Sanskrit Series No. 122, Banaras: Chowkhamba Sanskrit Series Office, 1936.

Srivastava, Shaligrama, *Prayāga Pradīpa*, Allahabad: Hindustani Academy, 1937.

Sumaṅgalavilāsinī, (eds.) T.W. Rhys Davids *et al.*, Pali Text Society, London: Luzac & Company, 3 vols., second edn., 1968-1971.

Sukul, Kubernath, *Varanasi Down the Ages*, Patna: Kameshwar Nath Sukul, Rajendra Nagar, 1974.

Swami Karapatri and Ojha, M.H., *Dharmakṛtyopayogitithyādi – nirṇayaḥ Kumbhaparva – nirṇayaśca*, Varanasi: Akhila Bharatiya Dharmasangha, 1965.

Taittirīya Saṁhitā (with the comm. of Sāyana), (ed.) Kashinath Shastri Agashe, Anandashrama Sanskrit Series No. 42, Poona: Anandashrama Press, 1946.

Tāṇḍya Brāhmaṇa (with Sāyaṇa bhāṣya), Bibliotheca Indica Series, Calcutta: The Asiatic Society of Bengal, 2 vols., 1870-1874.

Tatia, Nathmal (Gen. ed.), *Papañcasūdanī* (the comm. on *Majjhimanikāya)*, (eds.) U. Dharmaratana and U. Jagarabhivamsa, Nalanda: New Nalanda Mahavihara, Vol. I, 1975.

Thakur, Upendra, *The History of Suicide in India*, Delhi: Munshiram Manoharlal, 1963.

Tieffenthaler, Joseph, *Historisch-geographische Beschreibung von Hindustan*, Easter Band, (tr.) and (ed.) Johann Bernoulli, Berlin: ben dem Herausgegeber'/ Gotha: C.W. Ettinger, 3 vols., 1785-1788,

Tīrthacintāmaṇi of Vācaspati Miśra, (ed.) Kamalakrishna Smrititirtha, Bibliotheca Indica New Series No. 1256, Calcutta: The Asiatic Society of Bengal, 1912.

Tiwari, B.N., *Prayāga Darśana*, Allahabad: Vidya Prakashan Griha, 1976.

Triṣaṣṭiśalākāpuruṣacaritra of Hemacandra, (tr.) Helen M. Johnson, Baroda: Oriental Institute, 6 vols., 1931-62.

Tristhalīsetusāra of Bhaṭṭojī Dīkṣita, (ed.) S.N. Shukla, Princess of Wales Saraswati Bhawan Texts No. 65, Allahabad: Government Printing Press, 1936.

Tristhalīsetu of Nārāyaṇa Bhaṭṭa, (ed.) Ganesh Shastri Gokhale, Anandasharma Sanskrit Series No. 78, Poona: Anandashrama Press, 1915.

Tristhalīsetu Sāmānya-praghaṭṭaka (The Bridge to Three Holy Cities) of Nārayaṇa Bhaṭṭa, (ed.) & (tr.) Richard Salomon, Delhi: Motilal Banarsidass, 1985.

Tuan, Yi-Fu, 'Sacred space: explorations of an idea', in *Dimensions of Human Geography*, (ed.) K.W. Butzer, Chicago: University of Chicago, Dept. of Geography Research Paper Series 186, 1978, pp.84-99.

Tucci, Giuseppe, *The Theory and Practice of Mandala*, London: Rider and Co., 1969, 3rd impression, 1971.

Turner, Victor, 'The Centre out there, Pilgrim's goal', *History of Religions*, Vol. 12(3), 1973, pp.191-230.

Upadhyaya, G.P., 'The Origins and Functions of Tīrthas: Some Epic and Purāṇic Testimonies', *Indian History Congress Proceedings*, Calicut : 47th session, 1976, pp.126-130.

Uttararāmacarita of Bhavabhūti (with the comm. of Ghanaśyāma), notes and tr. P.V. Kane & C.N. Joshi, 5th edn., Delhi: Motilal Banarsidass, 1971.

Vaidya, C.V., *History of Medieval Hindu India*, Poona: The Oriental Books Supplying Agency, 3 vols., 1921-26.

Vaijayantīkośa of Yādavaprākāśācārya, (ed.) Pt. Haragovinda Shastri, The Jaikrishnadasa Prachya Vidya Granthamala No. 2, Varanasi: Chowkhamba Sanskrit Series Office, 1971.

Vājasaneyī Saṁhitā (with the comm. of Uvvaṭa and Mahīdhara), (ed.) Pandit Ram Sakala Mishra, Kashi Sanskrit Series No. 34, Benares: Chowkhamba Sanskrit Book Depot, 1912-15.

Vāmana Purāṇa (text and English trans.), (ed.) A.S. Gupta, Varanasi: All-India Kashiraj Trust, 1968.

Varāha Purāṇa (text and English trans.), (ed.) A.S. Gupta, Varanasi : All-India Kashiraj Trust, 1981.

Varun, D.P., *Uttar Pradesh District Gazetteers : Saharanpur*, Lucknow: The Govt. of U.P. Dept. of District Gazetteers, 1981.

Vāsavadattā of Subandhu, (ed.) Shankaradeva Shastri, Vidyabhavan Sanskrit Series No. 2, Varanasi: Chowkhamba Vidyabhavan, 1967.

Vasiṣṭha Dharmasūtra, (ed.) A.A. Fuhrer, Bombay : The Dept. of Public Instruction, Varanasi: Indological Book House, 1914, reprint, 1983.

Vāyu Purāṇa Bombay: Venkateshwar Steam Press, 1933.

Vikramāṅkadevacarita of Bilhaṇa, (ed.) Shastri Murali Lal Nagar, Benares : The Prince of Wales Saraswati Bhavana Texts Series No. 82; 1945; (tr.) S.C. Banerji and A.K. Gupta, Calcutta : Sambodhi Publications Pvt. Ltd., 1965.

Vijayadharma Sūri, (ed.) *Prācina Tīrthamālāsaṅgraha*, Part I, Bhavanagar : Shri Yasovijaya Jain Granthamala,Samvat 1978.

Vikramorvaśīyam of Kālidāsa, (ed.) H.R. Karmik and S.G. Desai, Bombay: Booksellers Publishing Co., 1959.

Vinayapiṭaka, (tr.) T.W. Rhys Davids and H. Oldenberg, Sacred Books of the East Series Nos. 13, 17, 20, Delhi: Motilal Banarsidass, reprint, 3 vols. 1965.

Vipākasūtra, Bombay: Agamodaya Samiti, 1920.

Vīrabhānūdaya Kāvya of Mādhava, (text and trans. in English), (eds.) K.K. Lele and Anant Shastri Upadhyaya, Rewa: Rewa Darbar, 1938.

Vīramitrodaya of Mitra Miśra, Vol. ix : *Śrāddhaprakāśa*, (ed.) Nityananda Sharma Parvatiya, Benares: Chowkhamba Sanskrit Series Office, 1916; Vol. X: *Tīrthaprakāśa*, (ed.) Pandit Vishnu Prasad, The Chowkhamba Sanskrit Series No. 239, Benares: Chowkhamba Sanskrit Series Office, 1917.

Vishwakarma, I.S., 'Dūrion kī māpa : Yojana, Li and Farsaka', *Bharatiya Itihasa Sankalana Samiti Patrika*, Vol. 3, 1985, pp.228-234.

Viṣṇudharmottara Purāṇa, Bombay : Venkateshwar Steam Press, 1912.

Viṣṇusmṛti, (with the comm. Keśavavaijayantī of Nanda Pandit), (ed.) Pandit V. Krishnamacharya, Adyar Library Series No. 93, Madras : The Adyar Library and Research Centre, 1964.

Vṛhat Svayambhū Purāṇa, (ed.) Haraprasad Shastri, Bibliotheca Indica Series, Calcutta: The Asiatic Society of Bengal, 1900 .

Vividhatīrthakalpa of Jinaprabha Sūri, (ed.) Jina Vinaya, Shantiniketan: Singhi Jaina Jnanapitha, 1934.

Wadia, D.N., *Geology of India*, London: Macmillan & Co. Ltd., 1953.

Watters, Thomas, *On Yuan Chwang's Travels in India 625-645 C.E.*, London: Royal Asiatic Society, 2 vols., 1904; Delhi: Munshiram Manoharlal, First Indian edn., 1961.

Winternitz, M.A., *A History of Indian Literature*, Delhi: Motilal Banarsidass, Vol. I, revised edn., 1983.

Wheeler, R.E.M., 'Archaeological Fieldwork in India: Planning Ahead', *Ancient India*, No. 5, 1949, pp.4-11.

Yadav, J., *Jaina Dharma kī Aitihāsika Rūparekhā*, Delhi: India Academy, 1981.

Yājñavalkyasmṛti, (with the comm. of Aparārka), (ed.) Hari Narayana Apte, Anandashrama Sanskriti Series No. 46, Poona: Anandashrama Press, 1903-1904.

Yātrāprabodha of Dīkṣita Samarapuṅgava, (ed.) Pandit Kedarnath, Kavyamala No. 90, Bombay: Nirnayasagar Press, second edn., 1936.

Yajurveda Saṁhitā (Vājasaneyī - Mādhyandina Śukla), (ed.) Shripada Damodara Satavalekara, Paradi : Sradhyaya Mandala, 4th edn., n.d.

Yaśastilaka of Somadeva, (eds.) Shivadutta and V.L. Shastri Pansikar, Kāvyamala No. 70, Bombay: Nirnaya Sagar Press, 1916.

Yoginītantra, (ed.) Biswanarayan Shastri, Delhi: Bharatiya Vidya Prakashan, 1982.

INDEX

New Appendices*

* Added to the second edition

APPENDIX – 1

ARAIL: A HISTORICAL AND CULTURAL PROFILE

D.P. Dubey & Ashish K. Dubey

The village of Arail lies in lat. 25°25'N and long. 81°53'E, opposite the fort, on the right bank of the Yamunā river near its confluence with the river Gaṅgā and is about 5 km from Allahabad in U.P. It is of undoubted antiquity and also attracts large gatherings of pilgrims mostly from Central India during the Māgha Melā every year and two sectors for pilgrims are being laid out there from 2001 in Kumbh Melā, but little is known about its historical and cultural importance in the sacred complex of Prayāga in the religious world from early times. An attempt is being made here to bring out the historical and cultural profile of this place piecing together information gleaned from varied available sources.

In the Tarti copper-plate grant of 1117 CE, the Gāhaḍavāla king Govindacandra is stated to have granted a village in the Siṅgaraura (Śriṅgaverapura on the Gaṅgā, 35 km north-west from Allahabad) *pattalā,* after bathing in the Veṇi (confluence of the rivers Gaṅgā, Yamunā and the invisible Sarasvatī) while staying at Arela, to a brāhmana named Sīdhūśarmā of the Sāṅkritya *gotra* and Sankritya, Āṅgirasa and Gaurīvita *pravaras.*[1] Arela of this inscription has been identified by the editor with the modern locality of Arail, near the confluence of the rivers, the headquarters of the pargana of the same name in the Karchhana tehsil of the Allahabad district.[2] The *Vīrabhānū-dayakāvya* of Mādhava (composed in about 1555 CE) says that Alarkanagara or Alarkapur stood on the bank of the Gaṅgā near its confluence with the Yamunā and the invisible Sarasvatī.[3] Vācaspati Misra (15th century CE) and Mitra Miśra (17th century CE) mention it as

Alarkanagara.[4] The *Vīrabhadradevacampū* (composed in 1577 CE) refers to it by the name of Alarkanagarī situated at the junction of the rivers Gaṅgā and Yamunā[5], while Nārāyaṇa Bhaṭṭa (16th century CE) mentions it as Alarkapura.[6] But Vidyāpati (1368-1475 CE), the famous poet of Mithila, spells the name of this village as Arela near the villages Seraja (modern Sājī kā pūrā) and Cakoranayanī (modern Naini), which was located to the south of Prayāga and where a mud fortress existed.[7] In fact, 'Alarka' is a sanskritised form but neither of the two forms – Arela or Arail – would account for the term 'Alarka' linguistically. The correct and original form of the name, on the authority of the inscription referred above and Vidyāpati, appears to be *Arela* which in popular parlance is pronounced as Arail.

It was the locality plundered by the orders of Sikandar Lodi in 1491 CE, as stated by Niāmatullāh in his *Tārikh-i-khān-i-Jahān*.[8] The Baghela rulers of Gahora-Rewa used to go and live there at the confluence of the rivers Gaṅgā and Yamunā.[9] It was there that the Baghela chief Virasiṁha is said to have entered into a friendly alliance with the Mughal emperor Babur.[10] The accounts given in the *Humāyūn-nāmā*, written by the princess Gulbadan as well as by Jauhar, would make it clear that Raja Virabhānu (Pirbhān) Baghela who was staying at Arail, came to the rescue of the Mughal emperor Humayun against the pursuing Afghan army of Sher Shah Suri in 1537 CE. He entertained him at Arail for a few days, supplied his retinue with provisions and escorted him to Kara-Manikpur[11]. The Mughal emperor Akbar granted Raja Ramacandra Baghela (1555-1592 CE), son of the Baghela chief Virabhānu, the pargana of Arail and Piyāg (Prayāga), together with its dependencies, as *Jagir* in 1569 CE[12] after the latter surrendered the fort of Kalinjar in the Banda district of UP to the Mughals. In his elaborate note on the 'Chaurāsīs', Elliot writes that 'Raja Rāma Baghela is said to have given in gift 360 villages to the *brāhmaṇas* of Arail'.[13] Akbar changed the name of Arail to Handiābās[14], but the change was short-lived. The *Jaṇgamas*, a prominent Śaiva sect also known as Liṅgayatas of Varanasi, held some bīghas of land in *madad-i-māsh*, possessed one *gumbad* (bastion) and a *bāgh* (garden) in the *Qasbah* (town) of Arail/Arayal in the time of the Mughal emperor Akbar.[15] In 1735 CE Muhammad Khan Bangash laid seige of Arail, but he was defeated by the forces of Shah Nawaj Khan.[16] In 1751 CE Ahmad Khan Bangash, the Nawab Wazir of Farrukhabad, captured the town of Arail by attacking the fort of Allahabad from the south but was compelled to lift the siege by the forces of Nawab Safdar Jung of Oudh and the Marathas.[17] Firminger says that "in 1764 CE ... Allahabad and Terhar or Arel were conquered by the British arms".[18] Joseph Tieffenthaler (1766-67 CE) says that "Arel was a town, not far from the confluence, which formerly had a castle for defending the crossing of the Ganga."[19] He further notes that "the fortress of Arel was under the control of a Hindu Raja".[20] This fortress at Arail, also referred by Vidyāpati, was obviously in the control of the Baghela rulers, some of whom stayed there waiting for death during the old age, e.g. Vīrasiṁha died at the confluence of the Gaṅgā and the Yamunā[21] and Vīrabhānu, renouncing worldly pleasures, retired from public life to reside near the confluence at Arail.[22] Remains of an old mud fortress littered with brick-bats still exist there, but the site has been regrettably converted into a park named Triveni Pushpa by the insensitive local urban development authorities in 2001-02.

Some *farmans* and *parwanas* of the Mughal emperor Shah Alam II (1759-1771 CE) and the Nawab Wazirs of Oudh (Shuja-ud-daula of 1773 CE, Asif-ud-daula of 1778 CE and Safadarjung of 1785 CE) were sold by the family of Naipalgiri and Narmadagiri, the priests of Pātālapurī-Akshayavaṭa in the fort, to one Shambhunath of Chhapra. These documents now in the possession of the Khuda Baksha Oriental Public Library, Patna, mention the village named Koin in the 'pargana Arel' granted in *madad-i-māsh* to Shankara Gosain and Durga Gosain, disciples of Balakripagiri Gosain[23] who held three *biswā* rent-free residential land below the fort on the left bank of the Yamunā from the time of Shah Alam I[24]; the remains of his residence still being visible in the form of a surviving bastion in the premises of the modern Manakāmeśvara temple there.

The Purāṇas refer to some *upatīrthas* such as Agni-tīrtha, Anaraka-tīrtha, Naga Bahumūlaka and Soma-tīrtha on the southern bank of the Yamunā.[25] But Arail, so close to the confluence of the rivers, escaped the attention of the Purāṇic authors. The place also did not attract the attention of archaeologists and art historians for quite a long period. Alexander Cunningham extensively toured in the Allahabad region, but for unknown reasons he did not visit Arail. There are two mosques of the late medieval period and several shrines of which those dedicated to Ādi Veṇimādhava, Someśvaranātha and Sūlaṭankesvara are old. The earliest reference to the foot-prints of God Ādi Mādhava near the confluence is found in the *Vīrabhadradevacampū* of Padmanabha Miśra (composed in 1577 CE).[26] The present shrine of Adi Veṇimādhava contains a short stone inscription of seven lines fixed to the right side wall of entrance to the *garbhagriha*. It mentions that this shrine was built by Śivājī Viṭṭhala Vincūrakara in Śaka 1707 / Vikrama 1842 (= 1785 CE) and renovated by Girijābāi Vincūrakara, the daughter-in-law of Raghunātharāo Viṭṭhala alias Annā

Sahib Vincūrakara, the chief of Vincūra (Nasik district, Maharashra), in Saka 1855 / Vikrama 1990 (= 1933 CE).[27] This shrine has now been fully renovated with marble flooring by one Kundan Lal Dutta of Punchha (J&K) in 2002. The renovated shrine of Someśvaranātha, one km east of Arail, on the southern bank of the conjoint stream of the Gaṅgā-Yamunā possibly represents the Purāṇic Soma-tīrtha. The *Mastya Purāṇa* glorifies it as a dispeller of great sins and says that he, who bathes there, gets the deliverance of hundreds of his ancestors.[28] The *Śiva Purāṇa* says that the *darsana* of Someśvara wards off all adversities.[29] The *Brahma Purāṇa* as quoted in the *Tristhalīsetu* states that a person, who worships the Supreme Being after taking a bath there, is emancipated from rebirth.[30] According to a local tradition, the Moon-god became free from diseases by performing penance and worshipping Lord Śiva there.[31] Raja Mān Singh of Amber-Jaipur is recorded in a Sanskrit inscription, to have visited this shrine in 1600 CE.[32] The Mughal emperor Aurangzeb is said to have bestowed a Jagir of 75 villages for its maintenance, the *furman* possibly being preserved by the priest of the shrine[33] who failed to produce that during our enquiring visit. The shrine of Śūlaṭaṅkeśvara, "Śiva of the Spear and Hatcher", flanked by a Pipal tree on either side, is 100 metres to the west of the Triveni Pushpa at Arail. Architectural fragments of the earlier shrine of the seventeenth-eighteenth century lie scattered on an elevated site, 10 metres to the south-west of the present one. Sūlaṭaṅkeśvara is the most venerated *linga* of Prayāga which was replicated at Prayāga Ghat, the northernmost sector of Dasasvamedha Ghat in Varanasi.[34] This *linga* was originally located under the imperishable Banyan tree on the northern bank of the Yamunā near the confluence as is clearly depicted in the *Prayāgapaṭṭa* of *c.* 10th century CE.[35] According to the *Prāgaya-māhātmya-śatādhyāyi*, the site of Śulaankesvara *liṅga* was at a distance of ten *hastas* (about 3 metres) from the famous Banyan tree.[36] This God at Prayāga had also been noticed by Vidyāpati.[37] When in the last quarter of the sixteenth century emperor Akbar constructed the fort this tree fell within its four walls. By the command of emperor Jahangir, it was cut down and a cauldron of iron was firmly placed over the stump. Thus, when the celebrated Banyan tree completely withered away during the first quarter of the seventeenth century[38], the venue of Sūlaṭaṅkeśvara appears to have shifted to the southern bank of the Yamunā, opposite the fort, at the present site which still commands the veneration of local people. All these three shrines face north towards the confluence of rivers.

Arail had developed into a township with a mud fortress during the medieval period. Scholars proficient in the Vedas and the six schools of Hindu philosophy resorted to it during the sixteenth-seventeenth centuries.[39] It is said to have been surrounded by groves and forests full of natural beauty. Three kinds of basil (*tulasī*) plants gave the place an additional sanctity. Rose plantation was done there at a large scale on the southern bank of the river, but in 2008 the land was acquired by the Allahabad Development Authority for developing residential colonies, thus causing scarcity of flowers in Allahabad.

Vallabhācārya (1479-1532 CE), the propounder of the Śuddhādvaita philosophy, selected the place for his residence to the end of his days, a period of about 20 years. Most of his time passed there in writing his great works and in teaching his disciples the secrets of the new faith and daily reading of the *Bhāgavata Purāṇa*. Once Caitanya, the exponent of the Acintya Dvaitādvaita philosophy, while going from Bengal to Vrindavana, came to Arail to meet Vallabhācārya.[40] A *baithaka* raised in the midst of beautiful surrounding, close to Arail in the east-south in the village Devarakh is a testimony of Vallabhācārya's association with this place. During the British period in the 19th and first half of the 20th century this place, despite being the headquarters of the pargana, seems to have been neglected and bore a deserted look till 1953 when Kulānand Mishra popularly known as Succā Baba from the village Shahpur in the Madhubani district of Bihar settled and constructed his Ashrama there. He was followed by another Sadhu from Chail in the Allahabad district, who established Tapasi Ashrama close by. Some small ashramas such as Phalahari, Guphawale Hanuman and Satsang Mandir also came up during the 1970s and 1980s, one of Mahesh Yogi's big Ashramas being established there in 1989 and that of Asaram Bapu in 2007. The opening of the new Yamunā Road-bridge in 2004 and construction of an embankment in 2000-2004 along the southern bank of the Yamunā from the old Yamunā bridge to Someśvaranātha have paved the way for rapid urbanisation of this once sleepy village.

Though all the shrines there are shabby looking dating back to the late medieval or modern times, Arail has yielded two early medieval sculptures proving the existence of Śaiva and Vaiṣṇava temples there, which would have been plundered later on by the Muslim armies. A plum-coloured sandstone sculpture of Umā-Māheśvara, datable to the eighth century CE, is now preserved in the Allahabad Museum.[41] It shows Śiva seated in the *ardhaparyankasana* on Nandi whose head is seen in front. A *yogapatta* is seen around his pendent leg resting on a lotus flower. He holds a serpent and a trident in his right and left upper hands, the lower left hand caresses the goddess under the chin and the lower right hand is seen picking something from a plate held by a gana. Umā is seated on his left knee with both her feet placed on lotus flowers below and her face is turned towards her consort, resting her arm on his thigh. "To Umā's left is a guardian figure leaning on a mace, while below the couple, from left to right, are figures of guardian, seated Gaṇeśa, an ascetic with hands raised, Nandī and Kārttikeya riding on a peacock. Above are flying Vidyadharas". The image is slightly damaged. Another sandstone slab from Arail, also in the same museum, depicts Lakshmī-Nārāyaṇa on Garuḍa and is dated to the twelfth century CE.[42] The four-armed Viṣṇu, holding a lotus flower stalk, a mace and a discuss, is seated in the *ardhaparyaṅkāsana* on Garuḍa whose badly damaged head is visible. His fourth hand is also damaged. Lakshmi is seated on her consort's left thigh, the left hand holding a lotus bud while the right hand is thrown across the shoulder of the God. The backrest, decorated with plasters, has an incomplete quatrefoil arch.

Thus Arail has been a religiously and culturally rich locality in the sacred region of Prayāga at least from the early medieval period. But the vandalism carried out there during the medieval period and the process of rapid urbanisation there especially after the opening of the New Yamunā bridge in 2003 have played havoc with its cultural heritage. There is an urgent need for preservation and conservation of historically important vestiges in the form of surviving shrines, sculptures and sites for posterity. The local Development Authorities should seek the help of a cultural historian and an environmentalist to save whatever cultural heritage has been left there.

* Originally published in the *History Today*, no. 9, 2008, p. 40-44.

REFERENCES

1. ...अरेलावासे वेण्यां स्नात्वा...

   Dubey, D.P, "Tārti Copper-plate Grant of king Govindacandra of the Gahadavala Dynasty*", Journal of the G.N. Jha Kendriya Sanskrit Vidyapeetha*, Vol. LIV-LV, 1998-99, pp. 68-69, lines 23-28.

   The Goharwa copper-plates of 1047 CE inform that the Kalacuri king Karma issued the command from his *skandhavara* (victorious camp) at Karṇatīrtha that he, after bathing in the Gaṅgā at Arghatīrtha had granted the village Candapahā, situated in the Kauśāmba pattala, to the learned Āvasathika Mālhū (V.V. Mirashi, (ed.), *Corpus Inscriptionum Indicarum*, Govt. Epigraphist for India, Ootacamund, 1955, Vol. IV (i), pp. 258-259). Mirashi holds that Karṇatīrtha was probably a Ghat built by him at Allahabad, because the donated village was "situated not very far from Allahabad" (ibid, p. 254). If his view on the identification of Karṇatīrtha is accepted, Arghatīrtha, left unnoticed by him, may be identified with Arail on the basis of some phonetical similarity in names. In that case the earliest known name of Arail would be Arghatīrtha. But Karṇātīrtha and Anghatīrtha in Allahabad are unknown to the Purāṇic Māhātmyas and local traditions. The donated village Candapahā (modern Canpahā, about 5 km NNW of Kaushāmbī), not very far from Allahabad, is in fact 60 km west-west-south of Allahabad. Therefore, Karṇatīrtha in all likelihood represents Kara on the Gaṅgā, the headquarters of the Subah of Allahabad in medieval period, which is 30 km NNW of Kaushāmbī and 65 km west of Allahabad. Arghatīrtha possibly was the ghat below the north-west corner of the old mound of Kara, which is still being used for bathing by the devotees visiting the shrine of Shitala Devi there.

2. *Ibid*, p. 62
3. Lele, K.K. and A.S. Upadhyaya (ed. & tr.), *Vīrabhānūdayakāvyam of Mādhava*, Rewa Darbar, Rewa, 1938, II. 62, III. 2 (Alarkanagara), XII. 29 (Alarkapura).
4. Krishna, Kamala, Smrititiirtha (ed.), *Tīrthacintāmani of Vācaspati Miśra*, Asiatic Society of Bengal, Calcutta, 1912, p. 23.
5. तत्रैव च गंगायमुनयोस्तटनिषण्णाऽलर्कनगरी नयनपथमगात्/

   Sudyumna Acarya (ed. & tr.), *Vīrabhadradevacampū of Padmanābha Miśra*, Veda Vani Vitanam, Satna, 1996, p. 81.
6. Gokhale, Ganesh Shastri (ed.), *Tristhalīsetu of Nārāyaṇa Bhaṭṭa*, Anandashram Press, Poona, 1915, p. 15.
7. चकोरनयनीग्रामो तीर्थराजस्य दक्षिणे
   चकोरचकोरीपक्षिप्रख्यानं यत्र चाभक्त्//
   अरेलग्रामः सेराजग्रामोऽपि यत्र दुर्गञ्च मृण्मयम्/
   महाप्रयागप्रदक्षिणं कृत्वा भरद्वाजाश्रमं गतः//

   Munishwar Jha (ed.), *Bhūparikramanam of Vidyāpati*, Mithila Sanskrit Parishad, Calcutta, 1976, III 20-21.
8. Halim, Abdul, *History of the Lodi Sultans*, Idarah-i-Adabiyat, Delhi, 1974, repr., p. 68; K.L. Srivastava, *The Position of Hindus under the Delhi Sultanate 1206-1526*, Munshiram Manoharlal, Delhi, 1980, p. 85.
9. *Vīrabhānudayakāvyam*, III.2, XII. 29.
10. *Ibid*, II. 63.
11. Beveridge, A.S. (tr.), *Humāyūn-nāmā*, Low Price Publications, Delhi, 1996, repr., pp. 135-136; R.P. Tripathi, *Rise and Fall of the Mughal Empire*, Central Book Depot, Allahabad, 1956, p. 96.
12. George, S.A. et al. (tr.), *Muntakhub-ut-Tawārīkh of Abdul Qadir Badauni*, Asiatic Society of Bengal, Calcutta, 1898-1925, Vol. II, p. 124.
13. Elliot, H.M., *Supplemental Glossary of Terms used in the North-Western Provinces*, 1844 (edited by John Beames under the title "*History, Floklore and Distribution of the Races of the North-Western Provinces of India*", Gian Publications, Delhi, 1980, reprint), Vol. II, p. 56.

14. Jarrett, H.S. (tr.), *Āin-i-Akbarī of Abul Fazl*, Asiatic Society of Bengal, Calcutta, 1949, Vol. II, p. 172.
15. Ansari, M.A., *Administrative Documents of Mughal India,* B.R. Publishing Corporation, Delhi, 1984, pp. 2, 16-17; documents no. 2 and 3, dated 1574 CE .
16. Joshi, E.B. (ed.), *U.P. District Gazetteers: Allahabad*, Deptt. of District Gazetteers, Lucknow, 1966, p. 52.
17. *Ibid*, p. 54; A.L. Srivastava, *First Two Nawabs of Oudh,* Shivalal Agrawal & Co., Agra, 1954, second edition, p. 163.
18. Firminger, W.K. (ed.), *The Fifth Report from the Select Committee of the House of Commons on the Affairs of the East India Company, July 1812*, Asiatic Society of Bengal, Calcutta, 1917, p. 467.
19. Sinha, S.N., *The Mid Gangetic Region in the Eighteenth Century*, Gitanjali Publishing House, Delhi, 1986, second impression, p. 55.
20. *Ibid*, p. 22.
21. *Virabhānūdayakāvyam*, II 73.
22. *Ibid*, XII. 29.
23. Khuda Baksh Oriental Public Library, Patna. SL No. 287, HL No. 1887/5; SL No. 288-294, HL No. 1887/11-12; SL No. 295, HL No. 1887/24-25. In the *parwanas* of the Nawabs the pargana is referred to as Jalālabād alias Arel.
24. *Ibid*, SL No. 283, HL No. 1887/1, dated 11th Zakat of the first regnal year (1707 CE) of the Mughal emperor Shah Alam I.
25. Dubey, D.P., *Prayāga: The Site of Kumbha Melā*, Aryan Books International, New Delhi, 2001, pp. 30-31, 37-39.
26. तत्र च कृतस्नानेन दृष्टादिश्रीमाधवचरणारविन्देन मया ततः प्रस्थितेन पथि....
    Virabhadradevacampū, after V. 4, p. 81.
27. 1. श्री आदिवेणीमाधव मंदिर, प्रयाग

    2. शिवाजी विट्ठल विंचूरकर स्थापित शके 1707 वि. 1842 गो–

    3. ब्राह्मण प्रतिपालक श्री कै. रघुनाथराव विट्ठल उर्फ आण्णा

    4. साहेब विंचूरकर चीफ ऑफ विंचूर यांची स्नुषा श्री गिरिजा

    5. बाई विंचूरकर यानी आपले परमपूज्य श्वसुर यांचे

    6. स्मरणार्थ जीर्णोद्धार केला

    7. सन् 1933 ई. मि. का. शु. 11 रविवार शके 1855 वि. 1990 [/]

    Vincūra with adjoining villages, a small principality located about 70 km to the north-east of Nāsik (Maharashtra), was granted to Shivadeva (Shivājī) Viṭṭhala, an ancestor of Raghunāthārao alias Āṇṇa Sahib, by the Peshwa as a special land assignment to support government troops and maintain forts. Viṭṭhala Shivadeva had distinguished himself at the seizure of Ahmadabad by Marāṭhās in 1755 CE . Irina Gluskova, "Moving God(s) ward, Calculating Money: Wonders and Wealth as Essentials of Tirthayatra", *Journal of South Asian Studies*, NS, Vol. XXIX (2), 2006, p. 217, fn. 7.

28. *Matsya Purāṇa*, Mor Prachya Shodha Sansthan, Calcutta, 1954, 108.2.
29. *Śiva Purāṇa*, Venkateshvara Steam Press, Bombay, 1944, IV. 2.14
30. *Tristhalīsetu*, p. 60.
31. क्षेत्रस्याग्नेयदिग्भागे प्रान्तवेण्यामवाक्तटे/
सोमतीर्थ श्रुतिख्यातं त्रिषु लोकेषु विश्रुतम्//
यत्रागत्य पुरा सोमो पीडितो राजयक्ष्मणा/
शिवस्याराधनं चक्रे भक्त्या तदपनुत्तये//
Prayāga-māhātmya-śatādhyāyī, published by Shokaha Shyam Narayana & Shesha Narayana Sharma, Prayaga, Samvat 1981, 87. 2-3.
32. Sinha, S.N., *Subah of Allahabad under the Great Mughals*, Jamia Millia Islamia, Delhi, 1974, p. 34, fn. 7. The inscription engraved on a stone pillar is now completely obliterated due to the thick vermillion coat over the pillar lying in front of the shrine.
33. Joshi, E.B. (ed.), *op. cit.*, p. 371.
34. प्रयागतीर्थराजाच्च शूलटंको महेश्वरः/
तीर्थराजेन सहितः स्थित आगत्य वै स्वयम्//
Skanda Purāṇa, Venkatesvara Steam Press, Bombay, 1909, IV. 69.39.
35. Dubey, D.P., *op. cit.*, p. 106, p1.13.
36. वटस्य दशहस्तान्ते शूलटंकेश्वरस्थलम्/
उत्तरे वर्तते पुण्यं पुण्यातिशयकारकम्//
Prayāga-māhātmya-śatādhyāyi, 76.5.
37. *Bhūparikramaṇam*, III. 5, 13.
38. Dubey, D.P., *op. cit.*, p. 58.
39. वेदान्तसिद्धान्तविदो द्विजेन्द्रा वैशेषिका न्यायविदो महान्तः/
मीमांसकाः सांख्यानिविष्टचित्ताः पातञ्जलास्तं निषिषेविरे च//
Virabhānūdayakāvyam, XII. 36.
तस्यां तर्कार्कभाषा प्रतिहत–सुगताद्युक्ति–गाढान्धकारे
श्रौते मार्गे चरन्ती विगतभयमसौ ब्रह्मविद्या चकास्ति//
सार्धं वैशेषिकाद्यैरपि च सुमतयो यत्र विध्वस्तमोहा/
मीमांसाःसांख्य–पातञ्जलफणिफणिनी पाठयन्तो जयन्ति
Vīrabhadradevacampū, V. 4.

40. Parekh, Manilal C., *Śri Ballabhācārya: Life, Teachings and Movement*, Bhagavata Dharma Mission, Rajkot, 1943, p. 167.
41. AM 727; Pramod Chandra, *Stone Sculptures in the Allahabad Museum*, American Institute of Indian Studies, Poona, 1970, p. 103, pl. LXXXVII.
42. AM 856; Pramod Chandra, *op. cit.*, p. 102, pl. LXXXVII.

APPENDIX – 2

JAINISM AT PRAYĀGA

Prayāga/Allahabad, picturesquely situated at the confluence of the rivers Gaṅgā, Yamunā and the invisible Sarasvatī in the heart of the Gaṅgā valley, is one of the most renowned sacred places of India. It is known as Tirtharāja and is believed by the Hindus to be the holiest place in the three worlds existing in space (heaven, earth and the netherworld) and in time (past, present and future). It is one of the most frequented places of pilgrimage, where people come especially during the month of Magha for bathing in the sacred waters of the confluence and every twelfth year they come by hundreds of thousands to the largest mela of the world, the Kumbha Mela. This place has been serving for millennia as a meeting ground for different kinds of peoples and traditions and communicating with every corner of the country. The name Allahabad was given to it by the Mughal emperor Akbar who laid the foundation of the city and a fort at the confluence of rivers there in 1583-84 CE.[1] The word 'Prayāga' is derived from the root *yāga* meaning sacrifice and the prefix *pra* attached to it means 'great'. The *Mahābhārata* says that since Prajāpati performed a great sacrifice there, it is known as Prayāga.[2] The *Rāmāyaṇa* of Valmiki has also mentioned Prayāga near the confluence of the rivers, where Rāma together with Sitā and Lakṣmaṇa was welcomed by the sage Bharadvāja in his hermitage.[3] Some modern scholars on the basis of some Jaina sources have opined that prior to the performance of the great sacrifice by Prajāpati, this place was known as Purimatāla or Puṣpabhadrapura.[4] But how this priority has been maintained by them is not clear, as the Epics stand far older than the Jaina literature which was finally codified in the sixth century CE. Moreover, Purimatāla itself is mentioned as a suburb of Ayodhyā in the Jaina texts[5] and Puspabhadrapura has been identified with Pāṭaliputra/ Patna in Bihar.[6]

One of the most important pilgrimage sites in Prayāga is the famous Banyan tree, popularly known as Akṣayavaṭa. This tree has commanded the adoration of the people for more than 1500 years and is still an object of worship in the form of a bifurcated log in one of the corners of the underground Pātālapurī shrine inside the local fort. We have discussed the historicity and religious significance of this tree in detail elsewhere.[7] Here our focus is to examine its association with the first Tīrthaṅkara Ṛṣabhadeva, as claimed by the Jaina devotees. Jinaprabhasūri (14th century) in his *Vividhatīrthakalpa* refers to the Banyan (Vaṭa) tree at Prayāga, which sprouted forth again and again despite being chopped off by the Turks.[8] He also speaks about the drowning of the Jain monk named Aṇṇikāputra while crossing the river at Prayāga.[9] But he does not mention any affiliation of Jainism with the tree there. However, according to the *Sarvatīrthavandanā* of Jñānasāgara (16-17th century), the first Tīrthaṅkara Ṛṣabhadeva practised Jaina-yoga for six months under the Vaṭa tree at Prayāga and delivered a sermon there.[10] In the *Prācīna Tīrthamālā-saṁgraha* we find conflicting statements regarding the association of Ṛṣabhadeva with the tree. Haṁsasoma says that Ṛṣabhadeva's initiation took place there,[11] while Jayavijaya maintains that he delivered his first sermon there.[12] Saubhāgyavijaya says that he broke his fast there,[13] but Śīlavijaya is of the opinion that he practised penances for one year under this tree.[14] These statements of the Jaina saints of the sixteenth-seventeenth centuries are unacceptable due to their controversial nature. The evidence of the association of Ṛṣabhadeva with the tree at Prayāga, found in these late Jaina sources, shows that in medieval times the Jainas made attempts to associate their religion with this Brahmanical *tīrtha.* We know from early Jain sources that Ṛṣabhadeva (born and brought up in Ayodhyā) renounced the world under an Aśoka tree in a garden named Siddhārthavana at Ayodhya[15], broke his fast at Hastināpur[16], attained omniscience under a great *Nyagrodha* (banyan) tree in a grove called Sakatamukha at Purimatāla, the chief suburb of Ayodhyā[17], and delivered his first sermon in the *samavasaraṇa* assembly held there.[18] It is Purimatāla in Ayodhyā which was rechristened as Prajāga/Prayāga after the first Tīrthaṅkara performed the great sacrifice of penance renouncing the luxuries of worldly life there; this episode is not related to Prayāga/Allahabad at the confluence of the rivers.

Fanny Parks, who lived in Allahabad from 1827 to 1845 CE , writes, "This tree grows in or is enclosed within the walls of the fort, in such a manner that you cannot see it from any place. They take you into a room, which was formerly one of a hammām, or steam bath. This room is called Achibuṭ (Akṣayavaṭa) Chamber, and there with the eyes of faith, the pilgrims behold the everlasting tree; ... The door of this chamber has been blocked up, on account of a native in the Collector's office wishing to put up his idol there; the man is a worshipper of Pārisnāth (Pārśvanātha, the 23rd Tīrthaṅkara), the god of the heretical Hindoos (i.e. Jainas). No orthodox Hindoo will worship in a temple where there is an image of Pārisnāth; and as this man had raised an altar in the Achibuṭ Chamber, and wished to place his idol thereon, it caused a great commotion; to quell which, the Commandant of the fort bricked up the door, and has never allowed the people entrance since that time"[19]. She further records, "When the Achibut Chamber was blocked up, the Brahmans set up the stump of a *ber* (Vaṭa) tree in the Patala Pooree"[20].

Fanny Parks' account is based on her visit to the respective sites including the Pātālapurī shrine in the fort in 1831. She had made her residence near the fort on the bank of the river Yamuna and her husband, a high official of the fort, became the Collector of Allahabad in1836. Therefore, we may accept her account as true. Her account proves that the original site of the Banyan tree was not in the Pātālapurī shrine but somewhere else inside the fort. The attempt of the Jaina devotee to put up an image of the 23rd Tīrthankara Pārśvanatha in the Akṣayavaṭa chamber and its opposition by the Hindus reminds of a similar event that occurred in the reign of emperor Akbar. According to Haṁsasoma's *Tīrthamālā* (V.S.1565/ 1508 CE), there was the foot-print *(carаña-cihna)* of Ṛṣabhadeva under the Akṣayavaṭa (Banyan tree).[21] But the *Tirthamālā-s* of Vijayasāgara (V.S.1717/1660 CE), Jayavijaya (V.S.1664 / 1607 CE) and Saubhāgyavijaya (V.S.1750 / 1693 CE) record that subedar Rai Kalyāṇa removed the foot-print of Jinendra and established a Śivaliṅga there in Vikrama Samvat 1648 / 1591 CE in the time of emperor Akbar.[22] The image of Pārśvanātha, referred by Fanny Parks, seems to be the same 54 inches high sandstone image enshrined today in the Pārśvanātha Digambara Jaina Pañcāyatī temple of the Chāhcand locality in the city; it was obviously consecrated at the present site sometime during the third decade of the nineteenth century and the person responsible for this pious act possibly belonged to the family of the maternal grandfather of Dr. G.C. Agrawal, a retired Professor of Economics of the University of Allahabad. The present temple, judging from the architectural style, dates back to the first half of the nineteenth century. The claim of the Jaina devotees that this image was found in the course of digging inside the fort and removed from there to the present site has no historical groundings; it is not substantiated by the observation of Fanny Parks. Some divine images were recovered from the fort in 1906-07 and are now preserved in the State Museum, Lucknow, but they are all of Brahmanical pantheon; no Jaina sculpture from the fort has ever been reported.

Jinaprabhasūri refers to the shrines dedicated to Śītalanātha (the 10th Tīrthaṅkara), Kunthunātha (the 17th Tīrthaṅkara), and Aranātha (the 18th Tīrthaṅkara) near the confluence of rivers at Prayāga and mentions the presence of the Ādikara (the First Tīrthaṅkara's)- mandala at the confluence of the rivers Gaṅgā and Yamunā there in.[23] These shrines would have existed during the fourteenth century in the time of Jinaprabhasuri in the Daryabad-Baluaghat locality, a predomi nantly Muslim quarter from the sixteenth century near the confluence of the rivers which used to take place there before the construction of embankments along the Gaṅgā-Yamunā in 1583-90 CE by emperor Akbar for saving the newly founded city and fort from the fury of floods. No Jaina antiquity has been reported from Arail and Jhusi on either side of the present site of the confluence of rivers. Jaina remains and antiquities have been found at Kauśāmbi, Pabhosā, Bālakamau, Kaṛā-Shahjādpur in the district of Kauśāmbi (western part of Allahabad district till 1997) and Siṅhapur in the district of Allahabad, the last place has been referred to in the *Yaśastilaka-campū* of Somadeva (10th century).[24] The adherents of Jainism deserted Siṅhapur and moved to the nearby marketplace Kohḍār sometime in the Mughal period, where they are still found in majority. In the city and countryside of Allahabad Jainas of the Digambara order are in majority from early times, very few followers of the Śvetāmbara sect have come and settled in the city in the later half of the twentieth century.

Besides the Digambara Jaina Pañcāyatī temple and the Dharmaśālā shrine which contain over a dozen medieval images of different Tīrthaṅkaras in sandstone and marble mostly brought from Kauśāmbī-Pabhosā and Shahjādpur in Chāhcand locality on the Zero Road and the new Digambara Jaina shrine in Beniganj which houses three images of Tīrthaṅkaras (Ṛṣabhadeva, Neminātha and Padmaprabha) in marble consecrated at Pabhosā in 1824 CE from the village of Berui, a Śvetāmbara Jaina temple was constructed in the Bāi kā Bāgh locality in the 1970s and a large Digambara Jaina establishment of shrines and rest-houses has appeared after 2001 in the village of Andāwā on the GT road, 5 km east by north of the confluence, by the efforts of the Jaina Śramaṇī Jñānamati of Hastināpur.

* originally published in D. P. Dubey and Ashish K. Dubey (eds.), *Uttar Pradesh mein Jaina Purāvasesha*, SDS, Allahabad, 2013, pp. 90-94.

REFERENCES

1. *Āin-i-Akbarī* of Abul Fazl, vol. II, p. 169, vol. III, p.616; *Tabaqāt-i-Akbari* of Nizāmuddin Ahmad, vol. II, p.577.
2. *Mahābhārata,* III.85.14.
3. *Rāmāyaṇa*, II.54.7-36, II.90-91,VI.124.1-2.
4. B.N.Tiwari, *Prayāga Darśana,* Vidya Prakashan Griha, Allahabad, 1976, p. 25.
5. *Triṣaṣṭiśalākāpuruṣacaritra,* I.3.389-512; *Kalpasūtra*,7.212; *Harivaṁśa Purāṇa* of Jinasena, 9.205-6; *Āvaśyakacūrṇi,* I.181; *Vipākasūtra*, 15; *Ādi Purāṇa* of Jinasena, I.20.218-219; J. Yadava, *Jaina Dharma ki Aitihāsik Rūparekhā,* India Academy, Delhi, 1981,p.18.
6. J.C.Jain, *Life in Ancient India as Described in the Jaina canons,* New Book Co., Bombay, 1947, p.324.
7. D. P. Dubey, *Prayāga: The Site of Kumbha Mela*, Aryan Books International, New Delhi, 2001, pp. 51-73.
8. *Vividhatīrthakalpa* of Jinaprabhasūri, Eds. D. R. Bhandarkar & Kedarnath, Asiatic Society of Bengal, Calcutta, 1942, p.234.
9. *Ibid.*, p.233. The story of Aṇṇikāputra also occurs in the *Āvaśyakaniryukti* (1190-91), *Avaśyakacūrṇi* (II.36)*, Niśithacūrṇi* (II.231), *Dharmopadeśamālāvivaraṇa* (pp. 41-46), and *Pariśiṣṭaparvan* (VI.43-174) which refer to Prayāga as a *kutittha (= kutīrtha,* a sacred place not belonging to Jainism). These texts are earlier than the *Vividhatīrthakalpa* in date.
10. *Tīrthavandanā-saṁgraha,* Ed. Vidyadhar Joharapurkar, Jaina Samskriti Samraksak Samgha, Sholapur, 1965, pp.66-67, *chappaya* 21; Balabhadra Jain*, Bhārat ke Digambara Jaina Tīrtha,* Bharatavarshiya Digambara Jaina Tirthaksetra Committee, Bombay, 1974, Part I, pp.135-136, which wrongly ascribes the couplet to Nayanasāgara.
11. *Prācīna Tirthamālā-saṁgraha,* Ed. Vijayadharmasuri, Yashovijaya Jaina Granthamala, Bhavanagar, 1978, Part I, p.14.
12. *Ibid.*, p.74.
13. *Ibid.*, p.77.
14. *Ibid.,* p.108.
15. *Kalpasūtra*, 7.221; *Padma Purāṇa* of Raviṣeṇa, 3.280-282; *Ādi Purāṇa* of Jinasena, 17.181, 201.203; *Triṣaṣṭiśalākāpuruṣacaritra,* I.3.61-74.
16. *Harivaṁśa Purāṇa* of Jinasena, 9.157-189; *Triṣaṣṭiśalākāpuruṣacaritra,* I.3.249-295.
17. *Kalpasūtra*,7.212;*Harivaṁśa Purāṇa* of Jinasena,9.205-210;*Triṣaṣṭiśalākāpuruṣacaritra,* I.3.389-398,512; *Ādi Purāṇa* of Jinasena, 20.218-220, 268.
18. *Triṣaṣṭiśalākāpuruṣacaritra,* 1.3.422ff.
19. Fanny Parks, *Wanderings of a Pilgrim in Search of the Picturesque*, Pelhem Richardson, London, 1850, Vol. I, pp. 213-214.

20. *Ibid*., p. 215.
21. *Prācīna Tirthamālā-saṁgraha,* p.14, *pada* 4.
22. *Ibid.*, p. 3, *ḍhāla* 2, *pada* 2.
23. *Ibid.*, p. 24, *ḍhāla* 1, *pada* 11.
24. *Ibid.*, p.77, *ḍhāla* 3, *pada* 11.

    Rāi Kalyāṇa is mentioned as an important dignitary in the time of the Mughal emperor Akbar (1556-1605 CE) in the *Akbaranāmā* of Abul Fazl, Vol. III, p. 683 and *Muntakhab-ut-Tawārīkh* of Badauni, Vol. II, p. 49. According to Saubhāgyavijaya, the *Śivaliṇga* was destroyed in the reign of the Mughal emperor Aurangzeb (1656-1707 CE). *Prācīna Tirthamālā-saṁgraha,* p.77, *ḍhāla* 3, *pada* 12.
25. *Yaśastilaka-campū* of Somadeva, pp. 326-334; D. P. Dubey, *Triveni : Essays on the Cultural Heritage of Allahabad,* Society of Pilgrimage Studies, Allahabad, 1996, pp.114-117.